Religion and the State in Russia and China

RELIGION AND THE STATE IN RUSSIA AND CHINA

Suppression, Survival, and Revival

Christopher Marsh

continuum

2011

The Continuum International Publishing Group
80 Maiden Lane, New York, NY 10038
The Tower Building, 11 York Road, London SE1 7NX

www.continuumbooks.com

Copyright © 2011, Christopher Marsh

Library of Congress Cataloging-in-Publication Data
Marsh, Christopher, 1969–
Religion and the state in Russia and China : suppression, survival, and revival /
Christopher Marsh.
    p. cm.
Includes bibliographical references and index.
ISBN-13: 978-1-4411-0229-4 (hardcover : alk. paper)
ISBN-10: 1-4411-0229-9 (hardcover : alk. paper)
ISBN-13: 978-1-4411-1247-7 (pbk. : alk. paper)
ISBN-10: 1-4411-1247-2 (pbk. : alk. paper) 1. Church and state—Russia—History—
20th century. 2. Church and state—China—History—20th century. 3. Religion
and state—Russia—History—20th century. 4. Religion and state—China—
History—20th century. I. Title.

BR936.M3435 2011
261.7'20947—dc22   2010022745

ISBN: HB: 978-1-4411-0229-4
       PB: 978-1-4411-1247-7

Typeset by Newgen Imaging Systems Pvt Ltd, Chennai, India
Printed in the United States of America

To my grandmother, Ruth Evelyn Mathews, who raised me with faith, love, and a passion for knowledge.

Contents

List of Tables

Acknowledgments

A work such as this entails not only years of research, but also the assistance and insight of many colleagues, students, and friends. Having spent so many years working on issues related to Russia, China, and church-state relations, it is well nigh impossible to thank everyone who has been instrumental in the writing of this book. As usual, the bulk of my thanks must go to my students, for they are the ones who hear my ideas on a daily basis and are an endless source of feedback, inspiration, and insight. Over the years, students who have been particularly instrumental include Sun Jue, Xie Xiaheng, Zhong Zhifeng, Qu Li, Artyom Tonoyan, Lydia Tonoyan, Jennifer Kent, Jon Mizuta, and Brenda Norton, who had the thankless job of helping me edit the first draft of this manuscript.

On the research side of things, students such as Xie Xiaheng, Zhong Zhifeng, and Artyom Tonoyan were again indispensible (though Artyom's driving style in Armenia proved a little too reckless for my tastes!). My debt here, however, is greatest to my Russian and Chinese colleagues and friends. These again are innumerable, but certainly include Grigory Kliucharev, Sergei Filatov, Roman Lunkin, He Honghua, Guan Guihai, Wei Dedong, and Li Qingsi. Without their assistance, from obtaining sources to gleaning the proper interpretation, this project would not have been possible.

I must also thank my teachers, from grade school on through my graduate education, a list that is impossibly long. But I must mention by name those who impacted me most, especially in the subject areas covered here. This includes Gavro Altman, Alan Smith, David Blitz, Henry Krisch, Yanan Ju, and Natalia Peterson. And while I never took a class from them, so many of my colleagues have been my teachers as well, and remain so to this day. This includes Jerry Pankhurst, Michael Bourdeaux, Xenia Dennen, Slava Karpov, Elena Lisovskaya, James Warhola, Robert Weller, Fenggang Yang, and Wallace Daniel.

And just as "the last shall be first," a heartfelt thanks to Peter Berger who has helped me expand my theoretical and conceptual horizons beyond the field of political science, and at the same time has taught me what is most important in life. It is with that in mind that I thank my family for their support and understanding, especially my son Evan and daughter Ashlyn, who sacrificed more than a few days and evenings while daddy was traveling or writing. And to my wife, Melissa, for her support, encouragement, and understanding. I love you all immensely, and wish I could spend every minute with you.

Introduction: From Forced Secularization to Desecularization

The expropriation of church lands in 18th century France and the massive demolition of churches under Soviet rule were clear signs of secularization. Conversely, the restitution of church property and the large-scale restoration of old and the building of new churches in post-Soviet Russia are clear symbols of desecularization.

—Vyacheslav Karpov

One of the greatest ironies of the twentieth century must be that, while in the democratic West secularization was being proclaimed as the future of the world, in the Communist East untold millions were suffering for their faith as they resisted the onslaught of forced secularization in the name of science and progress. One by one, beginning in the 1970s, sociologists of religion began to abandon secularization theory in the face of mounting evidence indicating that the world was just as religious as it had ever been, and in some cases even more so than at earlier points in history. Today the debate remains far from resolved, and while the majority of scholars in the social sciences recognize the continued relevance of religion in the modern world, some are still holding out or developing "revised" theories of secularization.[1]

While certainly not a litmus test for secularization theory, analysis of the world's most comprehensive attempt at forced secularization has much insight to offer into the topic. In particular, the story of the failed attempt to create an atheistic society can shed light—in ways perhaps unlike any other human experience—on topics such as the religious nature of man, the relationship between religion and modernity, the lasting effects of disbelief, the origins of belief in secular societies, the ability of the state to alter the religious landscape of a society, and probably many more. Having spent so much time studying religion and church-state relations in the Communist and post-Communist world, I find it quite interesting that virtually none of the debate on secularization has considered the only part of the world where it actually became a state policy, and where tremendous amounts of resources were allocated to erasing religious faith and promoting atheism in its stead.[2] The failure of these policies—as well as their successes—is not only one of the most harrowing tales of faith, it is also one of the most interesting and insightful cases in the fields of sociology of religion and church-state studies.

The State Militant

Few subjects of church-state relations are more significant, relevant, and indeed interesting than the attempt to wipe religion from the face of the earth, as attempted by the Communist regimes of the twentieth century. In terms of scope, systemization, and force, the Communist attempt to eradicate religion from the world is unprecedented in human history. While Christians certainly suffered under the Roman Empire prior to the Edict of Milan in 313, while believers of other faiths even today suffer for their beliefs in regimes that refuse to tolerate their "heretical" or deviant religious beliefs and practices, history has no parallel to the religious persecutions carried out by Marxist regimes in the name of "scientific atheism" and liberation from superstition. Across the Communist world, untold millions suffered for their faith, from simply being deprived of the human right to believe to suffering pain and torture as political prisoners, or even being locked up in psychiatric institutions for their "abnormal beliefs." Millions also gave the ultimate sacrifice of their life due to their beliefs and their refusal to denounce them.

The fact that the landscape of religious freedom and practice in the world today has changed so dramatically might lead some to question the continued relevance of religion's battle with Communism. This line of thinking apparently was behind the decline of Oxford's Keston Institute, which during the 1970s and 1980s was the pre-eminent center for the study of religion under Communism. After its move to Oxford in 1990, from rural Kent, the university's support began to lag and the institute's membership to decline. Keston founder Canon Michael Bourdeaux lamented this chain of events, responding that "it is only now that Keston's true work can begin."[3] Not only can their work in promoting religious freedom only begin now, but we are only now really able to analyze this historic episode. Much like the Holocaust, this experience of inhumanity must be properly understood as a part of the larger phenomenon of religion's struggle with modernity itself.

Throughout the history of civilization, religion has always played a significant role in society, and one of the greatest questions in the sociology of religion concerns the nature of the relationship between religion and modernity. The once popular response was that the two were incompatible, and that science and progress would lead to secularization. While certainly not a proof against that thesis, an unforeseen reaction against modernity has been fundamentalism, which not only seeks to give religion a privileged position in society, but to establish a particular religious understanding as the underlying basis for politics. In so doing, however, it is very unmodern, as it seeks to silence or sequester scientific knowledge that could destroy what is taken to be the "traditional" and "fundamental" way of doing things. In this it is, of course, something very modern.

More common in the modern world have been challengers to religion's role in the public square, including secularism and its more aggressive cousin, atheism. In both cases, the goal is to limit or eradicate the role of religion in society, and to replace it with another form of legitimacy, most often science and reason. Atheism and secularism differ mostly in their methods of bringing about this change and their level of, if you will excuse the pun, zealotry. While secularism applauds the liberation of the public square from religion, atheists can take great offense at the beliefs of others and wish to see religion not only removed from the public square but even eradicated from society *in toto*. I recently came across an interesting discussion among some atheists who were strategizing about ways to eliminate religious wording and phraseology from their daily language. Some were very concerned that they still said "oh my God" or "Jesus Christ" when caught off guard or if they dropped something, but the most interesting person was the one who got terribly offended if someone told him "bless you" if he sneezed. Apparently, he liked to yell a vulgar expletive back at the person who just blessed him without his permission. It is interesting to note how much religious language the Bolsheviks left in Russian, including *Voskresenie* (resurrection) for Sunday and *spasibo* (from *spasii nas, Bog*; God save us) for thank you. The atheists above, however, would be happy that *bud' zdorov* (be healthy) was used instead of bless you when one sneezed.

Religion's battle with Communism must be understood from this perspective as well. Militant atheism takes as its starting point the presupposition that religion is a false consciousness and that man's attachment to religion is eroding in the face of progress and science. The greatest difference between them, of course, is that secularism is a belief that this process is occurring and perhaps even a joyful welcoming of it; militant atheism was the attempt actually to accelerate the process and guide it along. And much like fundamentalism, militant atheism was itself an absolute religion, with no room for other faiths. It alone was the one truth that could set man free. In sharp contrast to fundamentalism, militant atheism was the dialectical opposite, for fundamentalism is anti-modern, and militant atheism must be understood as hyper-modern, that is, it attempts to move society further into the future than it has already progressed.

The Sacred Canopy and Secularization

Before we can turn to topics such as forced secularization and post-Communist desecularization, we must first define secularization and articulate the concept. The term itself originally referred to church lands that were leaving ecclesiastical control and returning to public or private hands. It also referred to monks who left their orders and returned to society. In both examples, secularization is the process whereby something within the sacred realm is handed over to the profane world. Over the years, the term has been expanded and come refer to the overall process of the decreasing role of religion in public life, as society bifurcates along religious and secular lines. This is very much a part of the process Max Weber referred to as "differentiation." In following Weber's thinking closely, Peter Berger defined secularization in *The Sacred Canopy* as "the process by which sectors of society and culture are removed from the domination of religious institutions and symbols."[4]

More recent scholarship has come to identify several different, but interrelated, dimensions of this process. This includes a decline in the vibrancy of religious associational life, a decline in the salience of religion in the public square, and a decline in religious belief among members of society, or even its complete erosion. Perhaps the best definition is that offered by Jose Casanova, who points to the three-pronged process of secularization as religious decline, secularization as differentiation, and secularization as privatization.[5] While these three propositions are related, they may, in fact, trend in different directions depending on a number of social factors. Thus Casanova concludes in his *Public Religions in the Modern World* that secularization as structural differentiation between secular and religious institutions is an empirical reality, which in some cases may lead to a decline in religious belief and practice.

If we have to identify who it is that is evicting God from the public square, science is one of the usual suspects. If religion exists to provide answers about existence, then as science progresses and knowledge expands, scientific explanations will come to displace religious ones, and the need for religion will decline. Thus is established a link between religion and modernity, which is still the central nexus around which scholars focus their attention as they seek to understand the phenomenon of religion's decline and/or persistence, oftentimes in the very same society.

In his early work, Berger argued that the forces of modernity would inevitably lead to a collapse of religiously-based legitimations for the social order, and this would in turn bring about the secularization of institutions, culture, and consciousness. As he explained:

> It will readily be seen that the area of legitimation is far broader than that of religion, as these two terms have been defined here. Yet there exists an important relationship between the two. It can be described simply by saying that religion has been the historically most widespread and effective instrumentality of legitimation. All legitimation maintains socially defined reality. Religion legitimates so effectively because it relates the precarious reality constructions of empirical societies with ultimate reality. The tenuous realities of the social world are grounded in the sacred *realissimum*, which by definition is beyond the contingencies of human meanings and human activity.

Berger saw the greatest danger in this secularization of legitimation, which would bring about a crisis of meaninglessness. As he phrased it, this "danger is the nightmare *par excellence*, in which the individual is submerged in a world of disorder, senselessness, and madness. Reality and identity are malignantly transformed into meaningless figures of horror." Sanity is only attainable through society, which offers a shield against the ultimate "insanity" that would be brought on by anomy, which is "unbearable to the point where the individual may seek death in preference to it."[6]

A central element to Berger's thinking is that the social world intends to be taken for granted. Man's search for significance leads him to impose a meaningful order, or *nomos*, upon the world around him. This order is then sustained, albeit with mild tweaking by each generation, through the ongoing process of socialization. Berger asserts, "socialization achieves success to the degree that this taken-for-granted quality is internalized." As this order "attains the quality of being taken for granted, there occurs a merging of its meanings with what are considered to be the fundamental meanings inherent in the universe."[7] Here Berger returns to the theme of sanity only being attainable within society, with its *nomos*, while anomy remains in the realm of madness. He argues, it "is not enough that the individual look upon the key meanings of the social order as useful, desirable, or right. It is much better (better, that is, in terms of social stability) if he looks upon them as inevitable, as part and parcel of the universal 'nature of things.' If that can be achieved, the individual who strays seriously from the socially defined programs can be considered not only a fool or a knave, but a madman."[8]

It is in this way that humans construct religion as a "sacred canopy" that establishes an all-embracing sacred order of nothing less than cosmological significance. Legitimation is achieved through explanation and justification within a cosmic frame of reference, with religion thereby contributing to the maintenance of the social order.[9] The base upon which the social world and its sacred canopy are constructed, and therefore dependent for their existence, is its plausibility structure. It is the precariousness of plausibility structures that leads to religion's own instability in the face of modernity. For the *nomos* to remain taken-for-granted, the constructed order must remain plausible in the face of mounting scientific knowledge and accepted truths.

Just how precarious this socially constructed world can be, Berger argues, "is revealed each time men forget or doubt the reality-defining affirmations, each time they dream reality-denying dreams of 'madness,' and most importantly, each time they consciously encounter death." For in the end, it is man's awareness of his own finite existence itself that leads him to seek meaning and significance. In language that only the gifted Berger could contrive, every "human society is, in the last resort, men banded together in the face of death. The power of religion depends, in the last resort, upon the credibility of the banners it puts in the hands of men as they stand before death, or more accurately, as they walk, inevitably, toward it."

The plausibility and credibility of the established order is, therefore, crucial for man's existence in a norm-governed social world. Berger's early thinking of the subject, as articulated in *The Sacred Canopy*, was that modernity brings about the pluralization of worldviews, and that these competing orders would lead to an erosion of plausibility structures, which in turn would erode the taken-for-grantedness. This "crisis of credibility," in which the plausibility of traditional religious accounts of reality collapses would lead to the secularization of man's consciousness. Hence, the sacred canopy would give way, through the process of secularization, to a "profane" canopy, a new set of now more scientifically-verifiable plausibilities. We now know that religious worldviews have not succumbed so easily to modernity, science, and progress, and while a single sacred canopy may no longer exist for societies as a whole, individuals, and groups traverse the globe protected by their own "sacred umbrellas," smaller universes of meaning and order that withstand a continued onslaught of scientific discovery, sometimes in ways that defy the common knowledge of society (such as the belief in a young earth, one consistent with an Old Testament-based calendar).

Europe: Rule or Exception?

Secularization theory is a prime example of inductive reasoning, wherein only a limited number of observations is used to ascribe properties or a trend to a phenomenon in an attempt to formulate a law or build a general theory. In the case of secularization theory, the view was exceptionally narrow—both geographically and historically, positivistic, and teleological. It was geographically narrow in that it drew primarily upon the experiences of Europe and America, while historically it determined the fate of a phenomenon that is thousands of years old by only examining barely a century of supposed change. It was positivistic and teleological in that it saw man's liberation from religion as an endpoint of history, the ushering in of a new era.

Unfortunately, by placing Europe in the position of the norm and the United States in the place of the exception, secularity was seen as not only Europe's future, but the future of humanity itself. Andrew Greeley was one of the first sociologists to break from the pack and denounce secularization theory, or at least to articulate his dissent in writing.[10] Greeley's thesis was bold, stating bluntly that "the basic human religious needs and the basic religious functions have not changed very notably since the late Ice Age; what changes have occurred make religious questions more critical rather than less critical in the contemporary world."[11]

If it was Greeley's work that stopped secularization theory in its tracks, it was Stephen Warner's that alerted us to our mistake in placing Europe as the future of the world rather than America. In his "Work in Progress toward a New Paradigm for the Sociological Study of Religion in the United States,"[12] Warner not only posits that a new paradigm is emerging (which although it hasn't displaced the old paradigm, as he predicted, but rather has come to take its rightful place alongside it), he also points out that our previous theorizing stemmed largely from the European experience. The American experience, therefore, should be taken more seriously and not viewed as a deviant case. All of a sudden, modernity, and religion were compatible.

This change of tack meant that European exceptionalism now needed explanation, a topic that took some time to address convincingly. The three best explanations for Europe's secularity are offered by Grace Davie, Graeme Smith, and a team led by Berger and Davie. In Davie's study *Europe: The*

Exceptional Case, she examines the religious life of Europe in comparison with five other examples of Christianity, the United States, Latin America, sub-Saharan Africa, South Korea, and the Philippines. In each case, she asks in what ways the European trajectory differs from that of most other parts of the modern world, even the Christian world, in its relative levels of secularity. The answers are many, and there is no single pattern of distinction. While Pentecostalism characterizes religious vitality across much of the terrain she traverses, including Latin America, Africa, and the Philippines, she finds as much variation as she does pattern. Her answer to why Europe is different rests with the specificities of European history, including its economic, political, and cultural dimensions.

Rather than comparing the whole of Europe with a sizable portion of the Christian world outside Europe, Smith takes a different approach in his *A Short History of Secularism*, looking in depth at the United Kingdom. It isn't the length of his book that is short, but rather the lifespan of secularism itself. Using detailed analyses of religious life in Britain, Smith cogently argues that the contemporary situation in terms of religious adherence represents a return to normal levels of religiosity following an extraordinarily religious Victorian era.[13]

Unlike the United Kingdom, which saw a subsequent decline in church membership following World War II, the United States did not return to its previous levels of religiosity. During America's colonial period, organized religion remained fairly small with some scholars putting church membership as low as 5 percent. Even by 1850, less than 15 percent of the U.S. population were members of organized churches, and as late as 1900, by which time the U.S. population had reached 75 million, only 35 percent were members of churches. It was only on the threshold of World War II that the United States crossed the threshold of 50 percent of the population claiming membership in some religious denomination. And then, with World War II hardly over, religion began to establish itself as a fixture in the American public square. The U.S. Congress identified itself as far more religious than at any other time in American history, enacting resolutions, and laws of all sorts in order to ensure that it was understood that America was a religious—and for many a Christian—nation.

Davie's *Europe: The Exceptional Case* helped prompt an entire project on "Eurosecularity" that involved Davie with two of her longtime collaborators, Peter Berger and Danièle Hervieu-Léger. The three led a series of workshops with the aim of better understanding the exceptional nature of European religious life. This project resulted in a joint work, co-authored by Berger and Davie along with the able assistance of Efie Fokas. Their book, *Religious*

America, Secular Europe?, offers the most satisfying explanation yet as to the reasons for European secularity.[14] Like Davie's earlier work, it is the particularities of the European historical experience that help explain its exceptionalism. The list, now expanded and more clearly articulated, identifies the "culprits" as differences in church-state relations; questions of pluralism; different understandings of the Enlightenment; different types of intellectuals; variations in culture; institutional contrasts; and differences in the way in which religion relates to categories of social difference, including class and ethnicity. While not a succinct argument, it is a satisfying and convincing one, although it is as necessarily complicated as the phenomenon that it seeks to explain.

Scientific Atheism and Forced Secularization

So why this seemingly tangential investigation into secularization theory and exceptional cases in a book investigating the suppression, survival, and revival of religion in Russia and China? The answer is that the survival of religion must be understood as a response to state policies designed to eliminate religion, and those policies were put into place based upon theorizing that combined economic determinism with an early version of what must be understood as secularization theory. This understanding of religion had various proponents, but two thinkers who early on articulated ideas that would come to undergird secularization theory were Auguste Comte and Ludwig Feuerbach.

Comte, in his "Law of Three Stages," posited that knowledge passes through three successive stages, with the first being the theological or fictitious, evolving through the metaphysical, and finally resulting in the scientific.[15] The theological stage itself, he argued, evolved from animism to polytheism and finally to monotheism. Feuerbach, whom we will consider in greater depth in the following chapter, argued that the "course of religious development consists more specifically in this, that man progressively appropriates to himself what he had attributed to God."[16] In other words, Feuerbach understood history in terms of a gradual transition from the dominance of religious authority toward an inevitable rise of secularism. Together, and with others, Comte and Feuerbach laid the foundations for a theory that would not only lead us to interpret incorrectly the world around us, but once joined with the ideas of Karl Marx and Friedrich Engels, to be put into a set of state policies designed to accelerate the process. Unfortunately, the theory was wrong and the policies doomed to failure, but not without first causing the untold suffering of millions.

Here we have established the first connection between secularization and what would become the policy of forced secularization. But, if secularization theory is incorrect, and religion is a normal feature of human existence, we might also wish to conclude that forced secularization is doomed to failure. Despite the severity of religious repression under Communism, however, we cannot totally dismiss the possibility that state policy could—with the right resources, policies, and the time to implement them and let their effects become embedded into culture—eliminate religion from the face of the earth. After all, while religious belief is still prevalent across the planet, there are also more committed atheists than at any other point in history. Moreover, as the pages below will show, Soviet and PRC policies were not without their successes. While religion has revived significantly since the collapse of the Soviet Union and the liberalization of China's religion policy, decades of promoting an atheistic worldview was not without its converts and true believers.

What we can conclude is that forced secularization is not so easily achieved, and that the lengths to which the Soviet and PRC regimes went was insufficient to completely—or even thoroughly—expunge religion from society. Now that we understand the relationship between religion and modernity differently in terms of the inevitability of secularization, we might have suspected such an outcome to any attempt to eradicate religion from a society. But that would be presumptuous of us. As the following chapters will show, these regimes were willing to go to great lengths to eliminate religion in the name of science and progress, and the outcome at every stage was uncertain. This is what makes the story of religion's survival so important to our understanding of man's attachment to—even need for—religion.

The Desecularization of the Post-Communist World

While forced secularization is something of a mutated variant of secularization, post-Communist desecularization may be the example *par excellence* of desecularization. Upon initial inspection, the term desecularization is a strange one. Does it refer to a reversal of secularization? Does this mean that secularization took place and that now a reverse trend is occurring? Does it even imply that we are returning to some historical arrangement in which religion held a strong sway over the lives of individuals? Berger himself recognizes the limits to the term and admits that it lacks clarity.[17] Nevertheless, it highlights a very important process that is clearly underway in the world today.

The term "desecularization" was coined by Peter Berger as he articulated his recantation of secularization theory, arguing that the world is just as religious as it ever was, and in some cases, extremely so. His intent was not to articulate a theory, but simply to state a fact regarding the limits of secularization itself and highlight the process. It is more the persistence of religion that he is highlighting, not so much a religicization of a secularized world, which the term seems to imply. If we were to take Berger's early definition of secularization and invert it we would arrive at a definition of desecularization as *the process by which sectors of society and culture are brought under the domination of religious institutions and symbols.* This is clearly not what the concept is meant to describe, however, nor is it what Berger seemed to suggest.

Another method of operationalizing desecularization is that offered by Karpov, who recently suggested that it is "a process of counter-secularization, through which religion reasserts its societal influence in reaction to previous and/or co-occurring secularizing processes."[18] Karpov's definition is superior to simply inverting Berger's definition of secularization for at least two reasons. First, it more accurately describes the process as one of religion reasserting its formerly-held position, which is quite distinct from bringing sectors of society under the domination of religion. It accounts for the fact that desecularization may be at work even if no single sector succumbs fully to the pressure. Secondly, Karpov keeps in the equation the fact that the trends we are observing are counter-secularizing trends, that is, they are occurring as a response to secularization. This is a point Berger argued repeatedly in his seminal article. Moreover, in his excellent analysis, Karpov highlights several empirical referents to identify and distinguish cases of desecularization, including a rapprochement between formerly secularized institutions and religious norms; a resurgence of religious beliefs and practices; a return of religion to the public sphere; a revival of religious content in culture; and religion-related changes in society's substrata (including demography, economics, etc.).

One environment in which the concept of desecularization is fully appropriate is the post-Communist world. In territories controlled by Communist governments, policies of forced secularization were carried out, often with zeal and great success. In sharp contrast to places such as the former East Germany, which is today the most atheistic region in all of Europe, most other post-Communist societies witnessed a rapid return of religion almost immediately following the liberalization of religion policy. Perhaps no other societies are more useful for developing a body of evidence to support the development of a theory of secularization than these, including Poland,

Russia, Ukraine, and China. They exemplify well the process of rapid change, from forced secularization to a vibrant resurgence of religious belief. If a theory of desecularization can be developed, post-Communist societies will be critical cases.

Research Design and Structure of the Study

Social scientists are limited in their ability to test theories both by their imaginations and the limited selection of test cases that history provides. In terms of modern societies that have attempted to eliminate religion and spread atheism, unfortunately, the several examples history does offer the researcher only comes at a tremendously high cost in terms of human suffering. Nowhere was that cost higher than in the Soviet Union and the People's Republic of China, where untold millions suffered for their faith over a period of decades. While this is partly a product of numbers, in that these were the world's two most populous Communist countries, it also relates to the fact that the Communist revolutions of the Soviet Union and China were both indigenous, leading Moscow and Beijing to initiate and innovate policy at their own whims, and based on their own interpretations of Marxism-Leninism.

While China's policies across many issue areas took Soviet policy as their launching point,[19] in the area of religion China continually showed itself to be more independent-minded. In his study of how well theories of sociology of religion explain the Soviet experience with religion, Paul Froese states that the Chinese modeled themselves on the Soviet Union when formulating religion policy.[20] Indeed, this has been an assumption for a very long time, dating back at least to the publication of an article by Rensselaer Lee in 1964.[21]

I shared this assumption myself before I was asked to join a group of researchers organized by Bernstein and Li to show how pervasive the Soviet model was on the development of Chinese religion policy.[22] As I dug deeper, however, I found a paucity of evidence to support this idea. As a result of conducting interviews with Chinese specialists and gaining access to some rare and difficult to obtain Chinese materials, I have now concluded quite the opposite. In fact, the area of religion policy appears to be the one area where the Chinese *did not* draw many parallels between their experience and that of their Soviet comrades. This is true both for the development of their initial religion policies, and it holds true all the way through the period of reform, a process that is still very much underway in China (and in significant ways in post-Soviet Russia as well). The interesting question is, why?

While the religion policies of Russia and China mirrored each other in some ways, as they say, "the devil was in the details." Not only are Russia and China home to vastly different cultures, in the area of religion Russia has historically been home to exclusivistic, monotheistic religions, namely Eastern Orthodoxy and Islam, with the former dominating the country's religious landscape. China, on the other hand, is home to ancient belief systems that are the subject of debate in terms of their function as religions. While Buddhism is easily classified as a religion, the cases of Taoism and Confucianism are less clear. Although this author certainly appreciates the religious dimensions of these traditions, they also serve epistemological and philosophic roles, respectively. Nevertheless, in the Chinese context, these "three-teachings" (sanjiao) are non-exclusivistic and, although there were periods in Chinese history when they battled it out with each other, for much of their history they have flourished together and syncretized to great degrees. These quite different pre-Communist religious contexts meant that similar policies were destined to function differently in their respective environments. Chinese policymakers, when looking to Moscow for models for everything from the arts to zoology, recognized this fact. Additionally, to whatever extent policy approaches were mirrored, the contextual difference meant that these policies evolved differently and were reacted to differently by their respective populations. All of this provides the necessary variation to observe how context and policy interact.

Following this introduction, the book begins in Chapter 1 with an investigation into the theological and philosophical roots of atheism and Marxist-Leninist thinking on religion. Tracing the social nature of religion from Schleiermacher and Feuerbach to Marx, Engels, and Lenin, I attempt to explain how the idea of religion as a social product evolved to the point of policies aimed at the forced conversion of believers to atheism. After all, Marx himself never advocated using force to stop people from believing in religion, but in the end this is precisely what regimes did in his name. Berger said many years ago that "whenever a society must motivate its members to kill or to risk their lives, thus consenting to being placed in extreme marginal situations, religious legitimations become important. Thus the 'official' exercise of violence, be it in war or in the administration of capital punishment, is almost invariably accompanied by religious symbolizations."[23] In both the Soviet Union and China, those legitimations and symbols were provided by Marxism-Mao Zedong Thought.

The book then continues with chapters on the suppression, survival, and revival of religion in Russia. Chapter 2 focuses primarily on the period of 1917 to the 1960s and 1970s in the Soviet Union, though it begins with a brief historical discussion to provide context for the reader unfamiliar with Russian history. Unlike many other studies, the position taken here is that the Soviets were unsure of how to deal with religion and kept trying different approaches to generate the desired result, that is, eradication of religious belief. I also argue that different leaders had their own ideas on how best to "evict God," and their personal views impacted policy choice and implementation. Attention is also devoted to the atheist propaganda programs that were carried out to speed up the process of secularization.

The discussion then turns from policies to people, focusing on the courageous stories of those who fought to live lives of faith under a regime that mocked and persecuted them. While it is certainly far beyond the scope of this study to survey all of the evidence available and to shed an entirely new light on the subject of the Soviet and Chinese repression of religion, the accounts presented here have been largely left out of the social science literature on the topic. I attempt to provide as comprehensive an account as possible, drawing upon extensive materials in both Russian and Chinese, first-hand accounts, interviews, and survey data. Chapter 3 continues the examination of the Russian case, focusing on the resistance movements and survival strategies by those that defied Soviet policies aimed at eliminating religion. Emphasis is on the Orthodox Church, the Evangelical-Baptists, and the Pentecostals. In addition to group-level analysis, personal detail is also provided by examining the lives of such significant religious figures as Fr Alexander Men', Pastor Georgy Vins, and Aida Skripnikova.

After having analyzed the suppression and survival of religion, the task turns to examining the revival of religion after the collapse of the Soviet Union. The return to primacy of Russian Orthodoxy in a society that attempted to wipe out religion for seven decades is certainly one of the most interesting stories in the politics of religion. The Orthodox are not alone, however, nor are they even the fastest growing religion in Russia. While the majority of people identify themselves as Orthodox, only a small number of those actually engage in any sort of religious life. In this chapter, I explore the nature of belief in post-atheist Russia, as well as survey the religious economy and examine the role the state policy of differential treatment for certain religions plays in it.

The topic then switches to the case of China. Chapter 5 mirrors the first Russia chapter, only now focusing on China's initial period of religious persecution, from 1949 to 1978. Not only do I explore the role of policy borrowing, that is, the way in which the Chinese borrowed policies from their Soviet mentors, but how they also innovated and adapted in the realm of religion policy. I argue that China's terrible history of opium addiction and the role of the West in the opium trade tainted significantly their understanding of what Marx's phrasing of religion as "the opium of the masses" implied about religion. I argue that this led the Chinese Communists to be much less worried about promoting scientific atheism and more concerned with simply dispelling religious belief. I also show how they were just as brutal in dealing with indigenous forms of belief (Taoism, Confucianism) as they were with foreign ones (Christianity, Islam), and just as effective in eliminating them.

Chapter 6 then examines the resistance movements and survival strategies of religious groups in China. The focus here is on Buddhists, Catholics, and Protestants, though certainly others suffered as well. I consider both the officially-recognized churches, members of the Three-Self Patriotic Movement, and underground groups, including the Christian House churches and the underground Catholic Church that has remained loyal to the Vatican. Again, as in Chapter 3, the personal stories of those who suffered for their faith play a critical role, including Xu Yun, Cardinal Kung, and Wang Mingdao.

The final substantive chapter explores the revival of religion in China, where now more Catholics attend church on Sunday than in Ireland. Beginning with the liberalization of religion policy in 1978 and the amendment to the PRC Constitution in 1982, the concept of "opium of the people" began to evolve. Whereas it had previously been tied in people's minds with China's experience with the Opium Wars and religious opium thus being viewed as a narcotic pushed by the West in order to exert control over China, a major shift occurs whereby religious opium becomes an anesthetic that can help relieve the suffering of people undergoing hard economic and social times. This chapter continues by analyzing growth patterns of religious belief and practice among Christianity, Islam, Buddhism, and Taoism, as well as the political and social consequences of such belief.

In his *Institutes of the Christian Religion*, John Calvin explored what he termed "the religious propensity of man"—that is the phenomenon of nearly universal faith of some sort. While his study was theological, and the world has changed greatly since the sixteenth century, this study shows that there is more than a kernel of truth to this idea. In the concluding chapter, I therefore attempt to draw together the findings set forth in the preceding chapters and reach some general conclusions regarding the efficacy of Communist atheist policies, the contemporary religious economies of each country, and even the religious nature of man. Not only do I attempt to contribute to the project of developing a comprehensive theory of desecularization, but I also argue for the continued relevance of the "old paradigm" of the sociology of religion, one in which the human experience and social reality retain primacy of place alongside models of religious markets and competition. I also suggest ways to expand the old paradigm so that it can more fully explain religious behavior in the world today, perhaps contributing to the development of a neo-Bergerian body of theory.

Now that this experiment is over and has clearly failed, it is the right time—perhaps the only time—to go back and try to understand this episode in human history and its implications for the social sciences and the study of religion more broadly. There is perhaps no better way to understand the relationship of mankind to God than by examining the persistence of religious belief under conditions of severe religious repression and persecution. Just as Durkheim studied aborigines to determine the elemental forms of religious life, here an examination of religious life under Communist repression and its aftermath may help us to unlock the key to man's religious nature.

Notes

1. Steve Bruce, *God Is Dead: Secularization in the West* (Malden, MA: Blackwell, 2007), and David Martin, *On Secularization: Towards a Revised General Theory* (Burlington, VT: Ashgate, 2006).
2. A very early exception is Pitirim Sorokin's book *The Basic Trends of Our Times* (New Haven: College and University Press Services, 1964), especially Chapter 4.
3. Discussion with the author, Oxford, UK, June 3, 2009.
4. Peter Berger, *The Sacred Canopy: Elements of a Sociological Theory of Religion* (Garden City, NY: Doubleday, 1967).
5. Jose Casanova, *Public Religions in the Modern World* (Chicago and London: The University of Chicago Press, 1994), p. 7.
6. Berger, *Sacred Canopy*, p. 22.
7. Ibid., p. 24.
8. Ibid.
9. Ibid., p. 29.
10. Peter Berger has said that he abandoned secularization theory around the same time, only he just took a different tack in his research, rather than writing a book breaking with this school of thought. He did so later on, however, in his "The Desecularization of the World: A Global Overview," in Peter L. Berger, ed., *The Desecularization of the World: Resurgent Religion and World Politics* (Grand Rapids, Mich: Wm. B. Eerdmans Publishing, 1999), pp. 1–18.

11. Andrew Greeley, *Unsecular Man: The Persistence of Religion* (New York: Schocken, 1972), p. 1.

12. Stephen Warner, "Work in Progress toward a New Paradigm for the Sociological Study of Religion in the United States," *American Journal of Sociology*, Vol. 98, No. 5 (March 1993): 1044–93.

13. Graeme Smith, *A Short History of Secularism* (London and New York: I.B. Tauris, 2008).

14. Peter Berger, Grace Davie, and Effie Fokas, *Religious America, Secular Europe* (London: Ashgate, 2009).

15. Though first articulated in his "Plan of the Scientific Operations Necessary for Reorganizing Society" (1822), the idea is more fully explored in his *Cours de Philosophie Positive*, translated and published by Harrict Martineau as *The Positive Philosophy of Auguste Comte* (London: George Bell & Sons, 1896).

16. Ludwig Feuerbach, *The Essence of Christianity* (New York: Harper & Brothers, 1957).

17. Discussion with the author, September 1, 2009.

18. Vyacheslav Karpov, "Desecularization: A Conceptual Framework," *Journal of Church & State*, Vol. 52, No. 2 (2010).

19. Christopher Marsh, *Unparalleled Reforms: China's Rise, Russia's Fall, and the Interdependence of Transition* (Lanham, MD: Rowman and Littlefield, 2006).

20. Paul Froese, *The Plot to Kill God: Findings from the Soviet Experiment in Secularization* (Berkeley: University of California Press, 2008), pp. 194–6.

21. Rensselaer W. Lee, "General Aspects of Chinese Communist Religious Policy, with Soviet Comparisons," *The China Quarterly*, No. 19 (July–September 1964).

22. "The Soviet Impact on China: Politics, Economy, Society, and Culture, 1949–1991," conference held at Columbia University, June 22–23, 2007.

23. Peter L. Berger, *The Sacred Canopy: Elements of a Sociological Theory of Religion* (New York: Anchor Books, 1990), p. 44.

CHAPTER ONE

The Theological Roots of Militant Atheism

Religion is the sigh of the oppressed creature, the heart of a heartless world, just as it is the spirit of a spiritless condition. It is the opium of the people.
—*Karl Marx*[1]

Throughout the Soviet period, a philosophical investigation of the works of Marx, Engels, and Lenin was the natural starting point to a work that sought to explain the origins of any Communist policy. Whether it be the Soviet legal system or rural grain production, it was to these philosophical roots that scholars first turned to glean insight. Indeed, Marxist philosophy is so dense and comprehensive that it does have implications for just about every aspect of society, from the family to international relations. The problem is that, when dealing specifically with the Marxist critique of religion, scholars have followed this line of thinking, taking Marx's *philosophical* critique of religion as their starting point. Religious belief is quite distinct from a philosophical viewpoint, however, meaning that almost all previous studies have avoided serious consideration of the theological roots of militant atheism.[2]

While it is with Hegel that one must begin to understand Marxist philosophy, one must take a detour through the thought of Schleiermacher, Strauss, and Feuerbach before coming to an understanding of Marx's and Engels's critique of religion.[3] And this reading of these theologians/anti-theologians must be built upon a foundation that takes the critique of religion seriously as an exercise in theology. Writing as they were in the nineteenth century, the lines separating religion from the fields of economics, philosophy, sociology, and political science were blurred at best, and more often simply nonexistent. This requires us to approach the subject from an interdisciplinary perspective, such as the method of *religionswissenschaft* of Troeltsch, a sort of precursor to our modern understanding of the social scientific study of religion.[4] Such a reading, which takes religious questions seriously, will generate a more accurate picture of the Marxist critique of religion.

For all of its merits, the best book on the subject of Marxist-Leninist atheistic policies falls short in this regard as well. Thrower's *Marxist-Leninist*

'Scientific Atheism' and the Study of Religion and Atheism in the USSR offers an excellent review of the philosophical roots of Marxism, from Hegel, Kant, and Feuerbach on up, and even draws upon selections from Marx's writings that were not even available at the time the Soviets and Chinese were drafting their religion policies.[5] While he does this to give the greatest insight possible into Marx's thinking, he makes a serious error in separating Marx's writings on religion from the study of religion itself. Any investigation of Communist religion policy must begin from a firm grounding in Marx's critique of religion, and must understand that Marx's conclusion that religion is the opium of the people is not *sui generis*, but rather has deep theological roots.

While quoting on the opening page of his book from Marx's *Contribution to a Critique of Hegel's Philosophy of Right* that "the criticism of religion is the premise of all criticism," Thrower fails to take Feuerbach, Engels, Marx, and others seriously as critics of religion (and simply fails to even consider two of the most important theologians of their time, Friedrich Schleiermacher and David Friedrich Strauss, whose work influenced Feuerbach and was mentioned specifically by Engels in relation to his loss of Christian faith). In fact, all of the major Marxist thinkers—from Marx and Engels to Lenin, Gorky, and Lunacharsky—dealt with religion as a central concern to their communist thought. To them, religion was a major reason why world revolution was not yet occurring, because the opium of religion was keeping people docile and numb to the true pain of their existence.

Another mistake in reading Marx is the conclusion that he was proposing a violent approach to dealing with religion, and that this was the only course available for Marxists to take toward religion. Many even read force and violence into tracts that simply were not there. Bockmuehl, for instance, paraphrases the Fourth and Eleventh of Marx's *Theses on Feuerbach* as reading, "before one can change the world, one must first do away with opium and begin to see things clearly. As Marx says, the destruction [*sic*] of religion is necessary, so that man will discard his illusions and regain his senses, stop revolving around God as his illusory sun and begin to," now quoting Marx directly, "revolve round himself and therefore round his true self."[6] But Marx actually said nothing in that quote about resorting to force or violence, he only said that "the *criticism* of religion disillusions man to make him think and act and shape his reality like a man who has been disillusioned and has come to reason, so that he will revolve round himself and therefore round his true self".[7]

It is not that scholars such as Thrower and Bockmuehl do not have an excellent grasp of the literature, it is simply that they interpret Marx, as have many of their predecessors and successors, as working from a narrowly philosophical perspective and relying upon the hindsight of the Soviet and Chinese Communist experiences. Viewing nineteenth-century philosophy through the prism of the twentieth century distorts the picture grossly, however, while limiting one's analysis to the confines of philosophy prevents the drawing of insight that might be gleaned from the disciplines of sociology and theology. As I will argue below, it is precisely these, and particularly the latter, which must be used to understand the Marxist-Leninist critique of religion.

The Cultured Despisers of Religion

In reference to the work of Hegel, Karl Marx is said to have commented that "there is no other road...to truth and freedom except the fiery brook" (in German, *feuerbach*), suggesting that the work of Hegel can only be properly understood through the corrective offered by Feuerbach.[8] And, of course, Marx's own work built upon that of Feuerbach. But Feuerbach himself did not write in a vacuum, and his ideas have roots in the theological tradition of Schleiermacher, Strauss, and Daub. Indeed, all ideas are contingent upon the ideas that preceded them, and the Marxist critique of religion is no exception.

In the case of all of those mentioned thus far, each had been strongly influenced by Immanuel Kant. Of particular significant in this regard was Kant's positing of the view that the idea of God was necessary for morals, but that God did not actually have to exist, thus removing the need for the transcendent. For Schleiermacher, however, the transcendent was the feeling of "absolute dependency" which man feels intuitively. To the young theologian Feuerbach, such ideas would lead to his concluding that man himself created God in man's image.

Before Feuerbach turned theology into anthropology, Schleiermacher attempted to save theology and reintroduce religion to a generation of the "sons of the Enlightenment" who not only considered religion a backward practice for the lower classes, but a relic of the past that would soon disappear. It was to this group, the "cultured despisers of religion," that Schleiermacher addressed his speeches in *On Religion* (1799). As Schleiermacher phrased it, "art and science have so fully taken possession" of the minds of these people, that "no room remains for the eternal and holy Being that lies beyond the world."[9] Schleiermacher understood this phenomenon as one in which the intellectual class had become so preoccupied with science, art, and letters, and the advances of modernity, that they had come to think of themselves as gods of their own universe. As he put it, having "made a universe for yourselves, you are above the need of thinking of the Universe that made you."[10]

As he describes it in *On Religion*, Schleiermacher had early in his life experienced a spiritual crisis in which he had to abandon the "sacred darkness" of his mother, who raised him in her piety, and as he "sifted" through the faith of his fathers as he cleansed thought and feeling from the rubbish of antiquity. Once "the God and immortality of [his] childhood vanished from [his] doubting eyes"[11] it was this piety that remained with him. This was not a Biblical faith, for as he put it, of "all this I praise, all that I feel to be the true work of religion, you would find little even in the sacred books."[12]

"Religion is the outcome neither of the fear of death, nor of the fear of God. It answers a deep need in man. It is neither a metaphysic, nor a morality, but above all and essentially an intuition and a feeling." He is careful to remind us that feeling alone is "not an emotion of piety because in it a single object as such affects us, but only in so far as in it and along with it, it affects us as revelation of God."[13]

God seems to have a place, therefore, in Schleiermacher's theology, though this is one of the reasons for sharp criticism against him. At times he often seems prepared to discard him, however, as when he states that "God and immortality…as they are found in such doctrines, are ideas,"[14] or when he argues that "belief in God, and in personal immortality, are not necessarily a part of religion; one can conceive of a religion without God, and it would be pure contemplation of the universe."[15] It is logical then for Schleiermacher to define religion as "the miracle of direct relationship with the infinite,"[16] but the reader is not entirely clear on the role of God in such an arrangement. He tries to clarify this point when he states, had "I not presupposed God and immortality I could not have said what I have said, for, only what is divine and immortal has room in which to speak of religion."[17]

Schleiermacher diminished (or even outright denied) the importance of the sacred from the canonical works of the Bible and sacralized man's relationship with his creator. He thus removed the study of religion from theology, though this was not his intention. Schleiermacher was suggesting a new type of theology, one that could survive and thrive in modern times, while the old, scriptural theology died an inevitable death.[18] To some, Schleiermacher was attempting to evade issues surrounding the authenticity of the Bible, the historicity of the Biblical narrative, etc., while to others he was rejecting such things as essential to faith, if not outright denying their veracity. Either way, he was attempting to modernize faith in a way he thought it could better survive in the face of modernity, perhaps the only way it could survive, and apparently the way it had survived for him as he "sifted through the faith of his fathers."

Schleiermacher's thought and writings sparked a debate that probably did more harm to religion than good. First, there were his fellow Christian theologians, many of whom labeled him a pantheist at best or an atheist at worst. Then were the atheists themselves, for he probably did more to support their position than to bring them back to a life of faith.

Feuerbach: The Anti-Theologian

The work of Friedrich Schleiermacher anticipated the work of Ludwig Feuerbach, provided a great impetus to it, and is even responsible for much of its structure. Schleiermacher's influence on Feuerbach is almost always overlooked, however, especially by philosophers and historians, who are perhaps not very well acquainted with Schleiermacher's thought and his influence far beyond theological circles.

Much like Schleiermacher, Feuerbach began as a theology student, entering the University of Heidelberg intent on pursuing a career in the church. It was there that he was introduced to Kant, Hegel, and the other great philosophers of the time. It was Karl Daub, Feuerbach's professor at Heidelberg, who introduced him to the work of Hegel. Feuerbach then transferred to the University of Berlin to study under Hegel directly, but in so doing he must have come into direct contact with Schleiermacher himself, who held a chair in theology there. Schleiermacher's *On Religion* was already the most famous contemporary work in theology at the time, and he almost certainly was busy writing his *Der Christliche Glaube nach den Grundsätzen der Evangelischen Kirche*, in which he identified religious feeling as the sense of absolute dependence on God,[19] during Feuerbach's period in residence at the university.

Feuerbach never embraced Schleiermacher's thought as his own, however, and he even drifted away from Hegel himself. He then abandoned the study of theology altogether, writing to a friend, "I can bring myself to study theology no more. I long to take nature to my heart, that nature before whose depth the faint-hearted theologian shrinks back." He eventually found a way out of his philosophical impasse through the "young Hegelians" and their focus on Hegel's dialectic. By abandoning Hegel's concept of system and focusing on the dialectic alone, the young Hegelians interpreted Hegel's "march of spirit through history" to mean that the existing culture and institutional forms of the West, particularly Christianity, would be superseded in subsequent phases of history.

Feuerbach's critique of Hegel's idealism is significant, for it opened the way for Feuerbach to establish a connection between philosophical idealism and religion. Feuerbach had become a materialist, and began to emphasize man's biological nature, arriving at the idea that man's thought was purely reflective. This was the decisive step in Feuerbach's rebellion against traditional religion, and where he set off to replace Christianity with a truer religion of humanity. Drawing upon his Hegelianism, Feuerbach turns God on his head to find man. The antithesis of divine and human is nothing more than an illusion, he concludes, nothing more than the antithesis between human nature and the human individual. Religion is thus man's earliest and mistaken form of self-knowledge, in which he contemplates his own nature as extrinsic to himself. Thus God is nothing else than man. He is, so to speak, the outward projection of man's inward nature.

This theme in Feuerbach was clearly derived from Hegel's speculative theology, in which the Creation remains a part of the Creator, while the Creator remains greater than the Creation. When Feuerbach presented his theory to Hegel, his professor, of course, did not respond positively to it. How could he? Feuerbach had, in his own words, turned theology into anthropology, which, despite what Hegel's own detractors were claiming about him, was far beyond anything he had intended.

Hegel's speculative theology was thus itself subjected to the dialectic, with Feuerbach determining that it was not the Creator that remains greater than the Creation, but the Creation is itself the Creator. As Feuerbach would express it, "The course of religious development consists more specifically in this, that man progressively appropriates to himself what he had attributed to God."[20] As Luchte puts it, "religious man is alienated man, for religious man, the true creator, makes that which is his own creation—God—into an authority over himself, thus throwing away his natural sovereignty and reducing himself thereby into a servile and miserable being."[21]

This is what opened the door for Feuerbach's theology as anthropology, because if that is what religion is, and it is not divine revelation and the sacred communion between God and man, then God is nothing more than our best ideas projected outward. And if this were true, Karl Barth argues, he would be right. Barth thus labels Feuerbach the "anti-theologian," and warns us where his and similar theologies can lead, that is, to anthropologies.[22] Barth, whose neo-orthodoxy was a direct response to the theological liberalism of Schleiermacher, Strauss, and others, also argues that Feuerbach is partly right for blaming the church and seeing religion as false. "The church will recover from the sting of Feuerbach's question only when her ethics is fundamentally separated from the worship of old and new hypostases and ideologies. Only then will men again accept the church's word that her God is not merely an illusion."[23] While Barth joins Feuerbach in rejecting religion as an institution of human creation, he does so only in order for man to find faith in the true God. To Feuerbach, however, man is God.

> "God, I have said, is the fulfiller, or the reality, of the human desires for happiness, perfection, and immortality. From this it may be inferred that to deprive man of God is to tear the heart out of his breast. But I contest the premises from which religion and theology deduce the necessity and existence of God, or of immortality, which is the same thing. I maintain that desires which are fulfilled only in the imagination, or from which the existence of an imaginary being is deduced, are imaginary desires, and not the real desires of the human heart; I maintain that the limitations which the religious imagination annuls in the idea of God or immortality, are necessary determinations of the human essence, which cannot be dissociated from it, and therefore no limitations at all, except precisely in man's imagination."[24]

We will see below how these ideas were instrumental in the formation of Marx's critique of religion, and how one can almost hear the words of Feuerbach when reading Marx's famous paragraph referring to religion as the opium of the people.

Fallen Engels

Most discussions of the Marxist critique of religion begin with Marx himself, but in fact the largest part of Marx and Engels's writing on religion was penned by Engels, not Marx. Though perhaps the most famous quote of the pair are Marx's, Engels was much more concerned with religion than was Marx. This may be due to the fact that Engels had been a more passionate believer than had Marx. In fact, it was a reading on Schleiermacher by Strauss that was very instrumental in Engels's loss of faith. While it was Schleiermacher and Strauss that started Engels on the road to atheism, it was his later encounter with the writings of Feuerbach that finished the job and helped him systematize his own thinking on religion. In fact, it took several years for this well-versed Christian to abandon the Protestant faith of his childhood entirely and embrace Feuerbachian atheism.

Engels was raised in a family well-known for its strong Calvinist faith. The region of Germany in which he grew up—Barmen in the Wuppertal region of Eastern Rhineland—has been called a place where pietism and Lutheran faith were held in high regard and where "puritanical Protestantism" was well-entrenched.[25] Indeed, in his *The Protestant Ethic and the Spirit of Capitalism*, Max Weber himself refers to the Calvinists of Wuppertal as having done "more than others" in promoting "the development of a spirit of capitalism."[26] Though the region is mainly Catholic, the Pietist grouping among its Protestants comprised a "minority within a minority," to which, given their Reformed Christian faith, the Engels family belonged. Despite this degree of "pluralism," the veracity of Protestant Christianity was a strongly-established taken-for-granted reality. Upon his confirmation into the Elberfeld Reformed Evangelical Church in 1837, Engels penned an early poem, in which he wrote:

> Lord Jesus Christ, God's only son,
> O step down from Thy heavenly throne
> And save my soul for me.
> Come down in all thy blessedness,
> Light of Thy Father's holiness,
> Grant that I may choose Thee.[27]

Clearly Engels was very strongly socialized into the Christian community in which he was raised. It was in this community that Engels was steeped in Christian doctrine, scripture, and faith throughout his childhood and young adult years. His break with Christianity would only come after a period of considerable mental turmoil.

The story of Engels' loss of faith can be seen in his letters of the late 1830s to Friedrich Graeber, his childhood friend with whom he stayed in close correspondence at the time. By 1838 he was wrestling with such issues as God as "caused" (*Grund*) and "non-caused" (*Ungrund*), mocking a fellow he knew for arguing that God was both, "because He has no cause or beginning of His existence, but is Himself the cause of His own and all other life."[28] Engels had no patience for such seemingly illogical theological debates. Nevertheless, he still held reverence for God and scripture.

The decisive break for Engels was the year 1839. In the spring of this year, he wrote the *Letters from Wuppertal*, his first major publication. It is here that we see Engels' ability to write a brilliant critique of the harsh conditions that were accompanying industrialization in the region of Wuppertal and Barmen, including water pollution from dyes and air pollution from coal fumes, all mixed together with harsh social conditions, including drunkenness, syphilis, and terrible poverty. It is here, too, that we see his first anti-religious statements, criticizing "strict" Christians,

who "treat their workers worst of all," cutting wages to prevent drunkenness yet offering bribes when expedient, particularly if it will help get the
right preacher elected. These "hypocritical Protestants" exhibited "a most
savage intolerance," and were "little short of the Papist spirit," the young
Engels wrote.

It is later in this same year, however, that we can pinpoint the crisis of
faith that led the young Protestant[29] to abandon the Christian faith of his
youth, and eventually his belief in God altogether. In particular it was the
writings of such radical theologians as Schleiermacher and David Friedrich
Strauss that led him away from his faith. While Strauss's *Das Leben Jesu*
(The Life of Jesus) may have been instrumental,[30] Engels himself specifically
mentions his *Charakteristiken und Kritiken*. "See that you get it, the essays
in it are all excellent," he wrote Graeber in December 1839, referring to the
essay on Schleiermacher and Daub as "a masterpiece."[31] It was Strauss that
led Engels along the "straight road to Hegelianism," he wrote. "I shall not
become such an inveterate Hegelian as Hinrichs and others," he continued,
"but I must nevertheless absorb important things from this colossal system.
The Hegelian idea of God has already become mine."

Engels's understanding of a "Hegelian idea of God" was one that abandoned Church doctrine, rejected any divine inspiration of scripture, and
viewed much of the Bible—in particular the Old Testament—as myth.[32] He
told his old friend that his debates on the Virgin birth of Christ and his
divine-nature and human nature were "sheer sophistry" forced on him "by
the attacks on the necessity of supernatural generation." Likewise, he chas-
tised Graeber for preaching to him on the doctrine of redemption, "Dear
Fritz, please drop this hyperorthodox and not even biblical nonsense." In
particular the idea of sin seemed to be a major problem for Engels. Not only
did he reject redemption, he wrestled with how God created a man who
could sin. The "story of Adam can only be a myth," he wrote, "since Adam
either had to be equal to God if he was created so free from sin, or had to sin
if he was created with otherwise human powers." It was not a long journey
from there to his total rejection of the Old Testament. "Old Testament history," he wrote, is "in the realm of mythology, and it will not be long before
this is generally acknowledged in the pulpits."

Though he was a man struggling with questions of faith for some time, it
was clear that there was no turning back for him. While Engels felt remorse
over how his old friend must have felt toward him ("Your orthodox psy-
chology must necessarily rank me among the most wicked, obdurate sin-
ners, especially as I am now wholly and utterly lost"), he was emboldened by
his new-found faith in atheism. "I have taken the oath to the flag of David

Friedrich Strauss and am a first-class mythic." Engels also saw religion as an edifice which had lost all footing. Strauss "has taken away the ground from under your views, the historical foundation is lost beyond recall, and the dogmatic foundation will go down after it." Engels thus became the first of the Young Hegelians to proclaim atheism openly. "All the basic principles of Christianity, and even of what has hitherto been called religion itself, have fallen before the inexorable criticism of reason."[33]

The German critique, not only of Strauss and Feuerbach but Arnold Ruge and Bruno Bauer as well, was decisive for both Engels and Marx in the development of their own thought. Once Feuerbach published his *Essence of Christianity,* both thinkers picked up that critique at the point where Feuerbach and the young Hegelians had left it. Agreeing in many respects with Feuerbach, they sharply criticized the Young Hegelians, particularly Marx's old friend Bruno Bauer. This is most clearly seen in *The Holy Family* (which is examined more thoroughly below), the initial collaboration between the pair, written in the summer of 1844. Together, the two would develop a body of thought uniquely their own and set it within a radically new understanding of the world and of man.

Engels's Critique of Feuerbach

Barth wrote that Feuerbach was "made by Engels into the philosopher of religion of scientific socialism."[34] This is true in two regards. First, Feuerbach's thought gave a much-needed sense of order and logic to Engels's own atheism, and would help him systematize his thinking on the subject. But secondly, Engels found Feuerbach a mere "philosopher" of religion, in so far as Engels critiqued Feuerbach for his naiveté in terms of his understanding of society and for not arriving at a purely materialist conception of history.

Engels's adoration and criticism of Feuerbach is most clearly and succinctly articulated in his *Ludwig Feuerbach and the End of Classical German Philosophy*, published after Marx's death and near the end of his own life. "Then came Feuerbach's *Essence of Christianity*," Engels writes:

> "With one blow it pulverized the contradiction, in that without circumlocutions it placed materialism on the throne again. Nature exists independently of all philosophy. It is the foundation upon which we human beings, ourselves products of nature, have grown up. Nothing exists outside nature and man, and the higher beings our religious fantasies have created are only the fantastic reflection of our own essence."

Engels exaggerates the effect of Feuerbach on his own turn to atheism (after all, he had clearly broken with Christianity in 1839, and Feuerbach's *Essence of Christianity* was not published until 1841). With its appearance, Engels wrote, "The spell was broken; the 'system' was exploded and cast aside, and the contradiction, shown to exist only in our imagination, was dissolved...we all became at once Feuerbachians."

If they became "Feuerbachians" in terms of his theology qua anthropology, Marx and Engels recognized the limitations to his thought and how it would be at odds with their own developments of Hegelianism. Here is where Feuerbach's thought runs counter to the distinctiveness of the Marx-Engels materialist conception of history. "If Feuerbach wishes to establish a true religion upon the basis of an essentially materialist conception of nature," Engels writes, "that is the same as regarding modern chemistry as true alchemy. If religion can exist without its god, alchemy can exist without its philosopher's stone."

While they were indebted to Feuerbach for "breaking the spell" and showing that "the Christian god is only a fantastic reflection, a mirror image, of man," they rejected the answer of establishing a true religion based on man (we will see this debate somewhat resurrected in the God-builders debate later in this chapter). This idea, however, soon found expression by Auguste Comte as the "true religion of Humanity," which ended up as a total failure. "The cult of abstract man, which formed the kernel of Feuerbach's new religion," Engels wrote, "had to be replaced by the science of real men and of their historical development."

Given the centrality of historical materialism to Marxism-Leninism (and Engels's unique contribution to it), Feuerbach's assertion that "the periods of humanity are distinguished only by religious changes" would have to be rejected, and was labeled "decidedly false" by Engels. Engels then points to Marx as the one responsible for its correction and further articulation. "This further development of Feuerbach's standpoint beyond Feuerbach was inaugurated by Marx in 1845 in *The Holy Family*." "The step which Feuerbach did not take," he wrote, "had nevertheless to be taken." This they did in *The Holy Family*.

While *The Holy Family* was the earliest corrective the pair offered to Feuerbach, it never articulated what the role of religion in a materialist conception of history would look like. It would take until the publication of his *Ludwig Feuerbach and the End of Classical German Philosophy* for him to write such an account, only now, with the passing of Marx, the job was left to him alone. With history already having been broken down into its various phases based upon the historical dialectic and the conflicts between social classes, it was only a matter of fleshing out the role of religion during the respective historical epochs.

For the origins of religion itself, Engels could still rely upon Feuerbach, only offering up that religion "arose in very primitive times from erroneous, primitive conceptions of men about their own nature and external nature surrounding them." During both the Roman and Medieval periods (or the plebian and feudal periods), Christianity stood as a religious counterpart of empire. "The need to complement the world empire by means of a world religion" was already in evidence during the early Roman period, in which pantheism flourished. But "a new world religion" would not come about in this fashion, "by imperial decree." In the Middle Ages, Christianity, which "had already quietly come into being, out of a mixture of generalized Oriental, particularly Jewish theology, and vulgarized Greek, particularly Stoic, philosophy…grew into the religious counterpart to [feudalism], with a corresponding feudal hierarchy."

As contradiction emerged within the feudal system, with the bourgeoisie beginning to thrive, "there developed, in opposition to feudal Catholicism, the Protestant heresy." Protestantism—particularly Calvinism, with its subservience to secular authority and attachment to the newly-emerging nation-state[35]—emerged as the counterpart to modern capitalism. It was the "Frenchman Calvin, with true French acuity," who "put the bourgeois character of the Reformation in the forefront, republicanized and democratized the church." While Calvinism "served as a banner for the republicans in Geneva, in Holland and in Scotland," and "freed Holland from Spain and from the German Empire," it was in England that the "second act of the bourgeois revolution" was to take place. "Here Calvinism justified itself as the true religious disguise of the interests of the bourgeoisie of that time, and on this account did not attain full recognition when the revolution ended in 1689 in a compromise between one part of the nobility and the bourgeoisie."

It was here that Christianity entered into its final stage, having become incapable of "serving any progressive class as the ideological garb of its aspiration," and increasingly became "the exclusive possession of the ruling classes." Not only was Christianity the sole possession of the ruling class, they now utilized "it as a mere means of government, to keep the lower classes within bounds." It made "little difference whether these gentlemen themselves believe in their respective religions or not." In this way, religion was not only false, but a further set of chains binding the proletariat as the slaves of the capitalist system.

Marx's Opium

The Marxist conception of religion has been perhaps most succinctly expressed by Bertrand Russell, who argued that religion "in any shape or form is regarded as a pernicious and deliberate falsehood, spread and encouraged by rulers and clerics in their own interests, since it is easier to exercise control over the ignorant." Such a statement is clearly reflective of Engels's contribution to Marxism, particularly as articulated in his *Ludwig Feuerbach and the End of Classical German Philosophy* quoted above. Indeed, it takes an even more sinister approach to religion than Engels offered, moving from it mattering little "whether these gentlemen themselves believe in their respective religions" to being a "deliberate falsehood." But the Marxist conception of religion, as articulated by those other than Marx and Engels themselves, is an elaboration and reemphasizing of their ideas, a set of ideas that they themselves expressed in much less insidious and militant ways. Between the pair, moreover, it was Engels who took chief responsibility for religious questions, particularly after *The Holy Family*. The two were essentially in agreement, but it was Engels who brought passion to the emancipation of man from myth.

From the outset of his professional career Marx was a convinced atheist. He was raised, however, in a home in which religion—even of the lowest-common denominator variety—was something of a taken-for-granted reality. Johnson argues persuasively that Marx is at his core a scholar in the Talmudic tradition (he is descended on both sides from rabbis and Talmudic scholars), with his writings expressing a strong millenarian component,[36] while Rothbard labels him a "millennial Communist."[37] The family of Heinrich Marx (né Hirschel ha-Levi Marx), converted to Lutheranism while Karl was still young, however, as a means of improving their standing in the community (at this time in Germany, several professions were off-limits to Jews). To Marx, religion was little more than a set of myths and moral teachings, and had little or nothing to do with the religious feelings that Schleiermacher considered the essence of religion.

There is some evidence that he had moments of religious fervor during his childhood, however, even if somewhat sentimental.[38] At 17, as a school assignment, Marx wrote an essay on "The Union of Believers with Christ," in which he spoke of the warmth of the bond that tied all Christians together that was the result of Christ's sacrifice on the cross. Whether or not these were genuine feelings or his first parody of religion, we will never know.[39] In a letter to his father in 1835, the young Marx exhibited something of an evangelical outlook toward his career, though mixed with doubts. In this letter to his father, Marx wondered if his perceived occupational call might be nothing more than a "self-deception," not a true call from the Deity (he consistently used the term Deity in this letter, in capitalized form, rather than God).[40] By the time Marx was a student at the University of Berlin, however, to where he had transferred from Bonn in 1836, whatever early religious beliefs he may have held were apparently abandoned.

It is in Marx's doctoral thesis, *On the Difference between the National Philosophy of Democritus and the Natural Philosophy of Epicurus*, written in 1841, that we see the earliest expression of Marx's hostility toward religion. As he wrote:

> Philosophy makes no secret of it. The confession of Prometheus: 'In simple words I hate the pack of gods' is its own confession, its own aphorism against all gods who do not acknowledge human self-consciousness as the highest divinity. It will have none other besides.[41]

Here we see already the influence of Feuerbach and his apotheosis of man. But Marx's chief concern was not religion, but economics, and religion—as with all other ancillary social phenomena—was determined by the superstructure. Marx therefore saw economic life and not religion as the chief form of human alienation. Religion itself was not the disease, it was a mere symptom. This meant that the liberation of man could not be achieved through simply eradicating religion, for such would be treating the symptom and not the disease. "The 'liberation' of 'man' is not advanced a single step by reducing philosophy, theology, substance and all the trash to 'self-consciousness' and by liberating 'man' from the domination of these phases," he wrote. "An atheism which takes itself as an end in itself is only the negation of religion" and could not succeed in transcending the religious level.[42]

By placing the struggle against religion within the wider context of the liberation of man, "Marx and Engels showed that their outlook was positive throughout."[43] They were also "far from ascribing to the struggle against religion the importance that it tended to assume in the writings of the 'left' Hegelians," Thrower adds, and here we can point out that the same is true for later Marxists and Marxist political regimes. Thrower's insights here are worth quoting at length, for he points out that Marx and Engels were,

> continually surprised, and on occasion not a little annoyed, by the persistent attacks on religion of Feuerbach and Bauer. As they saw it, religion

in general, and the Christian religion in particular, were already *in extremis*, and the attacks on religion by the 'left' Hegelians reminded them, as Marx said, of Sancho Panza in Cervantes' novel, *Don Quixote*, who mercilessly beat the harmless attendants at a funeral procession.[44]

Any attack on religion, therefore, was for Marx and Engels "as unnecessary as it was misplaced—unnecessary, because religion was a spent force; misplaced, because the real enemy was not religion but the society which produced religion."[45] But just as religion was a product of social and economic conditions, it was a pernicious product, as its effects were real. As he wrote, "religious distress is at the same time the expression of real distress and also a protest against real distress." And as with all negative social products, it would have to be eliminated in order to liberate man. "The struggle against religion," Marx then concluded, "is therefore indirectly the fight against the world of which religion is the spiritual aroma."

It is here that we arrive at Marx's most famous articulation of his concept of religion and one of his very few references to mention "abolishing" religion. Based upon his materialist conception of history, Marx determined that religion was a lie used by the capitalist class to facilitate their exploitation of the working class. As he wrote in 1844,

"Religion is the sigh of the oppressed creature, the heart of a heartless world, just as it is the spirit of a spiritless condition. It is the opium of the people. To abolish religion as the illusory happiness of the people is to demand their real happiness. The demand to give up illusions about the existing state of affairs is the demand to give up a state of affairs which needs illusions. The criticism of religion is therefore in embryo the criticism of the vale of tears, the halo of which is religion."[46]

This profound and poetic articulation of religion offers great insight into Marx's conception of religion. Of its many components, there is the oft-quoted term "opium," by which Marx meant nothing more than that religion acted as a sort of narcotic to ease the pain and suffering of the devastating economic and social conditions he and Engels saw all around them. Bockmuelh points out that Marx knew that others were also using the phrase at this time, including Goethe, who was referring to a preacher's sermons as a narcotic,[47] while Johnson decisively ascribes Marx's precise phraseology of "opium of the people" to Heinrich Heine, though without any attribution.[48]

As with getting an addict off narcotics, Marx understood that freeing people from religion would not be an easy task. As economic conditions determined reality for members of society, religion was yet another component of man's false consciousness, distracting him from his true goal, and thus a further barrier to worker's self-consciousness. But this also means that, once economic and social contradictions were corrected, as they inevitably would be, and worker exploitation came to an end and the utopia of communism came into existence, not only would the state wither away, but so, too, would religion. As Grace Davie has pointed out, Marx claimed "that religion would disappear of its own accord given the advent of the classless society: quite simply it would no longer be necessary."[49] Unfortunately, this enlightened view of Marxist thought, though quite logical, was not the one to be arrived at by Lenin and his successors.

As Marx would argue later in his life, not only did religion distract man from his true goal, it was often used as such by those whose interests are best served by such distraction, that is, the capitalist class. Deep insight into this idea is offered by Sergei Bulgakov's reading of Marx, who himself was a Marxist in his youth, but abandoned Marxism and not only returned to Christianity, but grew into one of the most important Orthodox theologians of the twentieth century. While Feuerbach looked to God and found man, Bulgakov looked to Marxism and found religion. In his *Karl Marks kak Religioznyi Tip*, Bulgakov provides one of the first arguments that Marxism is in fact a secular religion.[50] In a fascinating argument, Bulgakov demonstrates that the denial of the individual human spirit is in fact a denial of religion, which is, according to Bulgakov, Marx's chief aim in his works. Contrary to Marx, Bulgakov argues that religion is an aspect of the human condition, and that all human beings are religious in some way.[51] Religion serves as the highest values that a person holds, and thus no person is nonreligious. This is very similar to the idea of Paul Tillich that faith is a person's "ultimate concern."[52] Socialism thus becomes a secular faith, since the "ultimate concern" of the Marxists is to inaugurate a socialist utopia (read: heaven). In this sense, Bulgakov argues, Karl Marx becomes the spiritual father of socialism.[53]

Marx and the 'Fiery Brook'

The influence of Feuerbach on Marx was substantial, despite the lack of a close relationship between the two men and the points of intellectual disagreement between them. Feuerbachian motifs are also clear in many of Marx's articulations of religion. Where Feuerbach writes, "I maintain that desires which are fulfilled only in the imagination, or from which the existence of an imaginary being is deduced, are imaginary desires, and not the real desires of the human heart," Marx pens, to "abolish religion as the illusory happiness of the people is to demand their real happiness. The demand to give up illusions about the existing state of affairs is the demand to give up a state of affairs which needs illusions."[54] While both viewed religion as an expression of and a protest against real distress, and as a means by which those who are distressed can find consolation, for Marx all religion was a false consolation. The real struggle was not against established religion, therefore, but with the world which needs and produces religion. What Feuerbach saw as a perversion of true religion, Marx saw in existing socio-economic and political relations and conditions.

Marx's criticism of Feuerbach was that, although he had correctly identified that religion is an alienation of the human essence, he had failed to identify the real cause of this act of self-alienation, and hence the true source of religion. If one believes, as Feuerbach did, that man is compelled to create the fantasy world of religion due to the very nature of the society in which they live, he could conclude that it would be sufficient for man to then get rid of the illusions of religion and man would then come to a true understanding of himself and reality. For Marx, of course, this would be insufficient. As he wrote in the fourth of his *Theses on Feuerbach*:

> Feuerbach starts out from the fact of religious self-estrangement, of the duplication of the world into a religious, imaginary world and a real one. His work consists in resolving the religious world into its secular basis. He overlooks the fact that after completing his work, the chief thing remains to be done. For the fact that the secular basis lifts off from itself and establishes itself in the clouds as an independent realm can only be explained by the inner strife and intrinsic contradictoriness of this secular basis. The latter must itself, therefore, first be understood in its contradictoriness and then, by the removal of the contradiction, revolutionized in practice.[55]

While Feuerbach had resolved the essence of religion into the essence of man, to Marx he had failed to see that this essence itself is no abstraction inherent in isolated individuals, but rather that is the product of social relations. As Marx phrased it, Feuerbach "consequently does not see that the 'religious sentiment' is itself a social product, and that the abstract individual that he analyses belongs to a particular society."[56] Marx and Engels accepted Feuerbach's analysis of religion for the most part, but concluded that he could not explain why it was that man created such an illusory world. Their search for the ultimate source of religion became subsumed under what was, for them, the more important question of "humanity's self-inflicted impris-onment in its own world"—that is, the problem of alienation.[57]

Luchte, in his "Marx and the Sacred," argues that Marx's "initial *phil-osophical* criticism of religion is greatly influenced by Feuerbach, and the humanist criticism of absolutist idealism." Marx's "*step beyond*, towards a materialist criticism of religion," was thus "a specification and concret-ization" of the insights offered by Feuerbach. Luchte finds that "Marx's deconstruction of religion abides the implicit possibility of a retrieval of a non-alienated sense of the sacred as a concrete human activity and reflex-ivity via *praxis*." This is possible for Luchte because he defines religion as something distinct from the sacred. It is religion that "becomes ideology, as it is, for Marx, an alienated *product* of an alienated *existence*. As an alien-ated activity," Luchte maintains, "amidst a matrix of systematic alienation, its own self-interpretation is divorced from any immediate awareness of the conditions of its emergence and maintenance." In this way, it "cannot be anything but a mask that shrouds the concrete truth of human existence." As he explains,

> the traditional grand referent "God" and the theological infrastruc-ture articulated on the basis of such a conjecture persists as a lost work of art—ultimately of human origin, but forgotten *in its genealogy*. Marx writes that religion is the "self-consciousness and self-esteem of man who has either not yet found himself or has already lost himself again." That which was created by human beings has attained an abstract agency over humans in that the origin of the work of art has been erased.

Some have dismissed the influence of Feuerbach on Marx and his con-ception of religion. Zvi Rosen, for example, has argued that there are almost no Feuerbachian motifs in Marx's conception of religion, and even suggests that the reference to "the fiery brook" in *A Contribution* was added somehow by Feuerbach himself to boost sales.[58] Again, it is Luchte who sets the record straight. He gets directly to the point when he points out that, "regardless of whether or not Marx himself coined this famous phrase it is quite clear from a reading of the *Economic and Philosophical Manuscripts*, *Theses on Feuerbach*, and especially *The Holy Family*, that Feuerbach acts as an essen-tial catalyst in the transformation" of Marx's thought, from the "idealism of Hegel and toward the notion of a non-alienated humanity." It is here that "the role of Feuerbach as that of a 'fiery brook'…is clearly evident."[59]

Not only has Shlomo Avineri offered us a clear and groundbreaking investigation of the role Feuerbach played in the philosophical development of Marx, but a reading of *The Holy Family* leaves the reader with little doubt surrounding the question of Feuerbach's influence on Marx and the latter's agreement with the former on significant points regarding religion.[60] In Chapter IV of *The Holy Family*, Marx—and it was Marx who contributed this chapter to the co-authored volume—criticizes Edgar's analysis of Proudhon, and points out that it "belongs to Feuerbach, who was the first to describe philosophy as speculative and mystical empiricism and to prove it."[61] He adds that all Proudhon is doing is following Feuerbach (the "German critic"), who, "finding that the proofs of the existence of God are based on the idea of man, argue from that idea against the existence of God."

Later, Marx continues his critique, but this time taking issue directly with Bruno Bauer. Marx criticizes Bauer for arguing that self-consciousness lies at the basis of all religious ideas, and is "the creative principle of the gospels." "Why then," responds Marx, "were the consequences of the principle of self-consciousness more powerful than self-consciousness itself?" Marx responds that "the answer comes after the German fashion, self-consciousness is indeed the creative principle of religious ideas, but only as self-consciousness outside itself, in contradiction to itself, alienated and estranged."

Lenin's Vodka

According to his own admission, Lenin was already a convinced atheist by age 16, several years before he had even heard of Karl Marx or Friedrich Engels. His atheism, rather, originates from Russia's own radical tradition, and one can clearly perceive in his thinking on religion the influence of such proponents of political atheism as Belinsky, Herzen, Pisarev, and Bakunin.[62] Lenin had become acquainted at an early age with such ideas through his brother Alexander, who was involved in a failed plot to kill Tsar Alexander III. This was an atheism that sprang, not from Feuerbach and Marx, but from the rejection of the historic interdependence of the tsarist autocratic state and the Russian Orthodox Church. This influence is seen clearly in Lenin's earliest pronouncements on religion, which were intended to expose and unmask the Orthodox church as the servant of the State.[63] He perhaps nowhere says it more clearly than when he said "Christianity had lost its value on the day when Constantine promised it revenue and a place at court."[64] From this point on, the church was nothing more than an institution in the service of the ruling class.

The fact of the non-existence of God thus firmly rooted in Lenin, he approached atheism with enthusiasm, for he had great confidence in science's ability to destroy the myths that religion used as sustenance. This component of Lenin's thought was established even before his acquaintance with Marxism,[65] but it was the writings of Marx and Engels that articulated for the young Lenin the relationship of religion to class conflict and its deleterious effect on society. Likewise, once exposed to Feuerbach, Lenin then had a fuller explanation of how religion had emerged in history. With all of his questions answered, Lenin was thus completely uninterested in probing deeper into questions of religion, and throughout his life he expressed great impatience toward anyone who sought to reinvestigate the issue. As Thrower points out, therefore, it is not surprising that in what is his most important single work on religion, his "Socialism and Religion," he devotes only a single paragraph to religion's origin and social function. As he wrote in 1905:

> Religion is one of the forms of spiritual oppression which everywhere weighs down heavily upon the masses of the people, overburdened by their perpetual work for others, by want and isolation. Impotence of the exploited classes in their struggle against the exploiters just as inevitably gives rise to the belief in a better life after death as impotence of the savage in his battle with nature gives rise to belief in gods, devils, miracles and the like. Those who toil and live in want all their lives are taught by religion to be submissive and patient while here on earth, and to take comfort in the hope of a heavenly reward. But those who live by the labour of others are taught by religion to practice charity whilst on earth, thus offering them a very cheap way of justifying their existence as exploiters and selling them at a very modest price tickets to well-being in heaven. Religion is opium for the people. Religion is a sort of spiritual moonshine (*sivukha*)[66], in which the slaves of capital drown their human image, their demand for a life more or less worthy of man.[67]

Though a mere paragraph in length, this representation of the Marxist argument against religion encapsulates all that Marx and Engels had sought to impart, and does so in a much more succinct manner. The Feuerbachian understanding of the origins of religion are clearly expressed here, as is the anti-clericalism of Marxism in general. While repeating the "opium of the people" idea, Lenin goes a bit further and adds a Russian cultural translation, with religion now being equated with home-brewed vodka. Although some have argued that Lenin added practically nothing to the articulation of the Marxist idea of religion (is not brevity a worthy contribution?), Lenin also introduced an important distinction between the function of religion for the proletariat and the capitalists. The former are taught to be submissive and seek their kingdom in heaven, while the latter are taught to engage in charity as they live off the labor of the proletariat. Such a distinction is never clearly made by Marx or Engels, and is an important distinction for Marxism's conception of religion.

Prior to the Revolution of 1905, Lenin's interest in religion was limited, and only caught his attention if it could provide him with the opportunity to expand his political agitation. It was only after the first revolution that Lenin's opposition to religion and the church took a more intellectual turn. Between 1905 and the Revolution of 1917, Lenin set forth a distinctive Bolshevik position on religion. The primary contribution to this was his article, "The Attitude of the Workers' Party to Religion," written in May, 1909.[68] It is at this time that we begin to see in his thinking some clearly Feuerbachian motifs. While it has been noted that in his comments on Feuerbach's *Lectures on Religion*, Lenin ignored completely all reference to the origins of religion that did not fit squarely with the writings of Marx and Engels,[69] Lenin did draw upon Feuerbach's insights regarding the role of human ignorance and superstition regarding the origin and persistence of religion. As he expressed it,

> The deepest root of religion today is the socially down-trodden condition of the working masses and their apparently complete helplessness in the face of the blind forces of capitalism, which every day and every hour inflicts upon the ordinary working people the most horrible suffering and the most savage torment, a thousand times more severe than those inflicted by extraordinary events, such as wars, earthquakes, etc. 'Fear made the gods'. Fear of the blind force of capital—blind because it cannot be foreseen by the masses of the people—a force which at every step in the life of the proletarian and small proprietor threatens to inflict, and does inflict 'sudden', 'unexpected', 'accidental' ruin, destruction, pauperism, prostitution, death from starvation—such is the root of modern religion.[70]

Although certainly sympathetic to the conditions of the proletariat and understanding as to why they would find religion appealing, Lenin rejects the idea that ignorance alone is the cause of religion among the more backward segments of society. He also loses his sympathy when it comes to the issue of dealing with religion and believers. As he also writes in the same article,

> We must combat religion—that is the ABC of all materialism, and consequently of Marxism. But Marxism is not a materialism which has stopped

at the ABC. Marxism goes further and says: We must know how to combat religion; and in order to do so we must explain the source of faith and religion among the masses in a materialist way. The combating of religion cannot be confined to abstract ideological preaching... It must be linked up with the concrete practice of the class movement, which aims at eliminating the social roots of religion... It means that Social-Democracy's atheist propaganda must be subordinated to its basic task—the development of the class struggle of the exploited masses against the exploiters.[71]

Here we can see how Lenin had already begun to relate religion more directly to class struggle than had Marx or Engels. Although Marx had said in his Eleventh Thesis on Feuerbach, that "Philosophers have hitherto only interpreted the world in various ways; the point is to change it," Marx himself had not given any real guidance for how a post-revolutionary state should deal with religion, that is, leave it to die, or attempt to kill it. Lenin was taking a natural step, therefore, but a step that would set the stage for the most vicious attack on religion in the history of the world.

The God-builders

Voltaire famously once wrote, that "If God did not exist, it would be necessary to invent him."[72] Ironically, he penned this phrase in response to an atheist tract that he despised, and found extremely dangerous, for he believed that religion played an important role in maintaining social order. Once Nietzsche came onto the scene, declaring that "God is dead," the result was a lethal concoction, with some attempting to elevate man to the place of God.

As Lenin was articulating his ideas on religion, a movement was underway within the Russian Marxist movement to invest Marxism itself with a religious aura. The two most important figures in this movement were Anatoly Lunacharsky and Maxim Gorky. Together and with their supporters, they sought to counteract the religious renaissance that was underway in Russia after the Revolution of 1905 by offering their own variant, a "socialist religion" of man. While drawing heavily on "the religion of humanity" expounded by Comte and Feuerbach, Lunacharsky and Gorky, as well as the movement's two minor spokesmen, Bogdanov and Bazarov, were very strongly influenced by Nietzsche. In fact, as Kline points out, they may be properly called "Nietzschean Marxists."[73] Nietzsche had asserted in *Beyond Good and Evil* that religious feeling was growing stronger in Europe will simultaneously rejecting theism. This Nietzsche praised, but a quarter of a century later Lunacharsky and Gorky would embrace the idea and tried to develop a religion in its guise.

The religious renaissance which began in Russia around 1903, and which was well underway a decade later, was referred to as *bogoiska-telstvo*, or "God-seeking." Gorky coined the term *bogostroitel'stvo*, or "God-building," to deliberately contrast their movement with that of the God-seekers. While Lunacharsky had already begun writing on a "religion of mankind" as early as 1905, it was Gorky who in 1907 expressed its central themes in an article in a Paris journal. "Religious feeling, as I understand the term," he said, "should exist, develop, and make man perfect."[74] Here Gorky spoke of man's "imperious and proud desire to rival, in his creations, the generations of the past, and to create examples worthy of being followed by the generations of the future."[75] But it was Lunacharsky's response and elaboration of Gorky's words where we begin to see its elements take on flesh. Lunacharsky distinguished between the cosmic and humanistic/anthropological elements of the new faith. It is in the former that man senses "the joyous and proud . . . a harmonious bond uniting man and the universe," while the latter comprised a sense of an "active bond" that unites past, present, and future generations, "faith in [man's] own powers," and "hope for his victory."[76]

The broad outline to these ideas had been first sketched out by Lunacharsky as early as 1904, including the use of specific Promethean themes. "The faith of the active human being is a faith in future mankind," he wrote, and "his religion is an aggregate of those feelings and thoughts which make him a co-participant in the life of mankind, a link in the chain which stretches toward the superman (*sverkhchelovek*, Nietzsche's *Übermensch*), toward a beautiful and powerful creature, a perfected organism."[77] To Lunacharsky, religion was the expression of desires and feelings that socialism should take over and ennoble, not destroy.[78] This was a religion of immanence, without a god, the super-natural, or personal immortality, only feeding man's need for community, his yearning to transcend himself, and his unity with nature and all mankind. This is how Lunacharsky viewed religion, as a means by which man sought to reconcile himself with his own existence and to find a sense of meaning and purpose. If this were religion's primary function, then it would not disappear with death of the church, as men would still yearn for meaning in their lives. *Bogostroitelstvo* was thus a means for socialism to provide this.

Lenin and Plekhanov, however, had no place for such views. Lenin immediately condemned God-building as a dangerous flirtation with religious obscurantism.[79] As for Plekhanov, he considered religious doctrines as essentially superstitions, intellectual errors due to ignorance or the weight of tradition. As such, all religious attitudes and feelings would "wither away" along with religious doctrines. Lunacharski found this view false, narrow, "pre-Marxist," and even "pre-Feuerbachian,"[80] for it failed to grasp the essence of religion beneath the veil of theology and liturgy.

Gorky's role in promoting the religion of "God-building" was primarily literary and rhetorical, celebrating the "building of God" while leaving to others—namely Lunacharski—the theoretical elaboration of the doctrine. Since it was Gorky who gave the movement its sense of currency and notoriety, he became the focus of Lenin's attack on the movement. Lenin's attack was comprised of two long letters written in 1913, and thereafter appended by Soviet editors as "a kind of ideological vaccine" to all editions of Gorky's *A Confession*. Lenin had very few philosophical or theoretical arguments against "God-building," but as Kline argues, he made it clear from the start that he detested it...chiefly because it was much more difficult to discredit than the plainer "old-time religions."[81] As Lenin phrased it, "The Catholic priest who seduces young girls (of whom I just now happened to read in a German newspaper) is far less dangerous...than a priest without a frock, a priest without a coarse religion, a democratic priest with ideas, who preaches the building and creating of god (*sozidaniye i sotvoreniye bozhenki*)."[82]

In his refutation against "God-building," Lenin denied that there is any essential difference between the theistic religion of the "God-seekers" and the "purified" humanistic religion of the "God-builders." His arguments centered around three points. The first was man's worship of mankind is Philistine and narcissistic, nothing more. Secondly, that Gorky's "sugar-coating" or "gilding" of the idea of God is a gilding of the chains the ruling classes have fastened upon the "ignorant workers and peasants." As Lenin stated, at this stage in history, "every advocacy or justification of the idea of god, even the most subtle, the best-intentioned, is a justification of reaction." Finally, Lenin argued that religious feelings do not, as Gorky was claiming, strengthen social solidarity or reinforce the cohesiveness of the collective. "The idea of god has always deadened and dulled 'social feelings'...and has always been an idea of slavery (the worst, hopeless kind of slavery). The idea of god has never 'bound the individual to society,' but has always bound the oppressed classes by a belief in the divinity of the oppressors."[83]

Kline argues that although Lenin's refutation of the position of the "God-builders" was clumsy and primitive, "he seems dimly to have grasped a pertinent truth," namely, that the utopianism and romanticism of both Gorky and Lunacharsky would be difficult to reconcile with hard-headed social engineering." We must also concede that Lenin was at least a consistent materialist throughout, and believing religion was false, was himself unwilling to lie to the people. Gorky became embittered (pun intended) by the experience, but Lunacharsky himself quickly dropped his advocacy of the movement and focused his attention on the revolution. We will see that once the revolution is over, however, and he becomes commissar of education, the issue will raise its head again, this time without a Lenin to refute it.

Dangerous Thoughts: Atheism from Theory to Praxis

Throughout the nineteenth century, speculating about atheism was simply a theoretical endeavor. With no regime in power intent on promoting policies in line with atheist theorizing, atheism was little more than dangerous thoughts with a limited audience. This rejection of religion, as we have seen, goes back to Hegel and his rejection of transcendence, focusing instead upon immanence. The idea that there is no transcendent principle or external cause to the world opened up a Pandora's box, and led to the idea that the process of life is contained in life itself. This line of thought evolved in the minds and writings of Schleiermacher and Daub, and their student Strauss. But Feuerbach traveled a different path, one that was much more dangerous, and beyond rejecting the historicity of Jesus and the supernatural elements of scripture, placed man at the center of religion rather than God. It is this path, that of the "fiery brook," that came to influence the most virulent atheist of the Marx-Engels team—that is, Engels, the lapsed Calvinist.

Theologies of immanence and theories of atheism suddenly became significant forces in history as Communist movements readied themselves to take power in capitals around the world. It would be these regimes that would attempt to engineer societies in line with historical materialism, dialectical materialism, and scientific atheism. The application of Marxist thinking on religion was henceforth not simply an academic pursuit, but as Communist regimes sought to build societies in line with such thinking it became a human endeavor with real-life consequences. In the hands of the Soviet and Chinese Communist regimes, those consequences were lethal. The roots of militant atheism, therefore, rest not so much in the theologies of Schleiermacher or Strauss or the theoretical expositions of Marx and Engels, but in the political atheism of Lenin, rooted as it is in the Russian radical tradition. It is this branch of Marxism, that of Marxism-Leninism, that will transcend theory and become praxis once the Bolsheviks seize control of the reins of power in October 1917.

Notes

1. Karl Marx, *Collected Works III*, p. 176.
2. An important exception is Francis Nigel Lee, *Communist Eschatology: A Christian Philosophical Analysis of the Post-Capitalistic Views of Marx, Engels and Lenin* (Nutley, NJ: Craig Press, 1974). See especially Chapter XXXIII, "Critique of Communist Eschatology of Religion," pp. 807–21.
3. The use of the possessive of both names here is intentional, for both Marx and Engels each had their own distinct—though largely compatible—critique of religion. I am currently exploring this further in a work on Engels's contribution to the Marxist (not to be confused with Marx's) critique of religion.
4. Ernst Troeltsch, *Religion in History* (Minneapolis: Fortress Press, 1997).
5. James Thrower, *Marxist-Leninist 'Scientific Atheism' and the Study of Religion and Atheism in the USSR* (Berlin: Mouton, 1983).
6. Klaus Bockmuehl, *The Challenge of Marxism: A Christian Response* (Leicester: Inter-Varsity Press, 1980), p. 58.
7. Karl Marx, *Collected Works* III, p. 176.
8. Rosen suggests that Marx never even wrote this phrase, and that Feuerbach himself somehow added it as a way to promote sales of his own book. See Zvi Rosen, *Bruno Bauer and Karl Marx* (Martinus-Nijhoff, 1977), p. 148. See discussion below for further examination of the issue of Feuerbach's influence on Marx.
9. Friedrich Schleiermacher, *On Religion: Speeches to its Cultured Despisers* (New York: Harper and Brothers, 1958), p. 1.
10. Ibid., p. 2.
11. Ibid., p. 9.
12. Ibid.
13. Ibid., p. 93.
14. Ibid.
15. Quoted in Elie Kedourie, *Nationalism* (Praeger, 1961), p. 26.
16. Ibid.
17. Schleiermacher, *On Religion*, pp. 92–3.
18. The author thanks Peter Berger for his help in clarifying these points in Schleiermacher's thought.
19. For an excellent critique of the common practice of referring to Schleiermacher's understanding of religious feeling as "a feeling of absolute dependence" (*ein Gefühl schlechthinniger Abhängigkeit*) rather than "an absolute feeling of dependence" (*ein schlechthinniges Abhängigkeitsgefühl (bewußtsein)*, see Georg Behrens, "Feeling of Absolute

Dependence or Absolute Feeling of Dependence (What Schleiermacher Really Said and Why it Matters), *Religious Studies*, Vol. 34 (1998), pp. 471–81.

20. Ludwig Feuerbach, *The Essence of Christianity* (New York: Harper & Brothers, 1957), p. 31. Translation used here, however, is from Marxist Internet Archive.

21. James Luchte, "Marx and the Sacred," *Journal of Church & State*, Vol. 51, 3 (2009).

22. Karl Barth, "Introductory Essay," in Feuerbach, *The Essence of Christianity*.

23. Ibid., xxvii.

24. Ludwig Feuerbach, "Lecture XXX: Atheism Alone a Positive View," *Lectures on the Essence of Religion* (Harper & Row Publishers, 1851). Marxist Internet Archive.

25. Terrell Carver, *Engels: A Very Short Introduction* (Oxford University Press, 2003).

26. Max Weber, *The Protestant Ethic and the Spirit of Capitalism* (London: Routledge, 1992 [1930], p. 11).

27. Quoted from Tristram Hunt, *Marx's General: The Revolutionary Life of Friedrich Engels* (New York: Metropolitan Books, 2009), p. 16.

28. Friedrich Engels, "To Friedrich and Wilhelm Graeber in Barmen," September 18, 1838. *Marx-Engels Collected Works*, Vol. 2.

29. Thrower refers to him as a "Fundamentalist," as does Carver (Loc. 102), but this is an anachronism, given that the concept was not developed until the early twentieth century. Moreover, they both consistently refer to him as an "Evangelical," which is an incorrect translation of the German word *evangelisch*, which simply means "Protestant," and is not synonymous with the English word "Evangelical" in the American sense.

30. Carver cautiously states that Engels "evidently perused such rationalist works as David Friedrich Strauss's *Life of Jesus*" (p. 5), but does not say so definitively, nor mention how he determined this. I agree this seems highly likely, but rely here upon Engels' own words from his correspondence with Friedrich Graeber.

31. Friedrich Engels, "To Friedrich Graeber," December 9, 1839. *Marx-Engels Collected Works*, Vol. 2, p. 487.

32. Friedrich Engels, "To Friedrich Graeber," October 29, 1839. *Marx-Engels Collected Works*, Vol. 2, p. 476.

33. Cited in Carver, p. 9.

34. Barth, p. xxvii.

35. I am referring here particularly to Calvin's *Institutes of the Christian Religion*, "On Secular Authority," and the subsequent development of

Calvinism in distinct political entities, such as Geneva, Scotland, and the Netherlands.

36. Paul Johnson, *Intellectuals* (New York: Harper and Row, 1988), pp. 52–5.

37. Murray Rothbard, "Karl Marx as Religious Eschatologist," *Mises Daily*, October 29, 2009. Available at: http://mises.org/story/3769

38. Thrower, p. 8.

39. Edward Hulmes, "Karl Marx's Attitude toward Religion," in *The Oxford Companion to the Bible*, Bruce Metzger and Michael Coogan, eds. (New York: Oxford University Press, 1993), p. 497.

40. Karl Marx, "Letter to his Father," Written between August 10 and 16, 1835. *Marx-Engels Collected Works*, Vol. 1.

41. *Marx-Engels Collected Works*, Vol. 1, p. 30.

42. *Marx-Engels Collected Works*, Vol. 5, p. 38.

43. Thrower, p. 19.

44. Ibid.

45. Ibid., p. 20.

46. Karl Marx and Friedrich Engels, *Collected Works* (London: Lawrence & Wishart, 1975), p. 38.

47. Bockmuelh, p. 57.

48. Johnson, p. 56.

49. Grace Davie, *The Sociology of Religion* (Sage, 2007), p. 27.

50. Sergei Bulgakov, *Karl Marks kak religioznyi tip* (St. Petersburg, 1907).

51. Daniel Payne and Christopher Marsh, "Sergei Bulgakov's 'Sophic' Economy: An Eastern Orthodox Perspective on Christian Economics," *Faith & Economics* 53 (Spring 2009), 40.

52. Paul Tillich, *Dynamics of Faith* (New York: Harper and Brothers Publishers, 1957), pp. 1–2. Paul Valliere notes this similarity as well: "On Tillich's view modern secular ideologies cannot simply be unmasked and dismissed, as traditionalist critics might be tempted to suppose; they must be taken seriously as *faiths*, encountered in a critical dialogue about faith." Paul Valliere, *Modern Russian Theology: Bukharev, Soloviev, Bulgakov: Orthodox Theology in a New Key* (Grand Rapids, MI: Wm. B. Eerdmans, 2000), p. 236.

53. Bulgakov, *Karl Marks kak religioznyi tip*, pp. 41–3.

54. Feuerbach, *Lectures on the Essence of Religion*; *Marx-Engels Collected Works*, Vol. 5, p. 38.

55. *Marx-Engels Collected Works*, Vol. 5, p. 7.

56. *Marx-Engels Collected Works*, Vol. 5, p. 8.

57. Thrower.

58. Rosen, 1977.

59. Luchte, fn. 11, p. 421.
60. The author wishes to thank Prof. Luchte for pointing him to the work of Avineri as well as *The Holy Family* as a work replete with references to Feuerbach and obvious Feuerbachian motifs.
61. Karl Marx and Friedrich Engels, *The Holy Family*, Chapter IV.
62. Bohdan Bocuirkiw, "Lenin and Religion, in Leonard Shapiro and Peter Reddaway, *Lenin: The Man, the Theorist, the Leader* (London: Paul Mall Press, 1967), p. 109.
63. Thrower, p. 10.
64. *Lenin's Collected Works*, Vol. 21, p. 353.
65. Thrower, fn. 9.
66. The word *sivukha* is often translated as "booze" or even "gin," in an attempt to make it more colloquial. I have corrected the translation here, since he is clearly referring to a home-distilled form of vodka, which was the meaning of the term at that time. Michael Bourdeaux also suggested the term "rotgut," which also illustrates the strength of the drink quite well.
67. *Lenin's Collected Works,* Vol. 10, pp. 83–4.
68. V. I. Lenin, "The Attitude of the Workers' Party to Religion," *Proletarii,* May, 1909.
69. Delos B. McKown, (1975), pp. 95–103.
70. *Lenin's Collected Works,* Vol. 15, pp. 405–6.
71. Ibid.
72. Voltaire, "Epistle to the Author of the Book, *The Three Impostors.*"
73. Kline, *Religious and Anti-Religious Thought in Russia* (Chicago: University of Chicago Press, 1968), p. 106.
74. Maxim Gorky, *Sobranie Sochenenie v 18 Tomakh. Tom 1* (Moscow: 1963), 109–14.
75. Ibid.
76. Kline, p. 111.
77. Kline, p. 119, fn. 29.
78. Thrower, p. 10.
79. Cf. Lenin's correspondence with Gorky; V.I. Lenin, *Religion* (London: Lawrence & Wishart, N.D.) pp. 49–54.
80. Kline.
81. Ibid.
82. Lenin, "Letter to A. M. Gorky," in *Religion*, p. 50.
83. Ibid., p. 47.

CHAPTER TWO

Evicting God: Forced Secularization in the Soviet Union

"Religion is the opium of the people"—this dictum by Marx is the corner-stone of the whole Marxist outlook on religion. Marxism has always regarded all modern religions and churches, and each and every religious organization, as instruments of bourgeois reaction that serve to defend exploitation and to befuddle the working class.

—V. I. Lenin

Following their seizure of control, the Bolsheviks embarked upon the ambitious quest to eradicate religion from their new socialist paradise. Rather than waiting for the forces of modernization to do the job for them, as those theorists discussed in the preceding chapter had predicted, the Bolsheviks launched a policy of forced secularization. As early as 1918 they promulgated a decree "On the Separation of the Church and the State and the Schools from the Church," and then immediately set about nationalizing church lands and confiscating church property. Soon thousands of priests, monks, and nuns would be rounded up and sent off to the Gulag, with the methods used making it seem as though they were taking Diderot's call that "men will never be free until the last king is strangled with the entrails of the last priest" quite literally.[1] Thus was launched the most intense attack on religious belief the modern world has ever seen.

Just as Prince Vladimir faced tremendous opposition to the elimination of paganism and the promotion of Orthodoxy a thousand years earlier, the tails had turned and now it was the Bolsheviks who were to face resistance to their Godless communism. Simply attacking the church proved insufficient to eradicate the masses' religious beliefs, however, so the Communists turned to atheist propaganda, attempting to both convert believers to atheism and inculcate Soviet citizens into atheism from their youth. Although it would evolve through several different phases, some less intense than others, the suppression of religion in the Soviet Union remained a constant state and party policy until Gorbachev's *perestroika* reform program, finally changing course in its second year of implementation.

This chapter opens by placing the phenomenon of Russian church-state relations in its proper historical and cultural context by beginning the story with the arrival of Christianity in medieval Russia and the role of religion in tsarist Russia, including the repression of religion by the government. It then traces the development of Soviet religion policy and follows its evolution through its various phases. As we will see in Chapter 3 concerning China, the repression of religion was nothing new in either country, having deep historical precedents. What was new was the attempt to totally eradicate religion, rather than simply control it or suppress certain sects. This attempt to evict God from both the public square and the private mind would ultimately prove a failure in these societies with millennia-old religious traditions, but a failure not without several significant successes.

Religion and the State in the Russian Empire

The Slavs that inhabited the area that we would today call the central Russian plain practiced a form of paganism similar to that of other peoples in the vicinity. This included a pantheon of gods, with Perun being the preeminent god to many. It is the Slavic god of love, however, Kupalo, who continues to be celebrated annually with the holiday of *den' Ivana Kupala*. While it is quite common for the story of Christianity in the region to begin with the "Baptism of *Rus'*" in 988, when Prince Vladimir accepted the Orthodox faith and received baptism, historical evidence is clear that Christianity already had a presence in the region long before this, probably for more than 150 years. We cannot be certain of the accuracy of the legend, discussed in *The Tale of Bygone Years* (*Povest' Vremennykh Let*), that records that the Apostle Andrew visited what would become the city of Kiev and erected a cross along the slopes of the river Dnieper (where today stands St. Andrew's Church, built in the eighteenth century), but such a story is well-known among the people and provides a direct link between Russia and the Apostolic Fathers. We need not concern ourselves with the historical evidence concerning this story, for as Greeley so accurately tells us, when it comes to religion myth trumps scientific history: "He who thinks that his work is done when he has established that myths are historically inaccurate according to the canons of modern scientific history simply fails to understand what religion is all about."[2]

What we do know is that Christianity was fairly well established by the ninth century. Patriarch of Constantinople, Photius, sent disciples of Cyril and Methodius to the region to evangelize, and in an encyclical of 867 he announced that there were enthusiastic converts among the *Rus'*. Other evidence documents that churches were already in existence and Slavic translations of the Gospels were in circulation by this time as well. The origins of Christianity become quite clear once Prince Vladimir's grandmother converted to Christianity in the early tenth century, followed by Vladimir's brother.

The Baptism of Rus'

For the purposes of understanding the deep roots of Christianity in the region, specific dates are not so important. What is crucial is an understanding of what this history means. In the case of both modern Russia and Ukraine, as well as of tsarist Russia, the "baptism of *Rus'*" was just that—the baptism of an entire people. The first clue to this understanding is linguistic. While translated as "baptism," which comes from the Greek *baptizo* (to immerse), in Russian the actual word used is *kreshchenie*. Rather than connoting an immersion in water, such as the word baptism implies, *kreshchenie* is related to the word *krest* (cross), with the verb for *kreshchenie* being *krestit'* (to Christen).[3] *Kreshchenie* is thus closer to the English word "Christening," with linguistic connections also to the words *Khristianstvo* (Christianity) and *Khristos* (Christ). Unlike baptism, which since it refers to an immersion, necessarily connotes a ritual usually carried out by an individual or small group, it is difficult for the Western mind to conceive of a baptism as applying to an entire people, while using the term Christening perhaps alleviates this problem.

Durkheim's understanding of religion and ritual lends further insight into how this event has come to be understood by the Russian people. As he states, religious beliefs and rites "are always common to a determined group, which makes professions of adhering to them... *They are not merely received individually by all members of this group; they are something belonging to the group, and they make its unity*" (emphasis added).[4] This statement echoes closely the sentiments of the great Russian Orthodox theologian and historian, Georges Florovsky, who argued that "to be a Christian meant just to belong to the community. Nobody could be a Christian by himself, as an isolated individual, but only together with 'the brethren,' in togetherness with them."[5] This communal dimension to faith, in contradistinction to Protestantism and "personal religious preference," is at the heart of Orthodox understandings of faith and the religious life, and colors the Russian religious experience.

Additionally, there is the shared historical memory of the events of 988 themselves. Following Prince Vladimir's conversion, he not only had his 12 sons and many *boyars* (noblemen) follow him, he also organized mass baptisms in the river Dnieper. In this way, the baptism of *Rus'* was a mass event, and once depicted in artwork (the scene became a very popular one), it thus entered the collective imagination and minds of the people from them on. As we will see in Chapter 6, the date of these events will have great significance, as Gorbachev's liberalization policies were put to the test as Christians sought greater religious liberties in connection with the millennial celebration of the baptism of *Rus'*.

Unlike in medieval Europe, in today's world we often think of religion as a personal preference. As Berger articulated in *The Sacred Canopy*, however, this is a phenomenon unique to modernity. In earlier times, such as those discussed here, religion was something that was taken for granted. Such apparently was the case with paganism in *Rus'*, for once he converted, Prince Vladimir faced strong opposition to Christianity, in some cases lasting centuries. Resistance persisted despite the fact that both the sword and fire were used against those refusing conversion. There was no religious preference for anyone other than the prince, who was acting on behalf of the society he ruled. In this sense, Vladimir's conversion and the resulting Christianization of *Rus'* is a very early expression of *cuius regio, eius religio*.

The culminating event in Russian history regarding Orthodox Christianity was the ascension to autocephaly of the Russian Church in 1448 (a mere 5 years before the fall of Constantinople in 1453), with Metropolitan Jonas given the title of Metropolitan of Moscow and All *Rus'*. Then, in 1589, Metropolitan Job of Moscow was raised to the position of patriarch and received the fifth rank in honor after the patriarchs of Constantinople, Alexandria, Antioch, and Jerusalem. Moscow had rather swiftly gone from a pagan land ripe for mission to the "Third Rome," the capital of the Orthodox World. This was a natural progression, for the Russian tsar was now the sole Orthodox ruler, and saw himself as the true heir of the Byzantine emperors.[6]

Although it certainly took some time, Vladimir and his successors were able to establish Orthodox Christianity as a taken-for-granted reality. This was achieved not only through forced conversions, but also by suppressing paganism and heresy and lending state support to Orthodoxy. Over a millennium this taken-for-grantedness became so firmly established that, on the eve of the twentieth century, Metropolitan Ioann of St. Petersburg was noted as saying, "if Russia is not your mother, God cannot be your father."[7]

Not only had Orthodoxy become a taken-for-granted reality, its synthesis with Russian identity was so complete that the latter had attained the former's salvific efficacy.

The End of Symphonia

In order to provide context for the rest of this chapter and to illuminate the Soviet experience with religion, one need not conduct a comprehensive review of Russian ecclesiastical and theological history. Great volumes have been devoted to every major issue therein, along with many excellent survey works on the entire period.[8] Certain historical events loom so large in the public consciousness, however, that they are necessary for a proper understanding of this context. Certainly one such contextual factor is the link between Orthodox Christianity and national identity mentioned above. For much of the tsarist period, the two were so closely intertwined that it was difficult to determine where one began and the other ended. This system worked rather well for centuries based on the longstanding tradition of *symphonia*, or "harmony" in relations between church and state. According to this ideal, the tsar ruled over the secular realm, whereas the church and its leadership ruled over otherworldly matters, both exercising their control in the name of God. This *symphonia* was changed under Peter the Great in 1721, however, when he eliminated the institution of the Patriarch of Moscow and put the church under the control of the state.

The subordination of the Russian Orthodox Church to the tsarist state is one of the most significant events in the history of Russian church-state relations, second only to the arrival of Christianity itself. As part of his Westernization program, Peter the Great revamped Russia's governing institutions, allowing the representative institutions of the zemskii sobor and duma to fall into disuse and establishing a Western-style parliament, the Governing Senate, in its place. Peter created the Governing Senate in 1711 as the highest agency of the state, and gave it the responsibility of administering the affairs of state while the emperor was away and engaged in military endeavors.[9] Besides the senate, there was a procurator general, who acted as an intermediary between the senate and the tsar, since the latter rarely participated in the senate's meetings. Instead, the senate communicated with the tsar by issuing reports and orders through the procurator general, who thus performed a role not altogether different from that of a prime minister at that time.[10]

When it came to his reforms of the church, however, as Basil argues, it was more than Peter's "West European imagination" that inspired his actions. Peter's "querulous experiences with the church early in his reign" also served as a major inspiration for his actions.[11] Whatever combination of factors motivated Peter, however, he clearly saw the Russian Orthodox Church as a vestige of the past and a competitor for supreme power in Russia, and he moved quickly in his reign to bring the church under his control. His first move in that direction was to delay the election of a new Primate of the Church after the death of Patriarch Adrian in 1700. After nearly 20 years without a patriarch, Peter finally abolished the position of Patriarch altogether in 1721 with the promulgation of the *Spiritual Regulation*, which established the Most Holy Governing Synod (hereafter, the Synod). Modeled after the state-controlled synods of the Lutheran church in Sweden and Prussia, this institution allowed the state to closely control the church, and left Peter in the supreme position of power of both the church and the state, thus doing away with the traditional model of *symphonia*.

The next year a supplement to the edict was enacted which, as Basil further observes, ensured that "a captive Orthodox priesthood was obliged to list loyal service to the state in first place among its duties."[12] The new edict also created the post of higher-procurator (*uber-prokurator*) of the Synod, a post to be held by an agent of the tsar's government. By the first half of the nineteenth century, this lay official would obtain ministerial rank and exercise effective control over the church's administration until 1917. This control was facilitated by the subservience of most of the higher clergy, and was especially marked during the procuratorship of Konstantin Pobedonotsev (1880–1905).

Despite the arguments of some to the contrary, it was not the tsar's intention to eliminate all vestiges of the church's power. In fact, the "capture of the church even brought to the tsar fresh obligations to support Orthodoxy, often in ways dictated by bishops rather than the ministers of state."[13] With Orthodoxy now so firmly established as the state church, the government was actually obliged to propagate and enforce Orthodox canons and dogma throughout the country—including observance of Sunday church services—a fact which led to growing intolerance toward non-Orthodox in the realm, a group whose number had swelled during Peter's military expansions.

The many non-Orthodox citizens of the Russian Empire were not the only ones unhappy with the Petrine synodal system. By 1905 discontent was emanating from all quarters, each with their own unique set of complaints, but all in agreement that the system was in need of reform.[14] Positions ranged from those who wanted to retain some role for the tsar, only expanding the realm of religious toleration, all the way to some who called for nothing short of complete separation of church and state. In his excellent account of church and state in late Imperial Russia, Basil shows that all evidence "indicates that the weight of opinion, divided and caustic though it was, searched for a moderate reform that included both a wider scope for religious toleration as well as an Orthodox Church that enjoyed government support."[15] Preparations for convening an All-Russian Council (*sobor*) of the Church were begun in the late tsarist period, although it was to be convened only after the 1917 Bolshevik Revolution. The Council was able to restore the patriarchal office of the Church, and elected Metropolitan Tikhon as Patriarch of Moscow and All *Rus'* (1917–1925). But in the end the reforms were nothing more than an ill-fated attempt to reform a system that had effectively collapsed. Now, under Bolshevik control, the scope of religious freedom was shut to nothing more than the smallest aperture, while state support was shifted to the promotion of scientific atheism—this in a society that had identified itself with Christianity for just shy of a millennium.

The Evolution of Soviet Religion Policy

For the Bolsheviks who came to power in 1917, the Russian Orthodox Church was public enemy number one. It was not only an institutional part of the tsarist government, it resolutely defended the old regime even after the October Revolution. Of course, it also represented a position diametrically opposed to that of the Bolsheviks; while the church promised salvation through Jesus Christ, the Bolsheviks promised a "salvation" of their own—freedom from the "opium of the masses" and the constraints of the false consciousness that religion spread to keep the capitalist class in power and the proletariat obedient, as they suffered in this world in order to inherit the next.

While such different positions would seem to the outside observer to necessitate immediate and swift action on the part of the Bolsheviks against the church, Lenin was a very calculating strategist, and recognizing the reaction such a move would provoke, he determined that the Bolsheviks first needed to consolidate their political and military position before turning to social policies such as religion. As discussed in the previous chapter, Lenin had laid the basis for such a strategy in his article "The Attitude of the Worker's Party to Religion," where he had argued that war must never be openly declared against religion, for such a move would be an unnecessary "gamble of a political war."[16] This is the same article in which he reminded his readers "Let us recall that the whole of Engels's *Anti-Dühring*...is an indictment of the materialist and atheist Dühring for not being a consistent materialist and for leaving loopholes for religion and religious philosophy." Lenin continued by urging his readers to "recall that in his essay on Ludwig

Feuerbach, Engels reproaches Feuerbach for combating religion not in order to destroy it, but in order to renovate it, to invent a new, 'exalted' religion, and so forth." Marx's dictum that "religion is the opium of the people," Lenin stated, "is the corner-stone of the whole Marxist outlook on religion." While his initial religion policy would seem, therefore, to be contradictory, Lenin rejected accusations that his approach was inconsistent, responding "Marxist tactics in regard to religion are thoroughly consistent, and were carefully thought out by Marx and Engels."

Besides an all-out attack on the church and religion, there were two possible alternatives available to Lenin and the Bolsheviks at this time. The first would have been to allow religion to continue in some general form, as Marxist theory predicted that it would die out on its own. After all, Lenin and the Bolsheviks were staunch believers in the idea that science and progress would eliminate the human longing for religion. As Soviet society was built, fewer, and fewer people would turn to religion, and more people would become atheists. There was no need to wage a war on religion at this time, especially while still waging a civil war and consolidating power in territories the Bolsheviks held. In an address to the first All-Russian Congress of Working Women in November 1918, Lenin expressed precisely this sort of view:

> We must be extremely careful in fighting religious prejudices; some people cause a lot of harm in this struggle by offending religious feelings. We must use propaganda and education. By lending too sharp an edge to the struggle we may only arouse popular resentment; such methods of struggle tend to perpetuate the division of the people along religious lines, whereas our strength lies in unity. The deepest source of religious prejudice is poverty and ignorance; and that is the evil we have to combat.[17]

In addition to attacking the economic causes of religion in order to bring about atheism, the second policy option available was to replace religion, "to invent a new 'exalted' religion." As we just saw, and as was examined in detail in the previous chapter, Lenin explicitly rejected the ideas of the "God-builders" such as Gorky and Lunacharsky, specifically because he opposed all religion so strongly, even one directed by the party. As we will see later in this chapter, however, components of this approach were implemented to a certain degree with the introduction and promotion of "communodoxy," or the "praise of Communism," during the Soviet era. These were not widely implemented, however, until after Lenin's death.

The initial Bolshevik policies toward religion were pragmatic, therefore, and were more about weakening the church as an institution and separating religion from state and societal structures, and focused primarily on the separation of church and state and the nationalization of church-held lands. The first move in this regard was the passing in 1918 of the decree "On the Separation of the Church and the State and the Schools from the Church" by the Council of People's Commissars (*Sovnarkom*). The separation of church and state was not aimed at simply establishing a secular state, void of any religious preferences and affording equal treatment to believers of all faiths—or of no faith at all. Rather, the new policy was designed to halt religious socialization by the schools and to isolate the clerical class. The latter was accomplished with myriad tactics, including priests and clerics being declared, under Article 65 of the 1918 Constitution, "servants of the bourgeoisie". They were thus disenfranchised, received no ration cards, or those of the lowest category, and their children were barred from education beyond the elementary level.

Part of the "pragmatic" policy of not waging an all-out war against the church right away was permitting random and wanton acts of violence against churches and clerics carried out by overzealous soldiers and hooligans. As Gabel points out, these early "acts against religion were not official acts at all, but instead were defilements of churches and clerics by overzealous revolutionaries, not necessarily even party affiliated."[18] Being well aware of the Bolshevik stance on religion, Bolshevik troops shelled many churches (ostensibly without orders to do so), including those in the Kremlin itself. The shear nature and extent of the vandalism and looting they carried out once inside was appalling, with the soldiers covering church walls with graffiti, defecating in the "holiest of holies," and gouging gems out of sacred objects, such as crosses and icons.

Gabel has explained this behavior by arguing that, liberated "from the social bonds that had restrained them and certainly not motivated by any understandings of Marxist anti-religious theory, long-suppressed youth, workers, and soldiers, all too often went wild."[19] But this is a naïve and incorrect interpretation. For one, those who engaged in such acts were well aware of the Marxist critique of religion, and as Bolsheviks they were drunk with victory and anxious to build the world's first communist society. Secondly, simply being liberated from "social bonds" does not lead one to defile a sanctuary. A more accurate interpretation is that these were people who had long resented the power of the church and the tsarist state with which it was so closely associated, and had already begun to express a militant atheism that would eventually bring the church near its total destruction.

If we cannot clearly blame acts such as these on Lenin and the Bolshevik leadership, pinning responsibility instead on lower-ranking individuals, the same excuse cannot be given for the early attacks against the clergy. During 1918–1919, the Bolsheviks executed at least 28 bishops and thousands of clergy and laity. This included Metropolitan Vladimir of Kiev, who was assassinated, Bishop Ephraim of Irkustk, Bishop Hermogen of Saratov, and Archbishop Vasily of Chernigov, all of whom were executed for "counterrevolutionary activities." Bishop Adronik of Perm was himself horribly tortured and killed. As Gabel explains the horrors of the initial purge, there "were incidents of eyes being gouged out and tongues being cut off before priests were paraded through the streets, then shot."[20] In April and May 1922, 54 Orthodox priests and laymen were tried on charges of counter-revolution in connection with more than 1,000 riots by peasants protesting the closing of churches and confiscation of church land. Five of the priests were executed, and a few months later the Metropolitan of Petrograd and three co-defendants were executed on similar grounds.[21] Struve records that during 1922 alone some 2,691 priests, 1,962 monks, and 3,447 nuns "were liquidated." These acts were clearly of a different order than the ransacking and defilement of churches discussed above, and part of a clear Machiavellian policy of eliminating important church leaders in order to weaken the church as an institution.[22] Even the most zealous Bolshevik soldier would not have engaged in such acts if not clearly given a signal by his superiors to do so.

The severity of these attacks prove that, with the Communists emerging victorious from the civil war, Lenin's tactic of "being moderate towards religion" was now turning into determined hostility. The first step in this direction was seen as early as 1921. Whereas a decree of January 28, 1918 only forbade religious instruction in schools, still permitting the "study or teaching of religious subjects privately," a decree of June 13, 1921, entirely proscribed religious instruction to those below the age of 18, including one's own children. Then on March 19, 1922 Lenin issued a secret directive through Molotov calling for increased persecution against the Russian Orthodox Church in relation to the collection of church valuables. Lenin calculated that it was "only now" during this time of famine and cannibalism that "we can be 99–100 per cent sure of complete success in knocking out the enemy" in carrying out a forceful confiscation of church valuables. Lenin was explicit: secret police should be sent into Moscow and certain "spiritual" centers to identify and arrest "as many members of the local clergy and petty-bourgeoisie and bourgeoisie as possible, no less than a dozen," in relation to the resistance of the confiscation of church valuables. After reporting back to the Politburo, a decree would be sent down to the local judicial authorities, "culminating in the shooting of a large number of the most influential and dangerous" of the group."[23]

If under Lenin, Bolshevik religion policy gravitated from one of relative moderation to severity, Stalin's pendulum swung in the opposite direction. Immediately upon consolidating his grip on power, Stalin carried out a policy of widespread repression of religion and oppression of religious believers throughout Soviet-held territory. By 1929 church activity was reduced to the performance of religious services, with churches forbidden "to organize special prayer or other meetings for children, youths or women, or to organize general bible, literary, handicraft, working, religious study or other meetings, groups, circles or branches, to organize excursions or children's playgrounds, or to open libraries or reading rooms." Then, on May 22, 1929, Article 18 of the Constitution was amended. Now, instead of reading "freedom of religious and anti-religious propaganda," the amended text read "freedom of religious worship and *anti-religious* propaganda" (emphasis added) —the right to religious propaganda had been erased from the Soviet Constitution, just as the faces of Stalin's detractors would soon be removed from photos. At the same time the Commissariat of Education—headed by Lunacharsky—replaced the policy of no religious teaching in schools with a policy to provide *anti*-religious instruction in schools. The Soviet policy toward religion had shifted from slowly choking religion to one of socializing youth from an early age into atheism. These measures quickly expanded in breadth and resulted in brutal state-sanctioned persecutions that included the wholesale destruction of churches, the arrest and execution of many clerics, and various measures to break the religious sentiment of the populace.

The Church's Golgotha

As with the initial phase of religious persecution in Russia, legal and constitutional changes only tell a very small part of the story. As with most other policy areas, beneath the appearance of relative toleration was hidden the true policy of control and humiliation. Once the Soviet government had declared the separation of church and state and nationalized all church-held lands, these administrative measures were followed by the wholesale destruction of churches and the arrest and execution of church clergy. While the Bolsheviks called for the "painless but full liquidation of the monasteries, as chief centers of the influence of the churchmen, as nurseries of parasitism, as powerful screws in the exploiting machine of the old ruling classes,"[24] in reality their methods were anything but painless.

Immediately upon the Bolshevik seizure of power, Lenin nationalized all land, which of course included the church's holdings, which alone were worth perhaps $4 billion.[25] But one must bear in mind, as Conquest points out, that the greater part of "church" lands were in fact held by individual parishes, with the priests often plowing it themselves or renting it to the villagers. The next summer, the government began emptying the monasteries of their monks and nuns, filling them instead with the prisoners of the Chekha-driven Red Terror. Their high walls and solid construction made the monasteries an excellent choice for conversion to concentration camps. An empty convent outside Nizhnii Novgorod was designed to hold a prisoner population of 5,000, while one in Ryazan' was to be used similarly. The Boris and Gleb Monastery in Torzhok became a transit camp to more distant camps, and then in 1921, when more and remoter camps were needed for the burgeoning prison population, a special purpose camp was built on the Solovetsky Islands in the White Sea. The remote Orthodox monastery there eventually became a favorite long-term holding facility for recalcitrant clergy.

Only 2 years into Bolshevik control, more than 2.3 million acres of monastery and convent lands had been appropriated by the state. Of the more than 1,000 monasteries that had been in existence before the Revolution, one-third had already been dissolved. In all, the state had stripped from the monasteries 1,112 leased houses, 708 hotels, 602 cattle sheds, 435 dairy farms, 311 beehives, 277 hospitals and asylums, and 84 factories.[26] By 1928, nearly another 100 monasteries were closed, leading *Komsomolskaya Pravda* to proudly proclaim, that "the monasteries are no more centers of propaganda preaching; they have been transformed into museums, established to preach against God," further boasting that many "excursions come to visit them."[27] In successive stages, the thirteenth-century Danilov Monastery, the patriarchal home of the Russian Orthodox Church, was closed between 1929 and 1932, becoming a prison for juvenile delinquents.

The Renovationist Schism

While the Soviet government was carrying out its attack against the church and religion, it added another tactical maneuver to its repertoire, that of attempting a coup that would bring to power church leaders who were sympathetic to the Communists.[28] The story began with a GPU report to Trotsky in March 1922, in which it was claimed that numerous Orthodox hierarchs and priests were dissatisfied with the Patriarch, but unable to do anything about it due to the obedience owed him by church canons.[29] Trotsky agreed to the GPU plan to instigate a coup within the church, and Patriarch Tikhon was quickly arrested and charged with "instigating bloodshed." Both the charges against him and the supposed grievances of the coup-leading faction related to the Soviet confiscation of church possessions. The Soviets demanded the handing over of these valuables, ostensibly to support famine relief, while in reality the funds were eventually used to support the schism itself, being used to support the new Renovationist Church.

The Soviet government quickly registered the schismatic church, and accelerated its persecution of the Patriarchal church, even putting Metropolitan Venyamin on trial. Despite the great attention and celebrity given to the proceedings, however, it was hard to find fault in the Metropolitan. For one, he had expressed his willingness to hand over church valuables to the state, only insisting that the chalices not be touched by the hands of laymen; instead, clergy would oversee an operation whereby they would be melted down and turned into ingots.[30] Moreover, at the trial, his lawyer Gurevich pleaded his case exceptionally well, even shaming a Renovationist priest, who was a witness for the prosecution, for his involvement in anti-Semitic acts prior to the Revolution.[31]

After accusing Patriarch Tikhon of dealings with foreign powers and counter-revolutionary activities, he was released. Thereafter, the schismatic church continually lost support, until finally the government gave up on the plan and forced the Renovationists to initiate talks with the Patriarchal church about reunification. Despite the threat of further imprisonment, the Patriarch refused. He would allow individual clergy to return to the mother church, but would not accept a "unification" of the Renovationist schism with the Patriarchal church. Although most returned to the mother church in this way, a small faction continued to exist until the reprieve of World War II allowed the Patriarchate to finally do away with the schismatic group.[32]

There was another change of tactics following Lenin's death in 1924. As if taking a page from Peter the Great's methods, the Soviet government refused to permit patriarchal elections to be held following the death of Patriarch Tikhon in 1925. This did not eliminate the problem, however. After Patriarch Tikhon's passing, power changed hands several times among temporary heads of the church. Of the 11 hierarchs named as *locum tenens*, ten were soon in prison. The final successor, Metropolitan Sergii, was also arrested and imprisoned. The stubborn resistance of the church must have impressed the government with the need for compromise, for the secession of imprisonment, torture, and execution failed to leave the church emasculated.

The Communists were able, however, to force a *modus vivendi* with the imprisoned Sergii. In order to secure the survival of the church, in 1927

Metropolitan Sergii agreed to sign a statement of "loyalty" to the Soviet government and promised to refrain from criticizing the state in any way. Metropolitan Sergii's "Declaration of Loyalty" stated that "We want to be Orthodox and at the same time recognize the Soviet Union as our civic motherland. Her joys and successes are our joys and successes, her misfortunes are our misfortunes." Though seemingly a capitulation to the Communist state, in fact Metropolitan Sergii was very careful about what he was signing, and went back and forth with the Soviet authorities over at least three drafts over a period of months.

The use of the pronoun "her" here is critical in understanding to what entity Metropolitan Sergii was actually declaring loyalty. The "her" refers strictly to the "civic motherland" [*grazhdanskaya rodina*], which is feminine in Russian, as opposed to the "Soviet Union" [*Sovietskii Soyuz*] which is masculine. Using this grammatical trick—apparently overlooked by the Soviet authorities—meant that Sergii was, as he himself later confirmed confidentially, declaring his loyalty to the native (*rodnaya*) land of Russia, not to the Communist state.[33] This subtlety was not only lost on the Soviets, however, but on other members of the Church as well, and Sergii's signing of the declaration of loyalty led to further divisions within the Church. Metropolitan Sergii's response, however, must be understood from the perspective of the necessity to maintain an unbroken, Apostolic succession of the Church. With the Church so devastated by the Communists already by this time, one can argue that he was taking on a personal sin in order to spare the church itself.

Collectivization and Secularization

In 1928 with Stalin's elimination of Trotsky as political rival, Lenin's New Economic Policy was dismantled, and the first Five-Year Plan was introduced. One of its components was a focus on the rapid collectivization of agriculture. This policy became inextricably linked with the eradication of religion, since the churches still held large amounts of land, though it was often dispersed among small tracks connected to local parishes. The collectivization of agriculture, therefore, often included the appropriation of these church lands, and almost always involved the closure of the local churches to which they belonged.[34] In many ways, collectivization became "the leading instrument of eradicating religion."[35] As church lands were appropriated, the rest of its property was also confiscated. Icons were taken and burned along with other sacred objects involved in administering the sacraments and conducting worship, such as priestly vestments. Once this had been completed, many locals would then ransack the place. Conquest gives an excellent account of the typical closing of a church during the collectivization drive. In the first phase, the church elders were arrested, then anti-religion activists would remove the cross and bells. Finally, an "anti-religious carnival" would break out, in which the church "was broken into and its icons, books, and archives burnt, while the rings and vestments were stolen."[36] Conquest also cites a particular incident from 1930 in which "drunken soldiers and *Komsomoltsy*" went around "arbitrarily closing village churches, breaking icons, and threatening the peasants."[37] Stalin himself would denounce such behavior as part of being "dizzy with success," and he particularly criticized the removal of church bells as excessive. It is most likely, of course, that this was simply orchestrated to stave off increasing Western criticism of the excesses of the collectivization drive.[38]

The closing of churches in association with the collectivization drive not only yielded large amounts of land for the Soviet state, but buildings as well. Commissar of Education Lunacharsky drafted a policy in December 1921 "On the Use of Buildings Formerly Religious," outlining for local Soviets how to properly utilize the new-found facilities. The Soviets found a whole range of uses for church property, including granaries, auto parts stores, cinemas, stables, clubhouses, libraries, children's homes, mental health asylums, health clinics, and restaurants. Those that were allowed to remain churches had to be available for public use during the other six days of the week, being used for political meetings, lectures, concerts, plays, dances, and cinema, even anti-religious propaganda. Many congregations, however, refused to hold services in their churches after they had been "desecrated" in this way, which only led to the government declaring that they had been "voluntarily" closed.

A favorite practice of the Soviets was to convert some of the finest churches into museums, particularly museums of atheism or science. The St. Sophia Cathedral and other churches in Kiev were converted in such a way, but none was as dramatic as the *Kazansky Sobor* in the newly-named Leningrad, which in 1932 was converted into the Museum of the History of Religion and Atheism, and adorned with busts of philosophers and great atheists. In this they were clearly taking a page from the history of the French Revolution, where the Notre Dame Cathedral had been notoriously converted into a Temple to Reason. While this practice certainly desecrated churches (the inscription "Temple of Reason and Philosophy" remains on the Cathedral of Notre Dame to this day), this act of desecration also saved the churches from destruction in the end. One can only wonder if this had somehow been a part of the motivation of the "atheists" that proposed such conversions.

Another great wave of church closings began in 1936 during the Great Purges. Despite various and repeated calls for the eradication of religion in the near future, the results of a massive survey of religious belief in the Soviet Union conducted in 1936, illustrated the Soviet's relative ineffectiveness thus far. In fact, as to be discussed in Chapter 3, belief had barely been affected at all. The only answer was to intensify repression in order to meet the plan. In the process, not only was the church reduced to a shell of its former self, steps were also taken to prevent prayer meetings, Bible study, and any sort of religious education in private homes after the local churches had been closed.

On the eve of the Bolshevik Revolution, there had been around 48,000 functioning Russian Orthodox Churches in the country (if chapels and monasteries are included, this number rises to 54,000).[39] On the eve of World War II, this number had been slashed dramatically. Probably only 100 or so Orthodox churches existed in the territory of the Soviet Union, and most regions only had one, while 25 regions were designated completely "church-less," with all of the churches having been totally eliminated. As Davis reports, in the whole of the Soviet Union at that time, there were probably no more than 200–300 open churches, with none in Belorussia, "less than a dozen" in Ukraine, and 15–20 in Moscow, with only 150–200 throughout the whole of the Russian republic.[40] By this time, 80,000 Orthodox clerics, monks, and nuns had already lost their lives at the hands of the Communists. This figure represents about half the total number of clerics, monks, and nuns serving before the 1917 Revolution. It also includes 13 archbishops and bishops who died in Soviet prisons between 1928 and 1938.[41] It is also dramatically male, for all priests were men, and the peasants were reported to have been especially reluctant to turn out nuns (and there were more than three times as many nuns as monks).[42] On the eve of World War II, there were only four active bishops in the whole of the USSR; Patriarchal locum tenens Metropolitan Sergii (Stragorodsky), Metropolitan Aleksii (Simansky) of Leningrad, his suffragan Nikolai (Yarushevich), and Metropolitan Sergii (Voskresensky). With the church seemingly so close to its demise, it must have taken a tremendous amount of faith to still trust in the scriptural promise that "the gates of hell shall not overcome it" (Matt. 16:18).

The Rise of Militant Atheism

Lenin recognized early on that attacking the church was only one part of the process of liberating people from the grip of religious belief. As he said after promulgating numerous Bolshevik laws on religion, "We have separated the church from the state, but we have not yet separated the people from religion."[43] Indeed, eradicating the religious faith of the Russian people was to take more than destroying their churches or emasculating the church hierarchy. The second prong of the Soviet attack on religion was to be the promotion of atheism.

From Trotsky's Tractors to Yaroslavsky's Nails

The initial attempts to promote atheism started considerably later than the forcible attack on the church. Lenin, as we have seen, was a firm believer in the power of atheism, and as a good Marxist, thought that weakening the church would liberate the people from its control, and once freed from the church's grip, the people would abandon their superstitious beliefs. Lev Trotsky, the one-time Menshevik and eventual military strategist of the Revolution, interpreted the situation a little differently. He argued that it was "anti-religious propaganda [could not be placed] on the level of a straightforward fight against God," for such would not be sufficient. Simply by closing the churches, "as has been done in some places, and by other administrative excesses, you will not only be unable to reach any decisive success but on the contrary you will prepare the way for a stronger return of religion." Trotsky interpreted the failure of the masses to abandon religion as attributable to their "traditional religious nature" which is "closely knit with the conditions of our backward agriculture."[44]

Trotsky, therefore, placed great confidence in the ability of science and technology to release the masses from mysticism. His belief was so strong, in fact, that he actually believed that distributing mechanized farming equipment to peasants would destroy their religious convictions. "We shall vanquish the deep-rooted religious prejudices of the peasantry," he wrote, through "the electrification and chemicalization of peasant agriculture."[45] In this he was in agreement with Lenin, who had thought that delivering 100,000 tractors to the peasants would turn them into Communists.[46] Just before his death, Lenin had entrusted Trotsky with overseeing work in the area of anti-religion propaganda, in the hope of keeping Stalin and, by implication, Lunacharsky under control.[47]

This faith in science did not mean that atheist propaganda was not necessary. To the contrary, both Trotsky and Lunacharsky thought that promoting a scientific-materialist *weltanschauung* through as many means as possible was the key to breaking the back of religion. One such method was through the dissemination of various forms of atheist literature. The Soviet state had already been active in publishing such literature, including

Revolutsiya i Tserkov, Nauka i Religiya, Tserkov i Religiya, and *Kommunizm i Religiya* between 1919–1922. Except for *Revolutsiya i Tserkov*, which had been published since 1919 and carried solid propaganda pieces by its editor, Petr Krasikov,[48] these came out sporadically and often had short print runs. This all changed with the appearance of *Bezbozhnik* (Godless) in late December 1922.[49] This daily newspaper was the first mass and sustained effort at promoting an atheistic worldview among the masses, and also provided guidance (and an outlet) for atheist agitators. Rather than ridiculing faith, as had been the earlier tactic, *Bezbozhnik* was an attempt at a more sophisticated approach, combining very short, basic articles on religion, coupled with information on agricultural techniques and even weather conditions.

Other, similar publications soon followed, including *Derevenskii Bezbozhnik*, aimed at the peasantry. Other more professional journals appeared as well, including *Ateist*, which offered philosophical and historical criticism of religion, and *Antireligioznik*, a "scientific-methodological" monthly journal aimed toward anti-religion agitators.[50] To complement these periodicals, the atheist publishing houses printed a million and half atheistic books and pamphlets by 1927.[51]

Despite the sheer number and volume of published material, the newspaper *Bezbozhnik* unquestionably played the most important role in promoting atheism. Its editorship from the start was in the hands of the "commander of the anti-religious front," Emelyan Yaroslavsky, Lunacharsky's protégé. With a circulation of 200,000 by 1925 (eventually reaching 350,000), the decision was made to complement the newspaper's effectiveness by organizing a Society for the Friends of the Newspaper *Bezbozhnik*. Founded in August 1924, they initially held a week-long conference in April 1925 to strategize and develop an organizational structure, and then in June formally changed their name to the League of Godless (*Soyuz Bezbozhnikov*). The League began to organize cells in schools, factories, collective farms, and the military—where they were particularly resented.[52] It was organized at the regional, district, and village level, and by 1927 they had organized 45 provincial organizations with 138,402 members.[53] By 1929 this number had already swelled to nearly a half million,[54] while it would reach 5.5 million by 1932. Though it would last until the start of World War II, by 1938 its membership had fallen to only one-third of that of its high point, despite the dissemination of at least 100 million copies of anti-religious literature.[55]

Yaroslavsky was entrusted with the responsibility of heading the League and using it as a vehicle for atheistic propaganda. While the League's early efforts were no better than those of the past (in Samara its members had quickly rounded up church bells and purchased tractors with the proceeds), its efforts were supposed to be better organized, orchestrated, and more sensitive to the religious sensitivities of the masses. In this it was an abject failure, simply becoming a vehicle for anti-religious hooliganism. It carried out pogroms of all sorts, conducted blasphemous parades with mocking figures of Christ, Allah, and the Buddha, and held book and icon burnings. The decision in 1929 to rename the organization the League of Militant Godless was not made for any of these reasons, but it was fitting all the same. Yaroslavsky was later to recognize that, "religion is like a nail, the harder you hit, the deeper it goes in."

The Children Are Our Future

In his *ABCs of Communism*, Bukharin listed the liberation of children from the influence of their reactionary parents as one of the highest priorities of the Soviet state, arguing "From the very onset the children's minds shall be rendered immune to all those religious fairy tales, which many grownups continue to regard as truth."[56] Trotsky held a similar view of the home, referring to it as a "close little cage…with its icon and icon lamp." Only by getting the people out of their homes could the Communists hope to free them from their religious prejudices.[57] It was imperative that the religious outlook taught in the home be effectively countered by a scientific outlook taught outside the home.

The Soviets recognized that getting to their citizens while they were young was crucial to developing the new Soviet man, who would be an atheist man. In addition to citizens who were clean, relatively free from illness, and did not beat their wives or children (commendable goals indeed), Marxist ideology demanded atheism. All of these were goals of the Communist youth leagues, including the Komsomol, the Young Pioneers, and the Octobrists, roughly equivalent to the American Boy Scouts, Webelos, and Cub Scouts, respectively. In 1928 Bukharin gave one of the key speeches at the first Komsomol Congress, where he talked about "the masked enemies" of socialist society. These were legally existing organizations that nevertheless were detrimental to the development of socialism, with Bukharin naming religious organizations as the most important in this group.[58] Once again, we can see the Soviet tactic of projecting an image of toleration publicly, while agitating for the church's destruction to insiders.

A study of youth socialization through the Komsomol and Pioneers, conducted in the 1920s, provides excellent illustrations of how these groups were used to achieve atheistic goals. The Pioneers were instructed to help around the house, wash their faces, and encourage their parents to read books and subscribe to newspapers. And if possible, "the Pioneer is to put a picture of Lenin on the wall, next to the sacred image [icon]." In this way, and "by emphasizing revolutionary holidays in opposition to the religious feast days, the Pioneer is to combat the 'prejudices of religion' in the family."[59] He is then to report back to his Pioneer brigade. It was crucial, the Pioneers were instructed, to combat the prevalent use of the "opium of the people" in the home.[60] If the parents beat the child for these offenses, the child is then instructed to issue a complaint at the parent's workplace. Just how far the Soviets would take such accusations is illustrated by the "myth" of Pavlik Morozov, a young pioneer leader who turned in his father for crimes against the state. While the senior Morozov was found guilty and later executed, the family was so enraged by the incident that they rounded up young Pavlik and murdered him. The story, almost all of which has been dismissed by modern historians, soon came to symbolize for Soviet youth that loyalty to the state should be held in higher regard than filial love.

Once young Soviets got a bit older they could become more actively involved in building socialism. Rather than relying upon subtle maneuvers, Komsomol members should join the League of Godless, attend their lectures, read their newspapers and journals, and take part in their traveling atheist theatres. They should also attend and take part in their rallies and parades, especially those associated with Komsomol Christmas and Komsomol Easter, Communist Party-directed "anti-holidays." These were meant to replace religious holidays, and provide workers with time off and an occasion to celebrate. But more than this, Komsomol members rode on floats dressed as pagan idols and the gods of various faiths, mocking religious believers and the event being celebrated itself. For instance, lectures on the impossibility of the resurrection were held to coincide with Easter, with the venue often being right along the path to the church, which was still being flooded with parishioners.

Though membership in these youth organizations was relatively high, obviously not every young citizen could be reached in this way. The answer was to get them in the schools. With primary and secondary education compulsory, every future Soviet citizen could be reached through the schools. The great irony is that, while it was illegal to instruct the youth in religious teaching even at home, it became part of the curriculum to teach atheism in the schools. While many teachers were willing, however reluctantly, to teach their subjects in a non-religious manner, most scoffed at the order actually to teach atheism. This is, however, precisely what was increasingly being demanded of them.

Catechumens of Atheism

At their second congress in 1929, the League of Militant Godless had demanded that the schools be converted into institutions for anti-religious instruction, and that all teachers become instructors of atheism. Many teachers logically reasoned, however, that if the influence of religion in society was to become less prevalent as socialism progressed, then they should focus their teaching efforts instead on the natural sciences. Helping to develop a scientific worldview in their students, rather than directly attacking their religious sentiments, was actually a policy closer in thinking to Marx and Lenin (and even Trotsky). But by this time all three were out of the picture, and Yaroslavksy and his League of Militant Godless were adamant that any teacher who believed in God should be fired.[61]

Getting Soviet teachers to teach atheism was a tall order; however, for at the time at least 50 percent of the country's school teachers were the children of priests, a group known for their resistance to atheism. Lunacharsky himself conservatively estimated at the time that 30–40 percent of all teachers in the country were still religious believers.[62] As he complained, "the believing teacher in the Soviet school is an awkward contradiction," and schools were obligated to use every opportunity to replace such teachers with new ones hostile to religion.[63] Prizes were even developed to reward the most innovating and enthusiastic teachers of atheism, with a prize given in each region annually. Meanwhile, it was still a common occurrence in the rural areas for teachers to lead their classes to local churches for services during school hours, and they continued the practice of singing religious hymns in the classroom. Of course, by this time the Soviet Criminal Code had formalized the punishment for teaching religion to children in public or private schools as "forced labor for a period not to exceed one year," but such a law was entirely unenforceable, for its implementation would have decimated the teacher corps.[64]

By 1934 Russia's Statute on Secondary Schools had dictated that "The primary schools and secondary schools shall secure an anti-religious upbringing of the students and shall build instruction and educational work upon the basis of an active fight against religion and its influence upon the student and adult population." The teaching of atheism became a necessity, and teachers slowly and grudgingly caved in. An atheist worldview eventually came to permeate the Soviet educational system. In its more innocuous

form, students were forced to draw pictures mocking religion, while it sometimes became quite aggressive, with teachers and school officials actually
questioning students on their religious beliefs and even kicking them out if
they professed religious faith.

Even those teachers who wanted to teach atheism faced obstacles.
According to one anecdote from a Soviet ethnographer, to the teacher's question, "why do you make noise in the school, but behave yourselves quietly at
home?" the students responded, "because here we can—there are no icons."[65]
Despite being inundated with atheism through the course of their day, the
home still played a powerful role in a child's upbringing. The icon corner
wasn't the only source of religious socialization in the home, however, as
most families had at least one parent or grandparent who was still a committed believer in the 1930s. Those teachers who did set about incorporating
atheism into the classroom, therefore, had to face the real threat of parents
marching on the school and demanding their dismissal, with the local Soviet
often siding with the parents.

The story in higher education was a bit different. Given the different
nature of the college curriculum, specific courses could be devoted to atheism, and atheistic components added to others, while some subject areas
could remain relatively free from the party's propaganda efforts. Scientific
atheism became a compulsory subject, and new textbooks were developed
for this purpose. As early as 1922–1923, Yaroslavsky himself had organized a "circle for the study of the history of religion" in the Y. M. Sverdlov
University in Moscow,[66] where he could put to use his anti-religious books,
Kak rodiatsia, zhivut, i umiraiut bogi i bogini (How Gods and Godesses are
born, live, and die) and *Bibliia dlia veruiushchikh i neveruiushchikh* (The
Bible for believers and non-believers), which had begun to appear in serial
form in *Bezbozhnik* in December 1922.

The tactic often used to get atheism taught in the countries prestigious
universities was to establish chairs of atheism, though termed chairs for
the "History of Religion." The chair holders were responsible for teaching courses in such areas as primitive religion, ancient Eastern religions,
Greek and Roman religious traditions, and Christianity's origin and development. Alongside the country's main universities, anti-religious seminaries were opened, with the first one opening in Moscow in November
1922. Their purpose was to train atheist propagandists and agitators to
take on a variety of leading roles in the field of atheism promotion and
education. The courses in these "seminaries" were taught by such leading
figures in the field of atheist propaganda (and friends of Yaroslavsky) Ivan

Skvortsov-Stepanov, Petr Krasikov, and Mikhail Gorev, editor of *Nauka i Religiya*. By the end of 1926 there were already 68 such anti-religious seminaries in Russia.

This seemingly undefeatable approach left the Soviet authorities convinced that religion would soon be relegated to the dustbin of history. So in 1938 they closed the All-Union Central Executive Committee of the USSR's Commission for Religious Questions, leaving only the local and regional authorities to handle religious matters. From this point on the church affairs department within the NKVD (People's Commissariat for Internal Affairs) would be charged with overseeing the church's activities. The German invasion of the Soviet Union on June 22, 1941, however, was to change the nature of church-state relations dramatically.

Reprieve, Renaissance, and Renewed Attack

World War II is known throughout the world for the harsh conditions it demanded from those who were on the defensive end of aggression, and the Soviet Union perhaps suffered the most in this regard, with more Soviet war dead than any other participant nation. But in one area—that of religious life—the war brought a reprieve and a relaxation of the Soviet Union's harsh religion policies. Two days after the German invasion, Stalin opened the Soviet press and radio to Metropolitan Sergii, who called on the faithful to rise in defense of the fatherland. This event not only marked the beginning of popular resistance to the German invaders, it also inaugurated a new era in church-state relations under Soviet rule.

At the time of the Soviet Union's entry into World War II, the Orthodox Church had been almost completely destroyed throughout the country. There were only a few bishops who remained free, managing to survive in remote parts of the country or under the disguise of ordinary priests. Only a few 100 churches remained open for services, and most of the clergy were either imprisoned in concentration camps or had already died there. Church property soon began to be restored, however, and churches that had been closed by the League of Militant Godless were allowed to reopen.

Russian Orthodoxy underwent a renaissance. Ten theological schools were quickly opened, and thousands of churches began to hold regular services, although the number of churches opened paled in comparison to the number of requests submitted by believers and the church. Many priests were released from prison, including bishops, and some of the priests who had been in hiding or who had been put to work in factories returned to their parishes. As Anderson described the situation, icons "reappeared from chests or under beds to hallow the common tasks of the household from behind the 'lampadka' in the icon corner."[67]

The Concordat

The rapprochement between church and state quickly began to develop into a "patriotic union." On September 4, 1943, Stalin received Patriarchal *Locum Tenens* Metropolitan Sergii, along with Metropolitan Alexii (Simansky) and Metropolitan Nikolay (Yarushevich) in the Kremlin. Four days later 19 bishops assembled and elected Sergii Patriarch, filling the office that had been vacant since Tikhon's death in 1925. Much as Sergii had written his "Declaration of Loyalty" upon his release from imprisonment in 1927, he now wrote "The Truth about Religion in Russia," in which he downplayed to the rest of the world the harsh suffering of the church under Soviet rule. Commenting on Soviet Constitutional guarantees of religious freedom, the new Patriarch said "...it may be said with complete objectivity that the Constitution, guaranteeing full freedom of religious worship, definitely in no way restricts the religious life of the faithful and the life of the Church in general." At the end of the war, Patriarch Alexii (who succeeded Sergii in 1944 following the latter's death) expressed similar sentiments, telling the world that "Russian Orthodoxy was never subjected to systematic persecution, the Christians were never killed as in ancient Rome...To speak about intolerance and persecution of religion in the USSR means opposing the truth."[68]

The church also returned the favor of its renaissance by lending material and spiritual support to the military. Metropolitan Sergii had penned a letter to the faithful on the very day of the German invasion in which he proclaimed that "The Church of Christ confers its blessing on all Orthodox believers in their defense of the holy borders of our motherland." The clergy continued this message, appealing to their fellow believers "to join this holy struggle."[69] Priests began to give lively sermons to groups of Red Army soldiers, while regimental commanders are known to have led prayers among their soldiers before going into battle.

The Russian Church did not limit itself to giving spiritual and moral support to the motherland. Early on, the Church had begun collecting a special offering for the war effort, and even received permission from Stalin to open an account in the Central Bank for this purpose. While these funds mostly went to assist hospitals, children's homes, and aid the families of soldiers, it also funded two military units, the St. Dimitry Donskoy Tank Column and the St. Alexander Nevsky fighter squadron, honoring two sanctified Russian historical figures known for their victorious battles against foreign invaders. For his role in these efforts, Patriarch Alexii would receive medals "For the Defense of Leningrad" and the order of the "Red Banner of Labor."

These policies represented a complete reversal of policy on the part of the Soviet government and the Communist Party. Instead of scattering the parishes, they were united, instead of permitting local governmental agencies to carryout arbitrary actions, centralized control was maintained by Moscow, and instead of congregations exercising independence, the Patriarchate maintained a centralized and disciplined hierarchy.[70] In terms of promoting atheism, rather than resurrecting the crude activities of the League of Militant Godless, efforts were placed on scientific education in the schools and the publishing of books, pamphlets, and magazines that portrayed religion as a phenomenon natural to the old, class-based society, but unnatural, even harmful, to the new classless, and scientific society.

There is still a lot of controversy over the reasoning behind Stalin's change of course, and even its extent, but for our purposes here we can safely conclude that, in the face of war against fascism, religion was allowed to play a limited public role and was even seen as being able to function as a patriotic organization. This is a major revision of the Marxist and Leninist tenets on religion, of course, for under socialism religion should have no role. One explanation that has been put forward to explain Stalin's turn in religion policy is the idea that he might have thought about the use of the churches as a tool of control in the new Communist regimes of Eastern Europe. As Pospielovsky argues, Stalin needed to "tame" the Catholic, Protestant, and Orthodox peoples of Western Europe, and he had to practice religious toleration at home in order to not scare them off.[71] Once these regimes were securely in the Soviet sphere of influence, however, the Orthodox Church once again was of little value to the regime.[72]

It would soon find its new role as one of improving the Soviet Union's image abroad, particularly in the international peace movement and its emphasis on avoiding nuclear weapons proliferation. Stalin had also seemed to hope for a while that the Patriarchate might be able to develop into a "Moscow Vatican," with the Russian Patriarch taking on a leading role not only in the Orthodox communion, but among all (non-Catholic) Christians in the world. Such would have allowed him access and leverage in the decolonizing societies of Africa, for instance, as well as helped develop a sympathetic voice in America. The Patriarch's efforts in this regard, which centered around the establishment of an Ecumenical Orthodox Center in Moscow, never materialized, because to the Eastern Patriarchs it smacked of an attempt to build a Third Rome. While no ecumenical council or even preconciliar council could be held, Moscow did eventually hold a conference for leaders of Orthodox churches in 1948 in celebration of Moscow's 500 years of autocephaly.[73]

The reprieve had led to a rapid revival of church life, the restoration of the ecclesiastical structure of the church, and the resumption of relations between the Moscow Patriarchate and the other heads of Eastern Orthodox Churches.[74] The church, however, remained always under state control, and any attempts to spread its work outside its walls were met with a strong rebuff including administrative sanctions. Patriarch Alexii recognized this, and himself held back some of the more ambitious plans of his bishops and clergy, not wanting to "overstep the limits" of their new-found rights.[75] It was already at the meeting between Stalin and Sergii in October 1943 that the Council for Russian Orthodox Church Affairs had been created. Under the leadership of Georgii Karpov and a network of regional commissioners, this organ would act as a liaison between the Patriarchate and the government, and oversee the opening of churches throughout the country. As Chumachenko points out, from this point on church-state relations developed primarily through this rather civilized framework between 1943 and 1957, despite two brief attempts to turn back the clock in 1948–1949 and 1954.[76] On the eve of Khrushchev's ascent, the number of open places of worship had rebounded to 25,000, with the Orthodox churches alone reaching 14,000.

No Thaw for the Church

Khrushchev's period in power, though short (1956–1964), is fraught with inconsistencies and perplexities that still have not been worked out by historians, including his rise to power, his relations with other members of the Politburo, and the Cuban Missile Crisis.[77] His simultaneous "thaw" of Soviet society and renewed attack against the church is another one of those seeming inconsistencies. Just as quickly as religious life had come back under Stalin, the Khrushchev era saw wide-scale attempts to reverse this development, and in terms of commitment to atheism, carrying it even further.

At the Twentieth Party Congress of the Communist Party, Khrushchev gave his "secret" speech denouncing the crimes of the Stalin era and the former leader's "cult of personality," placing the blame for the excesses and atrocities of the regime squarely on Stalin's shoulders. This marked the beginning of a period of limited reform intended to make the Soviet Union more productive and the populace more materially satisfied. Khrushchev allowed for reform of Soviet criminal and civil law procedures, emptied many of the Gulags, and permitted freer expression, particularly regarding literature, music, and cultural life. He also launched a new crackdown on religion.

Some have argued that the attack on religion under Khrushchev cannot be ascribed to him personally, but is more accurately attributable to Suslov, the Party's chief ideologist.[78] Attacking the church at this time, however, fit perfectly with Khrushchev's program of de-Stalinization, and his insistence on finishing off the remaining "manifestations of Stalinism." It also squared nicely with his confidence in communism, and his agenda to construct a communist—and atheist—society in the decades to come. Either way, even Khrushchev's acquiescence to these new measures illustrates the seeming contradiction between his attempts to enhance the rule of law in Soviet society while simultaneously violating the constitutional guarantees on religious activity.

This new and widespread attack on the church began in 1958, with thousands of churches throughout the Soviet Union rapidly shut down. In sharp contrast to the heady days of the militant godless and their blasphemous parades, however, this attack was intended to be more discreet. No party or governmental resolutions were published in the Soviet press, and Karpov informed his regional commissioners that "you must absolutely not conduct this work as a campaign." He also directed them to no longer approve any openings of churches, and to "systematically develop specific measures for limiting church activity."[79] In his meetings with the Patriarch, with whom he had enjoyed a long and even warm relationship, Karpov did his best to conceal the new line toward the church. The patriarch saw right through this, however, recognizing that he was clearly under duress.[80]

One of the main goals of this "non-campaign" was to alienate the youth from religion. Films and music were played near churches during their services, and applicants to the country's seminaries often found themselves drafted immediately into the armed forces. Efforts were spent on trying to convince clergy to renounce their ordination, sometimes with promises of good jobs, and other times under physical threat. They had nearly 200 successful cases, including a few who joined in the atheistic efforts by contributing to the propaganda brochure *My porvali s religiei* (We Broke with Religion).[81] The physical church was also attacked. Some churches were closed for "renovations," only to reopen as clubs or some other secular organization, while those that were to be destroyed often were first enclosed behind scaffolding which would hide from view the destruction that was going on. They were also swift. In one case, the Ovruch convent in Zhitomir was converted into a children's hospital in only 26 hours.[82]

The renewed onslaught against the church took a two-pronged approach, not only attacking the church and its clergy, but also drawing away its members. In fact, the promotion of atheism was perhaps more the goal of this period than of any other in Soviet history. The promotion of an atheist worldview reached far beyond the classroom, and through various other programs scientific atheism was promoted to society at large. Rather than staunchly militant and mocking religion, the approach this time around was more subtle and focused on the intersection between science and religion, including the publication of a monthly journal by that very name. The first issue of *Nauka i Religiya* appeared on newsstands across the country in September 1959. As fate would have it, a young British scholar had just arrived in Moscow as part of the first Soviet-British academic exchange program in time to see it appear. Although no one else seemed to think much of it at the time, including his contacts in the British embassy, the young Michael Bourdeaux immediately understood it as part of a renewed attack against the church.[83] A few years later he would return to see that attack at its height. Just after his arrival he made his way for one of the churches he was familiar with, and eventually he was caught by some older ladies who saw him peeking through the scaffolding hiding the destruction of the church behind. These ladies saw Michael as sent by God to tell the world what was happening. He would "be their voice," and spread awareness to the outside world about what was occurring behind the iron curtain.[84]

Destroying physical vestiges of religion was one thing, but combating the faith of people such as these would be a more difficult struggle and require different tactics. A primary approach was that of atheist propaganda, including the flagship publication *Nauka i Religiya*. This "journal" sought to use modern science to combat religion, apparently believing that new developments in science would demystify the world. Indeed, it was even thought that Yuri Gagarin's announcement that he did not see God during his space mission would provide a jolt to the movement away from religion. The entire publishing efforts of atheist propaganda became more professional and scientific at this time, with works such as *Ateizm, religiya, sovremennost*,' and *Istoriya i Teoriya Ateizma* offering the reader sophisticated understandings of man's experience with religion, based firmly in Western social scientific theory. *Voprosy Nauchnogo Ateizma* appeared as the journal of the newly-opened Institute of Scientific Atheism attached to the Soviet Academy of

Sciences, while works geared toward middle school and college students also appeared, such as *Osnovy nauchnogo ateizma*. To this list one cannot leave out the *Karmanni Slovar' Ateista*, the publishing of which surpassed any other religious publication.

While *Nauka i Religiya* replaced the old *Bezbozhnik*, *Znanie* (the All-Union Society for the Dissemination of Political and Scientific Knowledge, or "Knowledge"), replaced the League of Militant Godless. They gave public lectures, conducted evenings of "Q & A" regarding science and religion, and even conducted chemical experiments, through which "miracles were exposed." They also conducted miracles of their own, including the "scientific miracle" of reanimating a warm-blooded organism, a photograph of which was included in pictorial devoted to science and religion.[85] Together, these activities were not only less offensive to believers than the parades and traveling theatrical troupes of the 1920s–1930s, they were also much more effective, and even downright popular. Believers went back to their priests afterwards and asked questions.[86]

The parallels between the old League of Militant Godless and *Znanie* are not coincidental. As Delaney points out, the atheist propagandists and agitators of this period were looking back to Yaroslavsky for guidance. The entire early period of atheism and anti-religious agitation was singled out for study. These were motivated by a concern over the persistence of religion after a half-century of official atheism, looking to the past for lessons of success and failure. The trend toward using various academic disciplines, notably the social sciences, to study and combat the phenomenon of religion were based on the theories of Yaroslavsky.[87]

At the Twenty-Second Party Congress in October 1961, Khrushchev unveiled his new Party Program, replacing the one passed in 1919. Khrushchev declared that within 20 years the Soviet economy would catch up to and surpass the standard of living in the United States. The program marked the beginning of a period of "full-scale communist construction," including education efforts intended "to free consciousness from religious prejudices and superstitions that continue to prevent individual Soviet citizens from fully realizing their creative potential."[88] The Congress accepted the mission to construct a communist society by 1980, by which time the church would have ceased its existence, as all Soviet citizens would be atheists by that time. The fact that the number of Orthodox churches in the USSR would decrease by more than 5,000 between 1960 and 1964 (leaving less than 8,000 in the whole country), would have shaken the confidence of most any believer. Patriarch Alexii, however, did not lose faith. Speaking at a civil society conference in the Kremlin, he proclaimed to his audience, "The church finds comfort in…the words of Christ…'the gates of hell will not prevail against the church'."[89]

Notes

1. Jean-François De La Harpe, *Cours de Littérature Ancienne et Moderne* (Boston: Adamant Media Corporation, 2001 [Originally Published 1840]).
2. Greeley, *Unsecular Man*, p. 124.
3. A. A. Azarov, *Bol'shoi Anglo-Russkii Slovar' Religioznoi Lekciki* (Moscow: Flinta, 2004).
4. Emile Durkheim, "Search for a Positive Definition," in Louis Schneider, ed., *Religion, Culture, and Society* (New York: Wiley, 1964), pp. 32–3.
5. Georges Florovsky, "The Church: Her Nature and Task," in *Bible, Church, Tradition: An Eastern Orthodox View* (Buchervertriebsanstalt, 1987), p. 59.
6. A.V. Kartashev, *Ocherki po Istorii Russkoi Tserkvi*, Vol. 2. (Paris: YMCA Press, 1959), pp. 121–4.
7. Cited in Kevin Boyle and Juliet Sheen, eds. *Freedom of Religion and Belief: A World Report* (London and New York: Routledge, 1997), p. 338.
8. Pierre Pascal, *The Religion of the Russian People*, Trans. Rowan Williams (Crestwood, NY: St. Vladimir's Seminary Press, 1976); Jane Ellis, *The Russian Orthodox Church* (New York: Routledge, 1986); Paul Meyendorff, *Russia, Ritual, and Reform: The Liturgical Reforms of Nikon in the 17th Century* (Crestwood, NY: St. Vladimir's Seminary Press, 1991); Nicolas Zernov, *The Russians and their Church* (Crestwood, NY: St. Vladimir's Seminary Press, 1991); Glennys Young, *Power And The Sacred In Revolutionary Russia: Religious Activist in the Village* (University Park: Pennsylvania State University Press, 1997); Nikolas Gvosdev, *An Examination of Church-State Relations in the Byzantine and Russian Empires with an Emphasis on Ideology and Models of Interaction* (Lewiston, NY: The Edwin Mellen Press, 2001).
9. *Decrees on the Duties of the Senate*, in Basil Dmytryshyn, ed., *Imperial Russia: A Source Book, 1700–1917* (New York: Holt, Rinehart and Winston, 1967), p. 15.
10. For a more detailed discussion of Peter's reforms from the perspective of modern democratic institution building, see Marsh, Christopher, *Russia at the Polls: Voters, Elections, and Democratization* (Washington, DC: CQ Press, 2002), pp. 17–21.

11. John Basil, *Church and State in Late Imperial Russia: Critics of the Synodal System of Church Government, 1861–1914* (Minneapolis: Minnesota Mediterranean and East European Monographs, 2005), p. 1.
12. Ibid.
13. Ibid., p. 3.
14. James Cunningham, *A Vanquished Hope: The Movement for Church Renewal in Russia, 1905–1906* (Crestwood, NY: St. Vladimir's Seminary Press, 1981).
15. Basil, p. 5.
16. V. I. Lenin, "The Attitude of the Workers' Party."
17. Paul Gabel, *And God Created Lenin: Marxism vs. Religion in Russia, 1917–1929* (Amherst, New York: Prometheus Books, 2005), p. 117.
18. Gabel, p. 115.
19. Ibid.
20. Ibid., p. 116.
21. Robert Conquest, *The Harvest of Sorrow: Soviet Collectivization and the Terror-Famine* (New York: Oxford University Press, 1986), pp. 201–2.
22. In a secret letter to Molotov, Lenin actually refers to Machiavelli thus, "a clever writer on political matters rightly said that if, in order to achieve a known political goal, it is essential to use a series of harsh measures, then this must be done in the most energetic way and in the shortest time." "Letter to Comrade Molotov (March 19, 1922)," published as "Lenin Attacks the Church," in *Religion in Communist Lands,* Vol. 7, No. 1 (Spring 1979), p. 47. Cf. Nicollo Machiavelli, *The Prince and the Discourses* (New York: McGraw Hill, 1950).
23. Lenin, "Letter to Comrade Molotov," p. 48.
24. Gabel, p. 31.
25. Ibid., p. 7.
26. Ibid., p. 34.
27. *Komsomolskaya Pravda* (April 10, 1928).
28. While some earlier scholars have denied the Politburo and GPU's orchestration of the schism (cf. John Curtiss), as Pospielovsky points out, their role is now beyond doubt. Dmitry Pospielovsky, *The Orthodox Church in the History of Russia* (Crestwood, New York: St. Vladimir's Seminary Press, 1998), p. 209, 240.
29. Ibid., p. 232.
30. Arto Luukkanen, *The Party of Unbelief: The Religious Policy of the Bolshevik Party, 1917–1929* (Helsinki: Finnish Historical Society, 1994), p. 109.
31. Pospielovsky, pp. 233–4.

32. Tatiana Chumachenko, edited and translated by Edward Roslof, *Church and State in Soviet Russia: Russian Orthodoxy from World War II to the Khrushchev Years* (Armonk: M.E. Sharpe, 2002), p. 37.
33. Pospielovsky, p. 251.
34. Conquest, pp. 204–5.
35. William Husband, *"Godless Communists": Atheism and Society in Soviet Russia, 1917–1932* (De Kalb: Northern Illinois University Press, 2000), p. 66.
36. Ibid., p. 31.
37. Ibid.
38. Arto Luukkanen, *The Religious Policy of the Soviet State: A Case Study: The Central Standing Commission on Religious Questions, 1929–1938* (Helsinki: Finnish Historical Society, 1997), p. 94.
39. Gabel, pp. 38–9.
40. Nathaniel Davis, *A Long Walk to Church: A Contemporary History of Russian Orthodoxy* (Boulder: Westview Press, 2003), p. 13.
41. Conquest, p. 212.
42. Ibid.
43. David Powell, *Antireligious Propaganda in the Soviet Union: A Study in Mass Persuasion* (Cambridge: MIT Press, 1975), p. 22.
44. Leon Trotsky, "Leninism and Workers' Clubs," (July 17, 1924). From *Problems in Everyday Life and Other Writings on Culture and Science* (New York: Monad Press, 1973).
45. Ibid.
46. Conquest, p. 33.
47. Leon Trotsky, *My Life* (New York: 1930), p. 476.
48. Joan Delaney, "The Origins of Soviet Antireligious Organizations," in *Aspects of Religion in the Soviet Union, 1917–1967,* Richard Marshall, Thomas Bird, and Andrew Blane, eds. (Chicago: University of Chicago Press, 1971), p. 105.
49. Husband, p. 60.
50. Ibid., p. 61.
51. *Antireligioznik* 10 (October 1927); cited in Husband, p. 61.
52. Part of this resentment stems from the battle between Yaroslavsky and Trotsky, with the military quite loyal still to the latter, who was seen as the military strategist of the Bolshevik Revolution. Cf. Delaney, pp. 118–22.
53. Husband, p. 62.
54. Ibid.
55. Davis, pp. 10–11, fn 44.

56. Gabel, p. 8.
57. Trotsky, "Leninism and Workers' Clubs."
58. Samuel Harper, *Civic Training in Soviet Russia* (Chicago: University of Chicago, 1929), p. 59
59. Ibid., pp. 77–81.
60. Ibid., p. 81.
61. Pospielovsky, p. 264.
62. Gabel, p. 13.
63. Ibid., p. 14.
64. Ibid., p. 15.
65. Husband, p. 79, fn. 54.
66. Delaney says this was the precursor to the Society of Friends of the Newspaper *Bezbozhnik* (Delaney, pp. 111–16). Evidence certainly seems to support this position.
67. Paul Anderson, "The Orthodox Church in Soviet Russia," *Foreign Affairs* 39 (1961), p. 300.
68. Chumachenko, p. 53.
69. Ibid., p. 4.
70. Anderson, p. 304.
71. Pospielovskii, pp. 192–3. See also M. V. Shkarovskii, "Russkaia pravoslavnaia tserkov' v 1943–1957 godakh," *Voprosy istorii,* no. 8 (1995), pp. 36–41.
72. Chumachenko, p. 54.
73. Ibid., pp. 53–4.
74. Anderson, p. 300.
75. Chumachenko, p. 52.
76. Ibid., p. 6.
77. See, for example, A. I. Adzhubei, *Te desiat' let* (Moscow, 1989); S.N. Khrushchev, *Pensioner soiuznogo znacheniya* (Moscow, 1991); R.A. Medvedev, *N.S. Khrushchev: Politicheskaya biografiya* (Moscow, 1990).
78. Chumachenko, pp. 148–9.
79. Ibid., pp. 156–7.
80. Ibid., p. 158.
81. Dmitry Pospielovsky, *The Orthodox Church in the History of Russia* (Crestwood, NY: St. Vladimir's Seminary Press, 1998) p. 328.
82. Chumachenko, pp. 170–1.
83. Discussion with author, Oxford, UK, July 7, 2008.
84. Michael Bourdeaux, *Risen Indeed: Lessons in Faith from the USSR* (Crestwood, NY: St. Vladimir's Seminary Press, 1983).

85. N. Krasnikov, V. Andrianova, and S. Rutenburg, *Pravda o religii* (Lenizokombinat, 1963), p. 31. Keston Center Archive.
86. Chumachenko, p. 175.
87. Delaney, p. 104.
88. Chumachenko, p. 188.
89. Ibid., p. 182.

CHAPTER THREE

Faith in Defiance: The Persistence of Religion under Scientific Atheism

During the 23 years of the request to allow our families to leave this country, we have outlasted two leaders, Khrushchev and Brezhnev, and since the question is not resolved, we have to wait for the solution from you...God will force you...to resolve our case righteously as He did with the king of Egypt.
—Letter of the Vashchenko children to Yuri Andropov[1]

A group of 32 Pentecostals barged into the U.S. Embassy in Moscow pleading for asylum on a cold wintry day in January 1963. They had had enough of the Khrushchevite crackdown on religion, and were determined to leave their homes, possessions, and families behind in an attempt to gain religious liberty. The small group eventually left the embassy, however, when the Soviet regime promised better treatment and to protect their right to religious freedom. Instead they lost their homes and jobs. This group included Augustina Vashchenko, the wife of Pyotr Vashchenko, who himself was in prison for his religious beliefs. Both were imprisoned before long, and Pyotr was even later confined to a psychiatric hospital (a treatment for religious "fanatics" in the Soviet Union which became increasingly common at this time). The couple never gave up their desire to emigrate with their families and gain religious liberty, however, enduring severe hardships for their beliefs. Their children were ridiculed, beaten, and ostracized at school, and when the parents decided to home-school them, the Soviet state ruled them unfit parents and seized their children, raising them in institutions until they reached the age of 16.

While the Soviet regime was making quick work of turning back the clock on the liberalization of religious life after 1943 and persecuting such people as the Vashchenko's, Khrushchev soon found himself on the wrong side of the Kremlin wall. On October 14, 1964, an emergency meeting of the Central Committee was called at which Khrushchev was removed from his post and forced into retirement. "What can I say? I've got what I deserved,"[2] was about all he could reply. Unlike the Vashchenko's, who had done nothing wrong, the members of the Central Committee had a litany of complaints against Khrushchev, ranging from his capricious policies and misguided interventions in industry and agriculture to promoting members of his family and taking them on expensive trips with the government footing the bill. During the meeting, Leonid Brezhnev was already sitting in the chair of the Party First Secretary.

Brezhnev himself criticized Khrushchev for the unjustified replacement and transfer of personnel, and the development of his own cult of personality. Before the end of his reign, however, Brezhnev would be guilty of many of the things for which he was condemning Khrushchev, including nepotism and a cult of personality of his own. In the area of church-state relations, though, Brezhnev deviated only slightly from the status quo that Khrushchev had established during his brief tenure in office. When he came to power, the number of functioning Orthodox churches in the Soviet Union was only slightly more than 8,000, a reduction of some 5,000 churches in the brief period of Khrushchev's anti-religion campaign. This number would not change much at all over the next quarter century. While the Brezhnev regime suspended the open struggle against the church, they pursued a strategy of gradually displacing faith with atheism through the promotion of the latter, relying upon the press, publishing efforts, and the schools (it is at this time that the Institute for Scientific Atheism was opened). This pattern of church-state relations evolved little until the time of Gorbachev's rise to Party general secretary in 1985, and indeed it would take even two more years from that point before a substantive shift in policy would begin.

Soviet policies aimed at strangling faith and promoting atheism were not carried out on a complacent populace. Many individuals and groups resisted fiercely, and their story is one that is critical to any understanding of the phenomenon of forced secularization. Unfortunately, this dimension is largely absent from modern research seeking to understand secularization in general and forced secularization in particular.[3] By the late 1980s, estimates put the number of believers at around 20 percent of the entire Soviet population, or some 60 million people, almost the same as estimates from the 1960s.[4] This means each and every one of these people retained—or indeed came to—a life of faith against an onslaught of atheism and despite severe repression. These sheer numbers force the scholar to be selective, so in this chapter I place emphasis on the Orthodox Church, the Evangelical-Baptists, and the Pentecostals, groups that are not only important, but the life stories of some of their flocks are illustrative of the many dynamics involved in living a life of faith under an atheist regime.

Faith under Atheism

What distinguishes the 60s and 70s from the preceding period are not drastic changes in Soviet policy toward religion or innovative methods of promoting atheism, but rather the church's fight for survival and the battle waged by believers against the Soviet regime. Certainly resistance had been put up—often heroic—by those who refused to give in to the initial Bolshevik attacks against religion. Numerous sources are available, both from abroad as well as the Soviet archives, attesting to this resistance. This includes such noteworthy episodes as the teachers' strikes in 1917–1918 over the removal of religious instruction from the curriculum to the groups of peasants who were reported as almost universally rallying to the defense of village priests as they were being dragged off never to be seen again. Then, of course, there are the leaders of various religious denominations who fought vigilantly against Soviet repression, often paying the ultimate price for their efforts.

But there is another side of the story that must be considered, that of attempting to live a life of faith in an "ordinary" totalitarian state. One must understand from the beginning that the generation that came of age in the 1960s only knew Soviet life, they were thus not resisting a usurpation of power as was the case with the early forms of resistance, they were rebelling against the very system which had reared them. Soviet socialization methods had failed with them, as did the attempts to inculcate atheism into their minds and hearts. This may not have failed with everyone, but it did fail with a large percentage of society and with each stratum of it. Just as the secularists in the West are often dismayed to see their children turn toward faith, Communist Party members faced a similar predicament. In a letter to Pope Paul VI in 1968, the Russian Orthodox intellectual Anatoly Levitin-Krasnov commented on this phenomenon. As he wrote the Roman Pontiff, "there is a growing number of instances in which the sons of Communists, even of old Chekhists, are baptized." Occurrences such as these raised Levitin's spirits and invigorated his faith. "When we consider these young men and women, who came in as strangers to the church and who just a few years ago did not even have the faintest notion of religion," he continued, the Gospel is what immediately comes to mind.[5]

Bourdeaux, in his critically important work on the subject, provides an excellent example of Soviet citizens who, not raised in the church, nevertheless came to a life of faith in the face of atheism. A particularly telling story is of the young couple Ivan and Tatyana, who became Christians during their studies at Leningrad State University. Despite being raised without any religion and facing a daily onslaught of atheist propaganda, Ivan happened upon a young theology student in a park one day, and his interest in Christianity piqued, the young seminarian gave a manuscript copy of Matthew's Gospel to him. As he said of the experience, "it soon became obvious to me that I had discovered something here which was of infinitely greater value than any of the tomes of Marx, Engels, Lenin or Stalin...the following winter I went to a church secretly and the priest baptized me."[6]

Unlike Ivan and Tatyana, others were raised in faith since birth. Bourdeaux provides the example of the young Galya, who was actually named Marya (Mary), but had been forced to change her name and renounce her faith in a traumatic way. One day the teacher called her to the front of the class and said, "Children, what do you think little Marya has been doing? She's been going to church every week. She thinks that Lenin and Stalin aren't good enough for her. She wants God instead." After chastising the young girl in this way in front of her peers, the teacher continued, "Now, Marya, if I were you, for your own good I would change your name to a nice one, Nina or Natasha or Galya—one that's fit to belong to a good young Stalinist."[7] The young, impressionable girl did exactly that, and began to study hard for her exams on atheism and dialectical materialism, quickly becoming a top student in these areas as well as in her other subjects. But she also retained her Christian beliefs in secret the whole time.

Those like Galya who were raised in a family with religion became an increasingly rare phenomenon as the Soviet era progressed. While this was a somewhat understandable occurrence for the generation of parents who themselves had been raised in a family in which religion was adhered to, once religious belief became a subversive activity, raising one's children to be believers in a society proclaiming the coming of atheism became increasingly costly, dangerous, and rare. Nevertheless, it did persist.

Russian Orthodoxy

It was not only average, everyday Soviet citizens who found their way into the Orthodox Church despite the onslaught of atheist propaganda and the tight restraints placed on the church's evangelistic activities. Again, it was often the children of high-level Communist Party apparatchiks. Archbishop Nikodim, who became chairman of the Department of External Church Relations of the ROC in 1960 at the age of 31, is a prime example. The son of the First Party Secretary of Ryazan', Nikodim chose to be baptized in secret from his parents as a teenager.[8] As so many others, including Fr Vsevolod Shpiller of Moscow, coming to faith in a system that equated religion with drunkenness, debauchery, and backwardness took "a personal conversion experience." Although brought up in an actively anti-religious environment, in the words of Levitin, suddenly young people like these "perceived the Church in her truth and beauty...and joined her."[9]

The Right People will be Found: Fr Alexander Men'

Others, such as Fr Alexander Men', had been raised in the Orthodox faith from birth, being baptized by a member of the catacomb church. This group had gone underground after Sergii had signed his Declaration of Loyalty to the Soviet regime in 1927. They saw this as a betrayal of the Church and Christ, but also as an act with no legitimacy, since they held that Sergii did not have the authority to speak on behalf of the Church (for he was neither patriarch nor canonically locum tenens). One of the priests in this group, Fr Serafim (Batyukov), baptized Alik (as he was known as a boy) and his mother just after his birth in 1935, and both became Fr Serafim's "spiritual children." Alik was raised a believer his whole life, with many believing individuals around him who also instructed him in his religious teaching. He even began following the theological seminary curriculum on his own before he turned 18, being encouraged and guided by Anatoly Vedernikov, then director of studies at the seminary, and later editorial secretary of the *Zhurnal Moskovskoi Patriarkhii* (Journal of the Moscow Patriarchate), which would become an important outlet for Fr Alexander's writings.

Alik also became involved with the "Maroseikans," a group of intellectual and devoted believers associated with the former St. Nicholas Church on Maroseika Street in Moscow. Among this group was a former priest of the catacomb church, the historian and ethnographer Boris Vasilev, who had spent many years in the camps. After World War II, he and his wife were the center of this group, which is where the young and intellectually curious Alik was reared in an informal education in history. Years later a close friend of his said that "he used to say that books found their own way to him when they were needed, just like friends and relatives coming to a birthday party."[10] In these ways, Men' received an amazingly well-rounded and thorough education in history, philosophy, and theology.

Due to his Jewish ethnicity, he was denied acceptance to Moscow State University, and instead enrolled in the Institute of Fur, which nevertheless allowed him to study biology and remain in Moscow. In 1955 he went with the institute where he was studying as it transferred to Irkutsk, and it is from this time that he became roommates with Gleb Yakunin. In the last year of his studies, just before he was to take his examinations, he was dismissed from the program when school officials found out he was a believer. This only gave him the occasion to be ordained, however, which he did in 1958, being ordained a deacon by Fr Nikolai (Golubtsov) and appointed to a parish in the southwest of Moscow. In 1960 he was then ordained a priest in the Donskaya monastery in Moscow by Metropolitan Stefany.

Fr Alexander was only the priest of a small village parish, but his followers—who continue to grow to this day through the efforts of his spiritual children—are many. He became the "evangelist to the intelligentsia."[11] As Roberts and Shukman point out, all of his writing had but a single purpose: "to make the Christian faith real and accessible to those who had been deprived of all religion under Soviet rule."[12] Like himself, this generation of Soviet citizens had been raised as "Soviets," their lives from birth onwards were controlled and regulated by the Soviet system, and they knew nothing of what it was like to live in a society that did not persecute one for his or her faith.

It was here that Fr Alexander's writings on secularization and the separation of church and state are most significant, both to those who lived at the time and were in desperate need of such a witness, and also today, when Orthodoxy is once again struggling to find an appropriate way to deal with the state that is meant to govern the society in which both believers and non-believers live their lives. Fr Alexander taught that Christianity "guards against authoritarianism and paternalism, which are rooted not in the spirit of faith but in characteristics inherent to the fallen nature of humanity"[13] (Matt. 20:25-27; 23:8-12). Living in a regime that offered the dialectical opposite, Men' argued that "the separation of the church from the state is the most desirable situation for faith," and warned that there was great "danger inherent in the very idea of a 'state religion'."[14] While today this has a somewhat different meaning, at the time he was referring to idolatrous pseudo-religions, which to him scientific atheism was an example *par excellence*.

What makes Fr Alexander noteworthy is not that he defied the Soviet system, for it would be difficult to defend the position that he was a dissident. If one understands a dissident as one who engages in organized resistance against a regime, then this would not adequately describe Fr Alexander. He worked within the system, never trying to mask his faith or violate the laws of governing regime. But if one takes dissident to mean someone whose way of thinking, his taken-for-granted reality, stands in sharp contrast to not only the norms of the day but to the values propagated by the governing regime and its elite, then Fr Alexander was certainly a dissident in this respect. It is also this which makes him noteworthy.

Fr Alexander was a voice in the wilderness, a person whose whole life was in so many ways anachronistic with the time in which he lived. In some ways he was a vestige of the past, a product of the thinking of Berdyaev and Soloviev, whose work he devoured again and again. But in another way, he was truly the theologian of "Christianity for the twenty-first century," as some have called him. For here was a man fully aware of the secularizing tendencies associated with modernity and who still found the Christian message vital to the humanity of the modern world. He was a man of science, so clearly not just by his training as a biologist, but by his view of science as a reflection of God's magnificence. As he said, "God gave us two books, the Bible and nature."[15]

Unfortunately, due to the intolerance of some in the world in which he lived, Fr Alexander was not to remain in this world for the twenty-first century; his violent murder on his way to Sunday services in September 1990 assured that. But as he said in an interview near the end of his life, perhaps sensing that he himself would not be here to take part in the critical reform efforts of the 1990s, he knew that nevertheless, "the right people will be found."[16]

A Voice Against Church and State: Fr Gleb Yakunin

In many ways, Fr Gleb Yakunin lived a life parallel to that of Fr Alexander. Both were born in Moscow within months of each other, and the two were even roommates during their studies at the Irkutsk Agricultural Institute in the 1950s. Once back in Moscow, they both were ordained and served as parish priests in the Orthodox Church, and remained extremely close friends. While Fr Alexander would not live to see the drastic transformation in religious life in Russia after the Soviet collapse, Fr Gleb would himself play an important role throughout the 1990s, criticizing the church for its unscrupulous economic activities and even serving as a deputy in the Russian Duma. In the roles of deputy and priest, Fr Gleb found himself in the awkward position of being a critic of the two institutions to which he belonged, the church and the state.

It was during the turbulent 1960s, however, that the different paths of these two great men began to unfold. Shortly after the Orthodox Church's new regulations were issued in 1961, which drastically altered the role of the priest in relation to his parish, removing him from its administrative affairs and leaving him simply as worship leader and spiritual guide,[17] a dozen or so young clergy serving in Moscow began to meet for discussion and share their experiences. This group was the brainchild of Fr Alexander, and included not only his old roommate, but also Fr Dmitri Dudko and Fr Nikolai Eshliman, with Anatoly Levitin-Krasnov frequently joining the conversation. Soon Metropolitan Ermogen, at the group's request, began to serve as their bishop and spiritual guide.

One of the central themes of the group's discussions was what he called "Sergievshchina" (the more contemporary term is *Sergianstvo*), a pejorative reference to the proclamation of loyalty by Sergii to the atheist state in 1927.[18] The group was not only dissatisfied with the 1961 regulations, but was also becoming increasingly opposed to the Moscow Patriarchate's failure to resist Khrushchev's anti-religion campaign. In 1964 the group decided to stop talking and to start writing, eventually drafting a detailed and lengthy pair of letters to the Politburo and Patriarch Alexii. This they did with the assistance of Levitin and the approval of Ermogen. By the time the letters were completed, however, it was already October, and Khrushchev had just been removed from power. Ermogen cautioned the group that it was not an opportune moment to submit the letters, and while Fr Alexander obeyed the spiritual instruction of his bishop, Yakunin and Eshliman proceeded and submitted the letters on their own. This not only illustrates the great degree of Christian obedience observed by Fr Alexander, but it also marked what was probably a decisive turning point in the life and career of Fr Gleb. From this point forward, Fr Gleb was a dissident.

The letter to the Politburo, sent to Podgorny, criticized the Soviet regime for abrogating its own laws on church and state. In particular, criticism was directed at the illegal transformation of the Council of Russian Orthodox Church Affairs, which had "radically changed its function. From being an official department for arbitration, it became an organ of unofficial and illegal control over the Moscow Patriarchate." The intrusion of its leaders and officials into the internal life of the Church "must be regarded as a flagrant violation of the very principles of socialist justice and Soviet legislation on religion and the church."[19] The "open letter" to Patriarch Alexii described the pressures under which members of the church were living, appealing to the Patriarch to be more resolute in standing up against state interference in church affairs. But it also pointed out that "such a situation in the church could occur only with the connivance of the supreme ecclesiastical authorities, which have deviated from their sacred duty before Christ and the church and have clearly violated the apostolic command by 'compromising with this world'."[20] Patriarch Alexii pointed out in his response that the young priests had themselves violated apostolic command to obey church rules and the directives of their superiors, which they vowed to do upon their ordination. This is, of course, precisely what kept Fr Alexander from adding his name to the letters. The Patriarch then disciplined both Frs Gleb and Nikolai, and while they were permitted to remain priests, their sacramental authority was suspended.

Yakunin refrained from dissident activity for most of the next decade, performing various functions in several Moscow parishes, serving as a reader and even watchman. But then in 1974 he began writing more letters to clergy both within the Russian Orthodox Church and outside, including the World Council of Churches. In 1975 he penned another letter to the Politburo, this time protesting their decision to make Easter Day a work day for all Soviet citizens. The next year, Yakunin formed the "Christian Committee in Defense of the Rights of Believers in the USSR," which from this time until his arrest in 1979 published hundreds of documents, letters, and other materials documenting the mass violation of religious freedom in the Soviet Union. These activities led to his arrest on charges of "anti-Soviet propaganda and agitation."

Yakunin was put on trial in August 1980, and for 3 days was tried in a half-empty courtroom, with multiple guards and secret police outside to prevent the many protestors from interfering. As monk Inokenty reported, Yakunin's right even to have a state-appointed defense attorney was violated, and only witnesses for the prosecution were permitted in the court proceedings. These, including A. Osipov and Metropolitan Igumen (Pustoutov), both of the church's department of external church affairs, acted as "false witnesses" according to Inokenty. The court was able to prevent witnesses for the defense from appearing by withholding their court summons, which they only received days after the sentencing had already been handed down.[21] Yakunin was sentenced to the Gulag, and was finally amnestied in 1987 at the start of *perestroika*.

Soviet Baptists

As with those who found the Orthodox Church during Khrushchev's thaw, estimates are that probably more were drawn to Protestant churches. As Levitin-Krasnov himself lamented in his letter to Pope Paul VI, "We have cited examples of conversions to Christianity in the Russian Orthodox Church. But the Baptists can pride themselves on an even greater number of conversions." Quite significantly, he also pointed out that "in every case…the conversions take place among those young people who were previously unchurched."[22] While this is a point to which we will return in the conclusion, for now we can take note of the fact that, for a variety of reasons, religious seekers were turning to "foreign" religious traditions in greater numbers than a religious tradition with a millennium-long history in their native land.

On the one hand, religious traditions that were understood as having a "Western" or "American" origin (many in Russia still believe that Protestantism is an American phenomenon), were attractive for a number of reasons, including their "halo of martyrdom"[23] and perception of foreignness and opposition to Soviet power, which rendered such faiths "not just attractive, but even fashionable."[24] On the other hand, more experiential and charismatic forms of religion have been popular in Russia throughout its history, even giving birth to several such sects itself. Indeed, Kolarz rightly points out that Protestantism among Russians and Ukrainians must be understood as "a synthesis of Western Protestantism with Russian-Ukrainian piety."[25] Claims that Protestant forms of belief and practice are "unnatural" to Russian culture are not firmly rooted in Russian religious history.

Baptists: Origins and Survival

The Baptists entered the Russian Empire in the nineteenth century through three separate streams, the Caucasus, Ukraine, and St. Petersburg. While the baptism of Nikita Voronin in the river Kura, outside Tbilisi, on August 20, 1867 is typically taken as the beginning of the Evangelical Baptist brotherhood in Russia, in fact on September 22, 1861 the Latvian Baptists were born when pastor Adams Gertner baptized 72 people in the Ziros river near Vindava.[26] In Ukraine Baptists became known as "stundists," since their roots were related to German Baptists who had organized "Bibelstunden" (Bible-studies). In St. Petersburg they were often referred to as "Pashkovtsy," after Colonel Pashkov, a member of the local intelligentsia who had converted after encountering a Bible group organized by the Englishman Lord Radstock. As an aide to the tsar and wealthy landowner, Pashkov became associated with the Baptist movement that grew rapidly in the capital,[27] and he was especially influential in spreading the movement among the poorer classes of society.[28] Though the League of Russian Baptists began its existence in 1884, the group did not officially exist until the 1905 proclamation of religious liberty made by Tsar Nicholas II.

During the Bolshevik Revolution and on into the 1920s, the Baptists, along with other evangelical groups, grew rapidly. One method of their spread was through their youth organizations, which came to be known as the "Bapsomol" or "Khristomol," meaning Baptist or Christian youth league. A *Pravda* article from 1921 complained that the Baptist youth organization had more new youth members than the party's Komsomol.[29] Such a trend aggravated Bukharin, and in an address to the eighth All-Union Congress of the Komsomol in 1928, he criticized these "replica" organizations as well as the Komsomol itself for not competing more effectively against the religious youth organizations. The Baptists had a good explanation for their success: "We begin our work where you end. You work in the clubs and in meetings, and we in the streets outside the clubs and after your meetings."[30] At a Komsomol conference the following year, another Politburo member, Rudzutak, even quoted the example of a Russian girl who had left the Komsomol to join a "Khristomol" because, as she put it, "she had met finer people there" than in the Komsomol.[31]

The Baptists also became connected with the government strategy of weakening the Russian Orthodox Church, with the Bolsheviks seeing the Baptists as a way of weakening its power by competing against it for believers. The Baptists had several characteristics which made them less offensive to the Communists. For one, they had been persecuted by the tsarist regime as they had, and since they had not been in any way an instrument of tsarist autocracy, they were not seen as counter-revolutionary. Moreover, the anti-religion measures of the early Bolshevik regime, such as confiscation of church property, removal of church bells, and closing of churches, had very little affect on them. As Kolarz points out, they were able to say, "The communists are quite right about the Orthodox Church; but look how different we are—no pomp, no icons, no relics and no priests."[32] After the 1929 law was passed and Stalin began to impose greater restrictions on religion again, however, this period came to abrupt end and the Baptists suffered as all other religious groups would.

Soon after Stalin's concordat with the Russian Orthodox Church in 1943, the regime changed its strategy toward the Baptists and other Evangelicals, including Pentecostals—to unite them all into a single organization that could be used to monitor, co-opt, and infiltrate them, the All-Union Council of Evangelical Christians—Baptists (AUCECB). In many ways, this organization was to function similarly to the Council on Russian Orthodox Church Affairs. While the Soviets clearly saw the differences between the Baptists and the Pentecostals, apparently they concluded that the common theological belief in believer's baptism was sufficient to warrant uniting these two groups who differ so much in theology and ritual. The Baptists struggled with the Pentecostals for leadership of the Council, and once some 50 percent or so of the Pentecostals failed to join or left the Council, the Baptists emerged as the leaders of this group.

By the time Khrushchev came to power, the official number of Baptists in the Soviet Union stood at 545,000, but such a number is a gross underestimation for a number of reasons.[33] First, we know that only about half of all Protestant congregations in the Soviet Union were officially registered.[34] Additionally, Baptists only count those who have received a believer's baptism as members, meaning that those seekers involved in the church, as well as the youth, are not counted. At this time a more accurate estimation of the number of Baptists in the Soviet Union was approximately 3 million, with registered communities in every corner of the USSR.[35] Contemporary observers described the Evangelical Christians and Baptists as "the most active Christian church in the Soviet Union."[36]

Khrushchev's renewed restrictions on religious groups would force a split within the Baptist camp, however, as a group that would come to be known as the *Initsiativniki* (initiative group) quickly split off from the Council over what they perceived as a "caving in" to the atheist state. This younger, more evangelical group refused to be servile before the authorities and their renewed pressure against the churches. This is precisely what the Council had done, they argued, when it had come up with a new set of policies and procedures in 1960 for the Baptist churches in the union, the New Statutes and Letter of Instructions, which included severe restrictions on their religious activities, and even pledged to keep the membership of younger people in their churches low. The parallel here with the Orthodox Church's regulations of 1961 is no coincidence, as they both stemmed from similar directives from the Politburo.

Under the leadership of such figures as Georgi Vins and Gennady Kryuchkov, the *Initsiativniki* were bold believers who were willing to stand up against the authorities, and they wished to convene a congress (this is the "initiative" from which their name derives) in order to get the union to support their position. After the leaders of the AUCECB and *Initsiativniki* met in 1961 and were unable to come to an agreement that would have kept the two groups together, the *Initsiativniki* went their own way, while the majority of Russian Baptists followed the AUCECB line. In 1965, they adopted the formal name of Reform Baptists, and they continued publishing their journal *Bratskii Listok*, their response to the AUCECB's *Bratskii Vestnik*.

Given their more radical stance, the Reform Baptists frequently found themselves in court, admittedly a better fate than had befallen many others during the Stalin and Khrushchev eras. Just how incompetent the Soviet criminal system was in dealing with such cases brought before them by the KGB and other state organs is illustrated by an exchange between a prosecutor and a subpoenaed witness. The prosecutor asked, "what do you know about the accused?" as he pointed to a group of Baptists who were on trial, to which the Baptist witness responded, "I know that their names are written in the Book of Life." The prosecutor quickly burst out "show us this book, we need documents!"[37] The Baptists themselves were quite savvy in their handling of their court proceedings. They were not afraid to defend their rights as Soviet citizens, even calling upon Lenin in their defense: "there is Lenin's law of liberty of conscience for believers," they would often point out to the court that was trying them for their beliefs.[38]

Fathers and Sons: Peter and Georgi Vins

There is probably no better personal history to illustrate the persecution and suffering of the Baptists in the Soviet Union than the "three generations of suffering" of the Vins family. The first imprisonment of Peter Vins coincides perfectly with the renewed Stalinist crackdown on religion in 1929, while the third prison sentence of his son, Georgi, brings us all the way to the final years of Leonid Brezhnev. Their story begins shortly after the end of the relatively mild treatment enjoyed by Baptists during the 1920s, which was marked by the passing of the 1929 law on religious associations. In Moscow in 1930 as an official representative of the Evangelical Christians-Baptists of the Far East region, where he was to take part in a church assembly, Vins was approached by an NKVD officer shortly after his arrival. He was "instructed" which two candidates he should support in the elections the next day for the leadership of the church council, but he refused. These candidates, of course, won their seats anyway, and a few days later Vins was arrested.[39]

After serving out his first term in prison, Vins returned to Siberia and set once again about conducting his work as a pastor, visiting believers, consoling those in need, and preaching scripture. He was arrested again during his time in Omsk, with the local NKVD suspecting him of living a life of luxury off the backs of other believers. When they arrested him they were astonished at the poor conditions in which he and his family lived. "I expected to see the luxurious flat of an American missionary," he said, "but here is poverty."[40]

His incarceration only lasted 9 months this time, and since he was in a local prison, his wife and son could deliver him packages on the weekend. And as soon as he was released, he immediately set back to his work of preaching, leading prayer meetings, and consoling other believers. Georgi recalls that their door was seldom closed, with people constantly coming and going. Despite the threat of arrest and hard labor in the Gulag constantly looming over his head, Peter Vins never stopped preaching and spreading the Gospel with others.

He would be arrested again before long, and he knew it. So did the young Georgi, for every time his parents began to gather warm clothes and sew pieces of the Gospel into the jacket collar and the pants lining, he knew the time was near. When crusts of bread and other non-perishable food were gathered up and put into a sack, though, he knew the day had arrived.[41]

As Stalin's second purge got underway, those around him tried to warn Vins and his long-time companion in evangelism, Anton Martynenko, to lay low and that they should be careful or soon they would find themselves back in prison. To this Martynenko fatefully replied "here we are guests, soon we will go home again—to prison!"[42] This is indeed the fate that soon befell them. Vins' wife, Lidia, gathered up a bag of crusts one day in 1937 as Peter Vins was being whisked off once again. He and Martynenko did not return from the camps this time, however, with Vins himself dying in 1943 in a Siberian labor camp.

In many ways, Georgi followed in his father's footsteps, both figuratively, as he became a Baptist leader himself and was persecuted and imprisoned on several occasions for his beliefs, but also literally, as Georgi once served in the very prison where his father had before him, that is, Solikamsk. From a very young age Georgi knew his calling was to follow in his father's footsteps. He watched as not only his father and friend were repeatedly whisked away, but "husbands and sons, fathers and mothers" were constantly being taken from their homes and placed in prisons for their religious activities. As Georgi later recalled in his memoir, "And so I came into communion with the persecuted Church of Christ in Russia!"[43]

During the period of relative relaxation of religion policy after World War II, Georgi Vins was able to live a life of faith and be an active pastor. But once the Khrushchev crackdown began, the fate of the younger Vins began to unfold. After the AUCECB published the "Letter of Instructions" and "New Statutes" in 1960, Vins was one of those who immediately protested, arguing that the policies betrayed the ideals for which his father so long and bitterly suffered.[44] Georgi became one of the leading figures in the *Initsiativniki*, though he was less radical than some of the others. The Reform Baptists, as they were now known, broke off from the Council in 1965, from which point they persistently asked the government for official recognition, being refused each time.

The Reform Baptists were not going to give up so easily, and they decided to hold a demonstration in protest. On May 16, 1966, some 500 Baptists from congregations all over the Soviet Union assembled in front of the Communist Party headquarters in Moscow. They then moved into the courtyard, carrying a letter listing their request for permission to hold a congress and to be officially recognized by the Soviet government. The group's leaders requested permission to see Brezhnev, and though they were allowed to enter the building, they were never to meet with the general secretary. Instead, the police descended upon the praying Baptists outside, who sang hymns as they were assaulted and rounded up.[45] Even more current Russian sources offer a different story, reporting that the leaders yelled as the KGB approached, "brothers and sisters, will we leave here or die?" to which the crowd responded, "we will die!" in unison.[46]

Although many of the demonstrators were already in custody, two of its leaders were not. When they walked boldly into the Central Committee offices the next day and informed them that they represented the suppressed demonstrators, Gennady Kryuchkov and Vins were arrested immediately and joined the other demonstrators at the infamous Lefortovo prison. That fall the two leaders were subjected to a long trial and subsequently sentenced to 3 years in prison.

After he returned from prison and regained his health, which deteriorated significantly during his period of incarceration, Vins was quickly sentenced to 1 year of forced labor, and summoned to the district's procurator's office. Vins refused to go, and instead sent a letter informing the procuracy that, as an elected member of the church (he was now secretary and Kryuchkov chairman) he should not be forced to work. So, he was leaving the factory and returning to his ministry. For the next 3 years Georgi was on the run from the KGB as he traveled throughout the Soviet Union preaching the Gospel and engaged in his church functions.

One day in 1974, while on a train in Novosibirsk, they caught up with him. He was quickly sent to Kiev where he was held and interrogated. Vins was asked by one of the KGB officers handling his case about what the Reform Baptists demanded in order to end their resistance to the Soviet state. Vins replied with a litany of demands, arguing that the state must abrogate the law on religious associations of 1929, give freedom to preach the Gospel, dismiss all Christians from prisons, camps and exiles, and return all children who had been taken from their parents because of giving them a Christian education. "That is impossible! That is an ultimatum!" replied the KGB officer, to which Vins responded, it was not an ultimatum, simply the only way to resolve the dispute. "I'm talking about the *minimum* terms which would return the confidence of the believers," he added, "there is no other way!"[47]

Vins was held for more than a year (a violation of the Soviet penal code) before being put on trial. Initially, a Russian-speaking Norwegian lawyer had offered to defend Vins at his trial. Vins demanded a believing attorney, and Alf Haerem was an answered prayer, but the Soviet Union would

not issue him a visa. In protest, and recognizing the trial would be a mock-
ery of justice anyway, Vins did not accept state-appointed counsel and also
refused to defend himself. He was ultimately found guilty of violating the
Soviet law on separation of church and state and of circulating deliberately
false statements which defamed the Soviet Union and was sentenced to the
Gulag once again. Four years later, however, he was released as part of a prisoner exchange and sent into forced exile in the United States, thus becoming
the only Soviet citizen imprisoned specifically for Christian activity ever to
be expelled from the USSR.

Aida of Leningrad

A young lady from Leningrad was present at Vins' 1966 trial, and she would
soon find herself in a similar courtroom, with her friends transcribing the
trial proceedings of this young outspoken Christian. Aida Skripnikova was
born in a small town in Siberia in the first year of the Nazi invasion of the
Soviet Union. She was raised in a home of deep Baptist faith, with her father
having been shot during the Russian Civil War for refusing to fight on religious grounds, and her mother raising the children in a "Christian spirit."
When she was only 11 years old, Aida's mother died as well, forcing the children to move to another town where they received a typical Soviet education.
As Tapley points out, she "did not so much lose her faith as she was bombarded with atheist propaganda." With the influence of her mother gone,
"Aida was no doubt confused and naïve, willing to believe the teachings of
the new authority figures in her life."[48]

Aida moved back to Leningrad in 1960, where her brother was already
living. One day while walking down Nevsky Prospekt the two young Soviet
citizens happened upon a house of prayer and went in. Thus began Aida's
reacquaintance with Christianity. Her brother Viktor was already a believing Christian, and his faith would strongly influence Aida, as did his passing shortly after she had moved to Leningrad. Viktor's unwavering faith
throughout his illness deeply influenced Aida, who began to regularly attend
a Baptist church after his passing, eventually being baptized after a considerable period of searching and growing in her faith. Once she had been
baptized, Aida longed to share her newly found faith with those around her,
proving fearless in her activities.

What probably caught the attention of the Soviet authorities more than
anything else was Aida's active attempts to inform Westerners of the plight
of believers in the Soviet Union. In sharp contrast to the period of Stalin's
liberalization of religion policy, which was promoted internationally with

great fanfare and church delegations, the crackdown of the 1960s was kept as quiet as possible, and remained largely unknown in the West for quite some time. Aida firmly believed that the Soviet government's actions toward Christians were a violation of their human rights, and she "toiled tirelessly to make the world aware of what life was like for Christians behind the Iron Curtain."[49]

In addition to calling Western attention to the plight of Soviet Christians and working tirelessly to increase the number of the latter, Aida also became involved with the *Initsiativniki*, which encouraged such missionizing efforts. They also rejected the AUCECB's passive acceptance of the order in the "Letter of Instructions" to "reduce the number of baptisms among those aged 18–25 as much as possible." Aida had experienced this practice first-hand when she was coming of faith, and this must have added to her feelings of identification with the *Initsiativniki*.

Aida was arrested for the first time outside the Museum of History and Science of Atheism on Nevsky Prospekt, where she stood on New Year's Eve in 1961 distributing a postcard with a poem about repentance and salvation she had written herself. The recent death of her brother must have surely weighed strongly on her young mind at this time, and started her thinking about the brevity and preciousness of life. Though this time she was released without a prison sentence, only losing her residency permit and job, the next time she would not be so lucky, and would be forced to serve 1 year in a labor camp in Siberia for residing in Leningrad without a residency permit, although the real reason was her involvement in illegal church meetings in the forests outside the city.[50]

Upon her return to Leningrad, Aida had difficulty finding and retaining employment. Once she was found out, she would be dismissed and have to find a new place to work in order to provide for herself. In one case, the secretary of the party organization offered to "take up the task of rehabilitating her through a 'proof-reading course'," but of course she refused.[51] Shortly thereafter Aida met a woman from Sweden, and began to supply her trial transcripts of believers and other information about the persecution of believers in the Soviet Union. Aida also gave her copies of the *Listok Spaseniya* and *Bratskii Listok*, while she received Bibles to be distributed among Soviet believers in exchange (some reports from this time state that Baptists and other Protestants were prepared to pay up to 300 rubles—a third of the monthly salary of well-paid worker—to get their hands on a Bible). When the authorities searched her home in April 1968, they found numerous copies of these two journals, as well as the transcripts of the 1966 trial of Vins and Kryutchkov.

Aida was charged with "systematically distributing among Soviet citizens and also among foreign subjects literature illegally published" in the USSR, as well as many reports and appeals which "contain deliberately false statements slandering the Soviet state and social order."[52] But unlike so many other trials which she had herself witnessed, at these court proceedings she was allowed to speak in her own defense as long as she wished. As she explained, this was because of "her contact with the West and their involvement in the case" and the court's suspicion that it was being monitored by foreigners. Aida used this opportunity to chastise the Soviet state for its appalling treatment of believers. As she later recalled in a 2000 interview, "I was able to tell the court that it was true that there was persecution in the USSR."[53]

Using this opportunity before the court, Aida surveyed the history of persecution of believers in the Soviet Union, particularly under Khrushchev, maintaining that anyone who truly believes in God will break the laws that forbade the teaching of religion to children, gathering for worship in people's homes, and missionizing. As Aida told the court, "believers cannot keep a law which forces them to deny the Gospel," and that while an atheist can be either militant or non-militant, "a Christian cannot be anything but militant."[54] As Tapley described her significance, Aida's struggles show "that one person can make a difference and overcome insurmountable odds if they have faith," with her story inspiring "not just family and friends but thousands around the world at a time when more and more knowledge of religious persecution in the Soviet Union was coming to light."[55]

Soviet Pentecostals

Despite their own battles against the Soviet regime, the Baptists resented the Pentecostals. They had been united with the Baptists into the AUCECB after World War II, but as a group they were extremely unhappy with the arrangement. For one, they held great disdain for centralized organization (which the Baptists favored), but they also perceived strong negative attitudes against them from the Baptists and others in the union. Most of the Pentecostal congregations eventually joined the union, but only after an agreement which was supposed to be a concession to the Pentecostals by the Baptists. Instead, it was used to encourage them to preach against and eventually abandon practices such as foot washing, *glossolalia*, and other "manifestations of the Holy Spirit that might destroy the decency and decorum" of Pentecostal religious services.[56] Essentially, the Baptists were trying to put an end to practices with which they were uncomfortable and disagreed theologically (for instance, the Baptists believed speaking in tongues was only a gift of the Holy Spirit to the Apostles themselves). Of course, this meant nothing short of eliminating the very practices that distinguished the Pentecostals from the Baptists.

In the end, Soviet authorities were able to force most Pentecostals to join the AUCECB. According to official figures, some 25,000 Pentecostals in more than 400 local congregations joined, with the majority coming from Ukraine, the Baltic republics, and Belorussia, while most Pentecostals in Russia preferred an illegal existence to AUCECB oversight. Those who were pushed into the AUCECB continually struggled with the Baptists who were its leaders. Even the Baptist journal *Bratskii Vestnik* (Brethren Herald) published articles critical of Pentecostals and their practices, singling them out for their unorthodox beliefs and rituals.

Pentecostalism: Origins and Survival

The origins of Pentecostalism in the Russian Empire can be traced back to the beginning of the twentieth century to two distinct streams. The first was introduced in 1911, when the first Pentecostal missionary, a Mr. Urshan (possibly of Norway), began work in Helsinki, then part of the Tsarist empire. It was here that N. F. Smorodin and A. I. Ivanov, preachers from a sectarian group, joined the movement and rapidly became its indigenous leaders. The fledgling church quickly moved into the Vyborg region and established Russia's first Pentecostal congregation, which then quickly spread farther afield, first to St. Petersburg and then to Novgorod, followed by Moscow. By 1915 they had reached the Caucasus.[57]

The more significant stream, however, entered a few years later in Ukraine when Ivan Voronaev, a Russian Baptist who had converted to Pentecostalism while pastoring a congregation in New York, returned to the Russian Empire as a missionary in 1921 and settled in Odessa. By 1924 he had formed the Union of Christians of Evangelical Faith, and within another 4 years was able to claim 350 assemblies with 17,000 members[58]

Pentecostals were able to spread rapidly during the advantageous political climate of the 1920s, when the Soviet authorities were less repressive toward religion in general, and even outright supportive of groups that could potentially attract members away from the powerful Russian Orthodox Church. The rapid rise of Voronaev's Pentecostals brought the attention of the Soviet authorities, and as the climate of religious tolerance changed under Stalin, Voronaev was imprisoned. He was released in 1935, but shortly rearrested during the height of Stalin's purges, never to return. Thus began the Pentecostals' long period of persecution and their fight for religious freedom.

Despite persecution, purges, and war, by World War II the number of Pentecostals in the Soviet Union had reached 80,000.[59] It is also estimated that the movement was already 50 percent non-Russian, with strongholds in Belarus, Ukraine, and the newly-incorporated territories along the post-war Soviet border, including the Baltics, eastern Poland, and Moldova.[60] Following the war and Stalin's liberalization on religion policy, they began to spread again, first throughout the black earth region and the Russian heartland, then moving east to Siberia and even to the Russian Pacific coast.

It was at the end of the war that the Pentecostals were joined together with the Baptists into the AUCEB. As mentioned above, most of the Pentecostal congregations eventually joined the union, but they continually struggled with the Baptists who were its leaders. The Baptists were trying to put an end to practices with which they were uncomfortable and disagreed theologically. More so than other Protestant denominations, the Pentecostals were "strange"—their speaking in tongues, love feasts, foot washing, and "shaking" (as they would shake while speaking in tongues; they were even known colloquially as *tryasuny*, or "shakers") all struck the average Soviet citizen as fanatical and bizarre. This was a fact the Soviet authorities played up, as they made a short "documentary" on them, "In the World of a Nightmare," which was shown before full-length features in theatres, much like the "support the war" films shown in the United States during WWII. A photo-documentary was also produced in magazine form and made available, showing some excellent examples of anti-religious propaganda and some really bad examples of Soviet photo-doctoring![61]

The Pentecostals behaved differently in more ways than just their rituals. Politically, Pentecostals were some of the first to engage in anti-Soviet political activities. As early as 1957, a full decade before the dissident movement in the Soviet Union was to get underway, a pipe-fitter in the Kherson shipyards and his Pentecostal brethren "crashed" an atheism propaganda lecture.[62] After the young atheist speaker (a former Orthodox seminarian), finished his lecture on religion as false consciousness, the Pentecostal elder responded that he did not believe only because he had never seen a genuine miracle, at which point he began trembling and speaking in tongues in front of the gathering. Behavior like this—coupled with Soviet propaganda efforts—did little to improve the image of Pentecostals among their fellow citizens.

Khrushchev's renewed attack on religion forced the Pentecostals to pursue a new strategy. Rather than face off with authorities, they migrated frequently, moving farther and farther east and eventually finding something of a refuge in Siberia. One account states that they moved as frequently as every 2–3 years, enjoying religious liberty upon settling in a new area unfamiliar with them and their practices, and then moving again as a group once local resentment and suppression became intolerable. This behavior must also be seen as part of their missionizing effort, if not as a strategy then as an added benefit.

The Pentecostals understood the means of repression being used against them and tried to use that knowledge to thwart Soviet attempts to curb their activity. They were known to spend months planning clandestine meetings in the countryside, frustrating attempts to monitor and track them. To avoid the eye of the authorities, they would pass on information using only word of mouth, not phones or written announcements. Then, at the predetermined date and time, they would descend upon a river embankment or hillside in droves, sometimes 10,000–20,000 of them, with hundreds of candidates for baptism. As they conducted their service, they would ignore the police and KGB who tried to disperse them. The Keston Archive is filled with photos of Pentecostals engaging in mass river baptisms while KGB and police attempt to intervene, with the gathered faithful hardly even acknowledging their presence.[63] Oftentimes, however, ignoring them was impossible, as the Soviet authorities would resort to more severe methods, such as water cannons and tear gas, tactics which proved more effective at breaking up the Pentecostal gatherings.

He Wrestles with God: Ivan Fedotov

Another way of curtailing the growth of the Pentecostals was to attack the movement's leaders. This was the tactic used against Ivan Fedotov, who eventually became a bishop of the Christians of Evangelical Faith—Pentecostals. Born in Tambov in 1929, nothing from this man's childhood signaled his eventual resistance against the Soviet regime. He had been a *Komsomol* member and even worked at a factory which supplied the army during his youth, then joining the Soviet Navy upon graduation (where he became a champion wrestler in the Soviet fleet). Ivan Fedotov's "career as a model Soviet citizen," however, "changed abruptly when he became a Christian."[64] During a brief visit to his mother in Moscow in 1954, he attended a Baptist church service with her, and there he became a Christian. He became an active member in the Moscow Baptist Church, where he attended for 4 years. But then he heard about the "baptism of the spirit," and he immediately sought to be baptized in such a way. He then began to witness to other members of his church and to speak in tongues, which led him and his growing group of followers to be excommunicated from the Baptist church.

Fedotov and the others joined a small Pentecostal house church in Moscow, but soon it began to grow, so large, in fact, that they began to hold outdoor meetings. This is where they came to the attention of the Soviet authorities, who immediately tried to get him out of Moscow. He lost his job and was sentenced to hard labor for 1 month for "damaging bushes" in the woods where the group met. Fedotov did not waiver, and soon the authorities took a drastic move to curtail the efforts of this charismatic Pentecostal leader.

The scheme involved a widow named Anna Krasina, whom Fedotov had allegedly told to sacrifice her daughter for the remission of her sins, including sending the young girl to a Young Pioneer summer camp. *Moskovskaya Pravda* reported the event in this way: "Ivan Fedotov yelled that the 'holy spirit' had come over him and that he demanded 'sister' Anna to lay her hands on her daughter and sacrifice her to god."[65] At his trial for "incitement for murder" the prosecution showed a film in which Mrs. Krasina ran up to the altar during one of Fedotov's outdoor sermons, begging not to have to sacrifice her daughter. The film had been shot by a member of the KGB who was hiding in the bushes waiting for the staged event to occur. Though Mrs. Krasina later recanted and attempted to withdraw her testimony, she was threatened with giving false testimony and changed her mind, while the film was shown at Fedotov's trial. In this way, Fedotov received the first of his eventual three prison terms, this one for 10 years.

Upon his release and relocation to the small town of Maloyaroslavets in Kaluga, Fedotov resumed his ministry. Again, the authorities quickly identified him as a trouble-maker and set out to persecute him and his church. One event, from 1974, resulted in his arrest for "slandering the Soviet state and social order." The church he led was growing fiercely, and its members wished to have a religious service for their weddings, rather than going to the state's marriage registration office for the event. In this particular case, many parishioners flocked to the house where the service was held, and the police and KGB prevented many from entering, cordoning off the entrance way and offering an intimidating presence by parking several police cars and trucks in front of the house, while officers went around with megaphones and cameras. Once these methods failed to disperse the event, they managed to get a "drunken hooligan" to enter the house, who ran around swearing and throwing his fists at the guests.[66]

The tactics used by Soviet authorities against Fedotov are symptomatic of those used against all Pentecostals. With their strange rituals, the

Pentecostals were a prime target. But focusing on such practices as foot washing and speaking in tongues was apparently not enough to sufficiently shock the Soviet population. So, the answer was to invent outright fabrications about them, in this case, seizing upon the myth that Pentecostals practiced child sacrifice. This myth was spread through workplace lectures on the danger of Pentecostals, and in the case of Fedotov even warning parents of school-children in the area that he practiced child sacrifice.[67] The brief clip from the outdoor service at which Krasina begged not to have to sacrifice her daughter eventually made its way into a KGB-directed film, "It Shocks Us All" (Eto trevozhit vsekh). This short film, which provided supposed "evidence" of child sacrifice among Pentecostals was also shown before full-length features in movie theatres throughout the Soviet Union.

The Siberian Seven

We began this chapter with the story of the Vashchenko's, the family that sought refuge in the U.S. Embassy in 1963. In the years that followed, the family continuously pleaded their case for immigration with Soviet authorities, eventually submitting 300 applications and appeals, including letters to Khrushchev and Brezhnev. All these efforts were to no avail. Meanwhile, their son Alexander was sent to the Gulag after conscientiously objecting to serve in the Red Army. He had been drafted right out of school, and told the conscription officer that "I am a believing Christian, and I fulfill God's commandment, 'You shall not kill'." The officer then grabbed the young man's father around the neck and told him, "you have taught your son to lose his head with his God. We are going to draft him and reeducate him. Then he will understand everything and he himself will deal with you."[68]

In June 1978 the Pentecostal family from Siberia once again barged into the U.S. Embassy, along with a fellow believer and her son. A Soviet guard attempted to stop them this time, and caught a hold of their youngest son, holding him down while the others ran through the gates and onto the embassy grounds. Another daughter later informed the parents that the young man had been returned home after a few days, apparently after having been tortured and beaten. He got "the full treatment, almost the electric chair," she exclaimed, "don't leave the embassy" she warned her parents.[69] Thus began the 5-year struggle of the group that came to be known as the "Siberian Seven." Once the embassy personnel realized they were not going to leave—and the embassy staff was not about to throw them to the wolves, so to speak—they were allowed to live cramped into small quarters in the embassy basement, performing odd jobs to make ends meet.

President Ronald Reagan discussed their plight during his presidential campaign, chastising the Carter administration for not using more aggressive means to get the Siberian Seven released. In 1980 several U.S. Congressmen, including Jack Edwards, Richard Shelby, and David Boren, visited them in Moscow, and shortly afterward nearly 50 members of Congress submitted an appeal to Brezhnev "urging" that they be granted visas in order to emigrate.[70] The media in the United States and throughout Europe were active in advocating on their behalf, including academics such as Kent Hill. Others, however, such as Paul Steeves, were less sympathetic. In a letter to *Christianity Today*, Steeves explained that this group was "very different from the 3 or 4 million Soviet evangelicals who, despite difficulties, are able to find a way of living as Christians within" Soviet society, even pointing out that Western attention "aggravates the conditions of life" for other Christians in the Soviet Union for they only "confirm the slander of the Soviet Communists who portray evangelicals as traitors and pariahs."[71]

In a letter of January 1983, the Vashchenko children wrote to the new general secretary of the CPSU, Yuri Andropov, reminding him that they "have outlasted two leaders" already, and were not going to go away. "God will force you…to resolve our case righteously as He did with the king of Egypt," they wrote.[72] Within 6 months of this appeal to the new General Secretary, the Vashchenko and Chmykalov families were free. After a protracted hunger strike inspired by the example of Andrei Sakharov, Lydia Vashchenko was wheeled out of the embassy in a wheelchair after Soviet authorities promised they would "look favorably" upon their application to emigrate. Within weeks the family was granted visas and emigrated, only finding the religious liberty they longed for abroad rather than in their native land. Within another 6 months, Andropov died of renal failure.

Ordinary Heroes

One must admit that the Soviet efforts at promoting atheism and killing the church had been successful to a considerable extent. Of course, they could boast that they had reduced the church to a shell of its former self, from nearly 80,000 churches on the eve of the Revolution to some 5,000 at the dawn of the Brezhnev stagnation. At the same time, the believing population had been halved, with estimates from the early 1960s suggesting that only about one-third of the population were still believers. This means that after a half century of persecution and atheist propaganda one in three people were still believers, retaining their faith despite daily exposure to propaganda and socialization efforts aimed at converting each and every member of society into an atheist.

If one considers views on religion themselves, rather than actual religious beliefs, we also see that, once the height of persecution had passed, attitudes relaxed as well. Data from a survey of workers in Leningrad indicates that, in 1970, 44 percent held a negative view of religion, with only 11 percent holding a positive opinion. By 1979 those negative views had declined drastically, down to only 14 percent, while positive views increased to 19 percent.[73] This suggests that the more mild and "professional" forms of atheist propaganda that Brezhnev carried out may not have been as effective as the more militant forms tried by his predecessors. It may also be that, as the dissident movement progressed during the 1960s and 1970s, especially as notable figures such as Solzhenitsyn and Sakharov became involved, liberal views became more respected along with dissident religious views.

The persecution of Christians certainly did not begin with the Bolsheviks, for ever since Jesus of Nazareth wandered the lands of Judea, his followers have faced discrimination, persecution, and suffering at the hands of others, and many millions have paid the ultimate price of martyrdom. As early as Roman times, Christians suffered under state persecution for their "strange" religious beliefs and the misconceptions surrounding their rituals. Accused of eating babies, committing human sacrifice, and engaging in incest, Christians were tracked down and murdered by the Roman Guard. Even those who were citizens of great respect and repute became outcasts once they accepted the faith.

Writing in the late second century, in his *Apology*, Tertullian pleaded with Rome to at least give Christians the same treatment as ordinary criminals, that is, a chance to defend themselves before being sentenced to death. The persecution of Christianity did not slow its spread, however, for as Tertullian recognized, "The blood of the martyrs is the seed of the church."[74] Separated by great expanses of time and space, innumerable citizens of the Soviet Union suffered in a similar way, as they resisted the state's secularization policies and suffered life and limb to remain true to their faith convictions.

The penalty paid for keeping their faith ranged from a loss of benefits and ostracism to forced placement in psychiatric hospitals, incarceration in the gulag, and—oftentimes resulting from the former—ultimately death. Although nearly two millennia after Tertullian's observation, the *modus operandi* of the state had changed little. So too had its effect. As Philip Walters phrased it, "As coal crushed under rocks turns to diamond, so the Christian faith grows strong and bright under persecution."[75] The stories summarized here attest to the fact that people of faith often stood up heroically against the Soviet attempt at forced secularization. And once that persecution began to subside, religion would quickly reemerge into public life in Russia and many of the former Soviet states, and often powerfully so.

Notes

1. Keston Archive, <SU/Pen/11/8>.
2. *Neizvestnaya Rossiya*, no. 1, p. 287. Cited in Robert Service, *A History of Modern Russia: From Nicholas II to Vladimir Putin* (Cambridge: Harvard University Press, 2005), p. 377.
3. The literature on secularization is so vast and this oversight so pervasive, that it is impossible to point out all the works that do this. The social scientific study of forced secularization, however, is not so vast, but the absence of consideration given to the personal struggles of faith is just as noteworthy. A case in point is Froese's *The Plot to Kill God*, which entirely neglects this dimension.
4. Cf. Paul Anderson's estimate of 64 million Soviet believers in 1964 with the VTsIOM survey from 1988 which found "18.6 percent." Paul Anderson, testimony before the Subcommittee on Europe, Committee on Foreign Affairs, second session. Recent Developments in the Soviet Blob, part I (January 27–30, 1964), pp. 100–1. Cited in D. Powell, *Antireligious Propaganda in the Soviet Union: A Study of Mass Persuasion* (Cambridge: MIT Press, 1975, p. 191; *Russkaya mysl'* no. 3725 (May 30, 1988).
5. Levitin-Krasnov, "Letter to Pope Paul VI" (Moscow: *samizdat*, 1967). Published in *Vestnik Russkogo studencheskogo khristianskogo dvezheniya*, No. 95–6 (1970), p. 86. Keston Archive Samizdat Collection, <Levitin-Krasnov/1970/1>.
6. Michael Bourdeaux, *Opium of the People: The Christian Religion in the U.S.S.R.* (New York: Merrill, 1966), pp. 149–50.
7. Ibid., pp. 145–6.
8. Pospielovsky, p. 318.
9. Ibid.
10. Elizabeth Roberts and Ann Shukman, *Christianity for the Twenty-First Century: The Life and Work of Alexander Men* (London: SCM Press, 1996), p. 7.
11. Ibid., p. 11.
12. Ibid., p. 71.
13. Ibid., p. 73.

14. Ibid., p. 71.
15. A. Belavin, "Svyashchennink Aleksandr Men'," in *Pamyati protoiereya Aleksandra Menya* (Moscow, 1991), p. 29.
16. Roberts and Shukman, p. 142.
17. Michael Bourdeaux, *Patriarch and Prophets: Persecution of the Russian Orthodox Church* (Mowbray, 1975), pp. 24–5.
18. Boris Talantov, "'Sergievshchina' or Compromise with Atheism (the Leaven of Herod)," cited in Bourdeaux, 1975, pp. 330–1.
19. Nikolai Eshliman and Gleb Yakunin, "Declaration to the Civil Authorities," in Bourdeaux, 1975, pp. 189–90.
20. Nikolai Eshliman and Gleb Yakunin, "Open Letter to his Holiness Patriarch Alexii," in Bourdeaux, pp. 195–6.
21. Inokenty, "Rasprava," (Moscow, September 1980). Keston Archive Samizdat collection, <Yakunin/1980/1>.
22. Winrich Scheffbuch, *Christians Under the Hammer & Sickle* (Grand Rapids: Zondervan, 1972), p. 10
23. Kolarz, *Religion in the Soviet Union* (New York: Macmillan, 1961), p. 338.
24. Catherine Wanner, "Missionaries of Faith and Culture: Evangelical Encounters in Ukraine," *Slavic Review* (Winter 2004), p. 742.
25. Kolarz, p. 283.
26. Vsesoyuznii sovet evangel'skikh khristian-baptistov, *Evangel'skie khristiane-baptisty v SSSR* (Moscow, 1979), p. 9
27. Scheffbuch, pp. 14–15.
28. Kolarz, p. 284.
29. Steve Durasoff, *The Russian Protestants* (Teaneck, NJ: Fairleigh Dickinson University Press, 1969), p. 55.
30. Kolarz, p. 301
31. Kolarz, p. 297–8.
32. Kolarz, p. 287. In this passage, Kolarz translated "*bez popov*" as "no popes," which I have here corrected to "no priests." Thanks to Xenia Dennen for pointing out Kolarz's translation error.
33. Bourdeaux, 1966, p. 153.
34. Scheffbuch, p. 9.
35. *Bratskii vestnik*, No. 3–4 (1954), p. 91.
36. Scheffbuch, p. 9.
37. *Vetsnik Spaseniya* 1 (1973), pp. 22–7.
38. Ibid., pp. 24–5
39. Vins, p. 37
40. Ibid., p. 48.

41. Ibid., p. 57.
42. Ibid.
43. Ibid., p. 57.
44. Ibid., p. 22.
45. Michael Bourdeaux, *Faith on Trial in Russia* (New York: Harper and Row, 1971), pp. 11–12.
46. N. Baturin, *Vestnik Istiny,* no. 4 (1988), p. 23. Given that Bourdeaux knew Vins personally, and was even flown to his debriefing in New York upon his arrival there as part of the prisoner exchange, I am relying more upon his account than that of Baturin.
47. Georgi Vins, *Evangeli v Uzakh* (Elkhart: Russian Gospel Ministries, 1991), p. 121.
48. Lauren Tapley, "Soviet Religion Policy through the Religious Dissidents from Leonid Brezhnev to Mikhail Brezhnev: A Comparative Study of Aida Skripnikova and Valeri Barinov," unpublished master's thesis, Department of History, Baylor University (May 2008), p. 26.
49. Ibid., pp. 29–30.
50. Michael Bourdeaux and Xenia Howard-Johnston, *Aida of Leningrad: The Story of Aida Skripnikova* (Berkshire, UK: Gateway Outreach, 1972), p. 68.
51. Ibid., p. 86.
52. Bourdeaux and Howard-Johnston, p. 47.
53. Dan Wooding, "Aida of Leningrad," *Assist News Service.* Cited in Tapley, p. 47.
54. Bourdeaux and Howard-Johnston, pp. 96–103.
55. Tapley, p. 53.
56. Sawatsky, p. 93.
57. Fletcher, p. 28.
58. Sawatsky, p. 43.
59. Durasoff, p. 55.
60. Kolarz, pp. 333–4.
61. Keston Archive, <SU/Pen/Kash>.
62. Kolarz, p. 337.
63. Keston Archive, <SU/Pen/11/8>.
64. KNS No. 126: "Biography, Ivan Petrovich Fedotov" (June 18, 1981). Keston Archive, <SU/Pen 8/2/fed>.
65. *Moskovskaya Pravda* (November 1960). Quoted in Daniil Shchipkov, "Stroiteli Tsarstva," *Nezavisimaya gazeta* (May 21, 2003), p. 4.
66. Information Service of the Pentecostal Movement, *Urgent Communication.* Keston Archive, <SU/Pen 8/2/fed>.

67. "Biography, Ivan Petrovich Fedotov."

68. "Faith on Trial," *Church Times*, November 23, 1979, p. 4. Keston Archive, <SU/Pen/11/8>.

69. John Pollack, *The Siberian Seven* (Hodder and Stoughton, 1979).

70. *Congressional Record*, Vol. 126, No. 108, part II (June 27, 1980). Keston Archive, <SU/Pen/11/8>.

71. Paul Steeves, "Inaccurate and Unbalanced Portrayal," *Christianity Today*, November 23, 1981, pp. 8–9.

72. Keston Archive, <SU/Pen/11/8>.

73. Dimitry Pospielovsky, *The Russian Church Under the Soviet Regime, 1917–1982*, Vol. 2 (Crestwood, NY: St. Vladimir's Seminary Press, 1984), p. 455.

74. Tertullian, *Apology*, p. 50.

75. Philip Walters, "Foreword," in *Light Through The Curtain*, Philip Walters and Jane Balengarth, eds. (Kent, UK: Keston College, 1985), p. 1.

CHAPTER FOUR

Russia's Religious Renaissance

Not everything has been easy and simple in the sphere of church-state relations. Religious organizations, too, were affected by the tragic developments that occurred in the period of the cult of personality. Now, under perestroika, mistakes that were made with regard to the church and believers in the 1930s and the years that followed are being rectified.

—*Mikhail Gorbachev[1]*

On November 4, 1990, the first Divine Liturgy to be held in nearly 60 years was celebrated in the Cathedral of Our Lady of Kazan. During the Communist era, the *Kazansky Sobor*, as it is commonly known, stood in the center of downtown Leningrad on Nevsky Prospekt as a sign of the triumph of atheism over religion. Shortly after the Bolshevik Revolution, the destruction of the Cathedral commenced, first with the martyring of the cathedral's dean and his two sons in September 1918, and then with the confiscation of the church's valuables in 1922. Finally, the church itself was closed and handed over to the Soviet Academy of Science in 1931. The next year it was reopened as the Museum of the History of Religion and Atheism, the greatest testament to atheism in all of the Soviet Union, and perhaps the world.

To Stalin, the *Kazansky Sobor* must have seemed like the ideal site for a museum of atheism. After all, it was in the cathedral square that the first ever political demonstration in Russia had been held in 1876. The Kazan Demonstration, which had been organized by the revolutionary group *Zemlya i Volya* (Land and Will), counted among its leaders the 19-year old Georgi Plekhanov, who would go on to found the Social-Democratic Movement in Russia and establish himself as the country's first Marxist theoretician. Indeed, it was here that the first red flag was raised in Russia, with both the one who unfurled it and Plekhanov finding themselves arrested and imprisoned. Nearly a century later it would be Aida Skripnikova who would find herself in prison shortly after standing before the cathedral and declaring her faith in Christ and calling others to the Lord.

The history of the *Kazansky Sobor* poignantly serves as a metaphor for Russia as a whole, and illustrates its rich history, horrific past, and uncertain future. The return of the *Kazansky Sobor* is symbolic of the larger trend in post-atheist Russia of the holy that was confiscated and made profane by the Communists being reconsecrated once again. Not only was the sacred site defiled, it was even held up as symbol of atheism. Perhaps now, after its suffering and martyrdom, it has attained a quality of even greater sacredness. In fact, the same can perhaps be said about the Russian Orthodox Church itself, which has risen from the ashes to return to playing a central role in Russian culture, society, and politics. While this is a sign of comfort for many Russians, not all welcome such an arrangement, particularly those who profess a different religious tradition or simply desire to see Russia develop into a truly secular state.

One of the Church's main justifications for assuming such a central role in Russian life is that the overwhelming majority of Russia's citizens identify themselves as Orthodox. Empirical evidence suggests that this is an exaggeration, and also suggests that those who think of themselves as Orthodox are only loosely affiliated in any way with the Church. Only a small percentage of self-identifying Orthodox actually attend religious services with any degree of regularity, though many do take part in other, less-institutionalized forms of religious observance, from simply wearing a cross as a symbol of Christian identity to taking part in pilgrimages and other "extra-church" activities. Nevertheless, many within the Orthodox community are intent on reversing the situation of the Soviet era, and placing Orthodoxy into a privileged position in Russian society. Other religious traditions, meanwhile, are treated little better than they were under Communist rule, subject to restrictions on their activities and enjoying a second-class status under the law. In society at large, the situation is even worse, with ethno-religious discrimination and even violence on the rise.

The return to primacy of place of Orthodoxy in Russia is also one of the most interesting stories in the politics of religion. In a society that attempted to wipe out religion for seven decades, the return of the church to the people and the people to the church is a complicated story, but one which offers great insights into the long-term effectiveness of forced secularization policies and the very nature of the interaction between religion and politics.

Perestroika of Religion

The celebration of the Divine Liturgy in *Kazansky Sobor* in November 1990 was not the first step toward the CPSU's liberalization of religion policy. Already in January of that year, on Christmas Day (celebrated according to the Gregorian calendar), a thanksgiving service and requiem had been held at the tomb of General Kutuzov. Mikhail Kutuzov's final resting place is in the *Kazansky Sobor* because, as Napoleon invaded Russia in 1812, Commander-in-Chief Kutuzov turned to the miracle-working Our Lady of Kazan icon for help. This event occurred in the midst of the cathedral's construction, and with the miraculous defense of Russia, the cathedral was named in her honor.

Russian history is strewn with such historical-religious coincidences, and it was perhaps the greatest of them all that led to the liberalization of religion in Russia. As Gorbachev launched his grand plan for restructuring economic, social, and political life in the Soviet Union in 1987, under the label of *perestroika* (restructuring), he initially showed little interest in liberalizing religion policy. His reforms, some thought, would perhaps differ little from those of Khrushchev, who liberalized much of Soviet life while simultaneously cracking down on religious belief. But the historical fact that 1988 would be the millennial anniversary of the baptism of *Rus'* excited many, both within the Orthodox fold and outside it—indeed even outside the Soviet Union itself.

The initial Soviet plan was to offer a counter-balance to the enthusiasm for the millennial jubilee, commemorating the seventieth anniversary of Lenin's 1918 law on separation of church and state. Chronologically, this would occur in March, before the millennial celebration planned by the Church for June, and it was hoped that this would diminish some interest in the latter celebration. By choosing the 1918 law, moreover, Gorbachev was following a similar strategy of justifying his reforms by linking them with Lenin-era policies, as he was doing already with the NEP and *perestroika*'s economic policies.[2] This was intended to signal to the growing number of his opponents, who questioned his ideological purity, that such reforms were squarely in line with the policies of the "architect of the revolution."

To the sophisticated observer, however, the elevation of the 1918 law, which legally had been superseded by later, more restrictive policies, such as the 1929 Stalin-era law and Khrushchev's reforms, indicated a willingness to liberalize Soviet religious life. One such "sophisticated observer" was the Russian Orthodox Church, which became an enthusiastic supporter of *perestroika*. This was a brilliant and pragmatic strategy on Gorbachev's part. Containing peaceful religious enthusiasm would have run counter to *perestroika* and *glasnost'* (roughly equivalent to "openness"), but by connecting the liberalization of religion policy to Lenin and interpreting believers' ambitions for greater religious liberty as support for *perestroika*, Gorbachev had effectively co-opted a potential opposition group and made it one of the strongest supporters of his reform initiative.

Glasnost' and the Gospel

On the part of believers, the millennium of the baptism of *Rus'* became an opportune moment not only to reflect on the nation's long attachment to the Christian faith, but also to redress the state for a greater sphere in which to practice that faith. Efforts in this direction began as early as 1980, when the Moscow Patriarchate formed a committee to prepare for the celebration, and then requesting in 1982 that various properties be returned to the church in order to hold a jubilee celebration in June of 1988. In 1983 the Danielovsky monastery compound, which had been a juvenile detention facility and was Moscow's oldest monastery (thirteenth century), was returned to the church and made the seat of the patriarchate. Once Gorbachev came to power, more facilities were handed over, including the Optina Hermitage and a monastery outside Yaroslavl' that was to house elderly clergy. It was at this time that the patriarchate began holding annual conferences in preparation for the jubilee, including a pre-council bishops' conference in March 1988 in the Novodevichy Monastery, where the final details of the millennium celebration were worked out.

While the church was cautious but persistent and consistent in using the jubilee to press open the sphere of their activities, other institutions and segments of society were slower and more guarded in their actions. All sectors of the intelligentsia, however, became interested in this almost prophetic historical commemoration, either embracing it or repudiating those who saw it as an opportunity to reevaluate Russia's religious past. Those in official positions in the academy as well as in the media were beginning to enjoy greater freedom through Gorbachev's policy of *glasnost'*, and they could explore the limits of this freedom as they researched the event from various perspectives. But even those who were the defenders of atheism became interested, such as *Znanie*, the organization whose purpose was to promote atheism. All would, however, have to broach the topic carefully.

Under the circumstances, the only way to open a discussion on the issue was to do so within the confines of accepted Marxist practices. Thus, one of the earliest investigations into the topic began with the requisite references to "religion as the opium of the people" and some quotes from Engels on the importance of studying religion in order to refute it. It then proceeded to pay homage to Soviet scholars of the "motherland" who had researched the great role religion played in Russia's past, but then argued that Soviet scholars must enter into discussions and research on the topic since the "imperialist" scholars were doing so. Rather than justifying the importance and significance of the millennial anniversary of the baptism of *Rus'* directly, Soviet scholars L. Emelyakh and Ya. Kozhurin argued that they were obligated to lead research into this area lest foreign scholars do it instead. "Our historians and philosophers," they argued "need to prepare current scientific works in order to get high-quality materials into the hands of popularizers and propagandists."[3] This would allow Soviet scholars "to repudiate the pseudo-objective" findings of the "bourgeois" Western scholars—as well as the émigré church—who had been active in "employing their own fabrications in the area of fatherland history."

This was no trite matter, Emelyakh and Kozhurin argued, for these "foreign foes" were at work "searching our past for the occasion to denigrate our present." Their intentions, they pointed out, were not lofty, but rather nefarious. They "are not interested in defending faith, or protecting those of different opinions from the progressive-minded," they continued. "With Jesuit hypocrisy and sanctimoniousness they stand up for all sorts of devils."[4] It was because of such sentiments that Gorbachev was wise to connect the *perestroika* of religion with Lenin's 1918 decree.

Such methods were probably necessary at the time, or at least inevitable. They were necessary in order to test the waters of *glasnost'* and its limits to freedom of speech, and they were perhaps inevitable because those in the position to publish their ideas were the model Soviet citizens, and therefore unlikely to wander too far from the old Party line. As repugnant as their justifications might be, these works did open a discussion on what would turn out to be a critical turning point in the history of church-state relations in Russia.

Politburo member Konstantin Kharchev, who would be one of Gorbachev's strongest supporters, himself wrote an article in *Pravda* in January 1988 partly justifying Lenin's decree of 1918, and partly arguing that a new direction must be pursued now. There are millions of believers in the Soviet Union, he acknowledged, "the majority of whom accept perestroika and hope with all others to actively participate in the renewal of our society."[5] "Now is the time," he continued, "to check our policies against those of Lenin and his approach to freedom of conscience." But Kharchev did more than simply argue that Lenin's position of 1918 was justified. He acknowledged that spiritual life has its own "current," and that "this current was impossible to liquidate administratively, or to meld it together with our ideology." Now under *perestroika*, "It is possible and necessary to unite these efforts to help people move toward more humane, moral, and spiritual values, toward peace, toward our common welfare." Kharchev, the representative of the Council on Religious Affairs for the Council of Ministers of the USSR, then called for nothing short of a reconsideration of Soviet policies regarding religion: "We should ensure the correctness of our legislation on religious cults," he stated bluntly, and "the juridical principles of freedom of conscience" and bring them into line with contemporary circumstances.[6]

Others in less secure positions, and perhaps more ideologically committed, were not as interested in embracing *perestroika* and offered a less positive view of religion.[7] Emelyakh and Kozhurin's own work intended more to prevent the West from overly-identifying *Rus'* with Christianity, and suggested that the Orthodox Church was simply trying to use the activities surrounding the celebration of the millennium of Christianity in order to "stir up interest among believers in these events of the deep past."[8] While offering a Marxist, class-based analysis of the baptism of *Rus'*, they did critique the Soviet regime of the 1920s–1930s, however, including Yaroslavsky, for its overly-ideological critique of Christianity, which denied the progressive nature of Christianity in comparison with paganism.[9] Others, such as Kurbatov, Frolov, and Froyanov, were even less generous toward Christianity, concluding that, if one were to ask whether Russia was either Christian or pagan, "the answer would be pagan, or at best *dvoeverie* (dual-faithed)," combining elements of both, but "in no case truly Christian."[10]

While such contributions to the public discourse did little to promote the tolerance of religion, they also did little to keep people from returning to the church in droves. While Gorbachev and Kharchev were consistently signaling that a new era in Soviet policy toward religion had arrived, alongside each negative publication on religion was another that offered a much more positive and sympathetic interpretation of Russia's historical connection to Christianity. There was perhaps no better contribution in this regard than the collection of essays published under the title *Kreshchenie* Rusi (The Baptism of *Rus'*) by the Moscow Patriarchate in early 1988, under the editorial direction of arch-presbyter (*protoierei*) Lev Lebedev. In discussing the decision to turn away from paganism and toward Christianity, the authors took a radically different approach to the topic than did their ideologically-motivated comrades. "*Rus'* made no mistake in its choice," they concluded, referring to Prince Vladimir's consideration of various faiths before choosing Orthodoxy, and the "Sun of Truth" shown upon the Russian land from that time forward.[11] Works such as these served as the necessary counter-balance to the more conservative publications, and soon the former would begin to flow—and has yet to subside—while the latter quickly slowed to a trickle that dried up in the Soviet Union's final days.

The Church's Jubilee

At the final jubilee preparatory conference in March, the assembled bishops not only considered the names of "martyrs of faith and piety" to be considered for canonization by the bishops' conference to be held in connection with the jubilee, they also recounted the many ways in which the church had been able to expand its activities in recent years. Churches that had been confiscated in early periods were being returned while new churches were being built. Church valuables in the possession of the state were being returned as well, and the church's publishing activities were expanding rapidly. Not only were 100,000 copies of a jubilee edition of the Bible prepared, hundreds of thousands of regular editions of the Bible had been published, including a Ukrainian edition and a half million copies of a Russian language prayer book.

Immediately following the conference, the participants were received by Kharchev, who told them how *perestroika* was going to help arrive at a solution of the problems concerning the activities of churches and religious associations in the Soviet Union, and he offered the assistance of his council in preparation for the jubilee.[12] For its part, of course, the church publicly proclaimed its appreciation for the assistance it was being given. In a manner reminiscent of the Stalin-era concordat, the church's press releases announcing their activities and new developments consistently concluded with gestures of humility and appreciation to the Soviet state for all of its assistance.[13]

Things on the church-state front were changing rapidly. As recently as 1986, the CPSU party program had listed religion among other "vices" such as corruption, alcoholism, and theft of state property. In Pospielovsky's phrase, "faith in God was still treated as a pathological deviation from the norm."[14] Though slow in addressing the issue of religion, in the first few months of 1988 Gorbachev quickly undid much of the restrictive Soviet policies toward religion from the past 70 years.

On April 29, 1988, Gorbachev met with Patriarch Pimen, along with five of his bishops, in the Kremlin. Gorbachev's speech to the assembled hierarchs began much as the articles cited above, with the requisite homage to Lenin and his 1918 decree. "Not everything has been easy and simple in the sphere of church-state relations," he continued, including "the tragic developments that occurred in the period of the 'cult of personality'."[15] Gorbachev then specifically stated that there had been "mistakes made with regard to the church and believers in the 1930s and the years that followed," and promised that "these are being rectified."[16]

Gorbachev then announced a new law on freedom of conscience, one which would not only guarantee the freedom of individual belief, which Lenin's 1918 decree was seen as dealing with sufficiently, but one that also "reflects the interests of religious organizations." The general secretary agreed to recognize the church as a legitimate public institution, thus ending the policy of official atheism that had stood in various forms for almost 70 years. The patriarch's response was an enthusiastic embrace of the promise and his support for Gorbachev and *perestroika*: "I pledge full support to you, the architect of *perestroika* and the herald of new political thinking." "We, the church people," he continued, "ardently pray for the success of that process and are seeking to do everything within our power to promote it." As archbishop Kirill of Smolensk (who would become patriarch himself in 2009) said shortly before this meeting, the "Russian Orthodox Church has pinned on *perestroika* its hopes for definite changes in its existence."[17]

The first 2 weeks of June 1988 were filled, from dawn and into the evening hours, with various events celebrating the jubilee. The bishops' conference at the Trinity-St. Sergius Monastery in Zagorsk (Serge'ev Posad) only lasted 2 days, but official celebratory activities went on for more than a week. These included a concert at the Bolshoi Theatre, numerous cultural activities each evening, art exhibits, colloquia, and cultural/spiritual excursions, including to the church's newly-renovated facilities in Kaluga and Yaroslavl'. The church, with state support, spent untold millions of dollars in promoting this event.

The state had reasons of its own, however, for spending so much money on promoting something that was only recently being rehabilitated. The Soviet government arranged for a U.S.-USSR arms summit to coincide with the event, as the church was once again seen as useful in the foreign policy realm. In a joint letter to Gorbachev and Reagan, Patriarch Pimen encouraged them in their growing cooperation, and said he and the Church were "praying for their success."[18] Patriarch Pimen then wrote to Soviet presidium chairman Nikolai Ryzhkov just following the summit, expressing the church's support for their work in disarmament. "Blessed are the peacemakers, for they shall be called sons of God," Pimen wrote the Soviet leader, quoting from the Beatitudes. He also pledged the church's continued support as the Soviet government worked to build peace among nations.[19] Finally, he also expressed the church's desire that, by the time of the bi-millennial celebration of the birth of Christ, the world would be entirely free of nuclear weapons.

Supporting the state in this way came with some expectations as to how the state would treat the church from this point forward. In a letter to Kharchev drafted at the jubilee, Patriarch Pimen wrote that the "Russian Orthodox Church, other churches, and all believers" were "greatly encouraged" by his meeting with Gorbachev and "approve the restoration of Leninist principles of the attitudes towards religion and the faithful, which provides for the strengthening of unity of our nation, the dignity and authority of our Motherland."[20] An implicit agreement had been reached between Gorbachev and the church by forging together *perestroika* and Lenin's decree on separation of church and state. It would still take some time, however, before this understanding could be codified into Soviet law, a development that would all too quickly be nullified by a legal arrangement that actually gives preferential treatment to the ROC.

The great fanfare surrounding the jubilee and the highly-publicized involvement of state leaders in the activities sent a clear signal that religion was rehabilitated. Similar strides had been made over the previous year in the area of *glasnost'* and the press, meaning that press coverage of the jubilee was largely free from ideological bias. The result was frank and open discussion on religion in the press, which quickly expanded to society at large. As *Novoe Vremya* reported shortly after the jubilee, "for many years in our country, there were not only subjects that were closed to criticism, but entire spheres" that were off-limits. "First in line," they were now able to report, "was religion."[21] This era was now part of the past. "Now priests have been given the right to speak before crowded auditoriums," on the radio, and on TV, addressing "even the most varied questions dealing with spiritual life and church history."[22]

A Religious Renaissance

In the first half of 1988 alone, 60 new religious communities had been registered in the Soviet Union, and seemingly wherever one looked a new cathedral was under construction. Moreover, with the legal restrictions being loosened on personal belief, no longer would it be listed in one's passport whether or not he or she had been baptized (a practice that was used for discriminatory purposes). From that point on, official persecution came to an end and religion in Russia underwent a renaissance. In 1988, a VTsIOM survey found that only 18.6 percent identified themselves as religious; within 5 years that number had more than doubled to 43 percent.[23] Another survey indicated that in Moscow—the Soviet Union's most developed city—the rate had jumped from only 10 percent in 1988 to 27 percent by 1990, almost tripling in only 2 years. At the time, the authors of that study assumed that the rapid rise in religiosity was a reaction against Communism and the persecution of belief and that it would subsequently level off.[24] As the years passed by, however, it continued to rise.

Belief in God continued to climb from *perestroika* to the post-Soviet period, reaching 34 percent in 1991, 46 percent in 1993, and 47 percent in 1996, which Kaariainen suggested might be a "normal" level of belief among Russians.[25] According to the 1999 World Values Survey, however, the last one in which the specific question "do you believe in God?" was asked in Russia, 59.3 percent agreed.[26] In 2006, which is the most recent wave of the World Values Survey, 65.3 percent responded that they considered themselves "a religious person." This suggests that religiosity's rise in Russia may not yet be over.

In the same 2006 survey, only 3.9 percent of Russians polled identified themselves as "a convinced atheist," while 19.5 percent simply answered that "they were not a religious person." In 1991, some 35 percent of Soviet citizens polled had identified themselves as atheists.[27] How did the number of believers rise so rapidly in such a short span of time, while the number of atheists virtually disappeared? Agadjanian has explained this phenomenon as the result of the liberalization of self-expression that made it possible for many to finally profess what they had believed all along.[28] Rather than having been true atheists who found God, they were probably believers who had denied their faith in order to make life in the Soviet Union more tolerable, or they may simply be embracing religion today as weakly as they had "embraced" atheism during the Communist era.

Of course, identifying oneself as a believer is not the same as actually living a life of faith in practice. While Protestants and Pentecostals seem to attend church quite frequently,[29] the vast majority of believers in Russia identify themselves as Orthodox, though many hardly ever attend church. Various surveys report self-identification as Orthodox among 55–70 percent of the population, although the Russian Orthodox Church frequently claims that 80 percent of the population is Orthodox (which is the percentage of ethnic Russians in the country). Whichever number is closer to reality is impossible to determine, as is what exactly it means to be "Orthodox." Of those who identified themselves as such in the World Values Survey, only 5.4 percent claimed to attend church services weekly, while an additional 11 percent claimed to do so at least once per month.

One must be careful not to conclude that this means Orthodox Christians are believers in name only, and do not participate in a life of faith. When asked about praying outside of religious services, 27.9 percent of Orthodox claimed to do so everyday, compared to only 3.8 percent of the non-religious segment of the population. Additionally, nearly 90 percent of Orthodox responded that they receive comfort and strength from their religion, suggesting that in contemporary Russia, a satisfying religious life can be lived without regular church attendance.

One way in which such people live out their lives of faith is through alternative forms of religious behavior. For example, many Russians frequent monasteries, meet with monks and nuns, pray before holy relics, and collect water from holy springs. These monastery-centered activities do not show up on church attendance statistics, of course. And while clearly connecting people to the Church, it seems to be acting as a substitute for regular church attendance, or at least it does not seem to be translating strongly into identification with a local parish and participation in its services. There is a close connection between churches and monasteries, of course, and the two do not compete with each other for patrons. But this leads to an interesting question: why is enthusiasm for alternative religious practices not contributing more strongly to the rise of a more robust parish life?

One possible explanation is that church attendance is not a very good indicator of Orthodox religiosity. Some have already suggested this idea, arguing that prayer frequency or participation in pilgrimages and church processions might be better indicators. One part of the explanation may be that the monasteries were not tainted by Communist-era co-optation the way the churches were. Whereas it is clear that the Church was co-opted to a significant degree, even if this is understood as a necessary strategy for survival, the monasteries are popularly seen as blameless and even the ultimate victims of the attacks. They are thus martyrs, as are the saints who resided inside their walls. They are also more other-worldly than the church, particularly given their isolation and often remote location. In general, monasteries, monks, and the processions have been able to retain much more of the mystical tradition in Russian Orthodoxy, and this is proving more popular in the post-Soviet religious economy than the local parish and Sunday church attendance.

The practice of one's faith beyond the church walls through such activities as monastery visits, pilgrimages, and processions can be understood as under-institutionalized forms of religious behavior. As Naletova has persuasively argued, pilgrimages to holy sites and processions are popular forms of religious behavior which give people a genuine and satisfying religious experience.[30] The Velikorestkii procession of the cross is an excellent case in point. As Rock points out, this procession had as many as 50,000 participants before the Bolshevik Revolution, but dwindled down to only a handful during the height of Khrushchev's anti-religion campaign. In the 1980s, it began to rise again, however, from a few hundred in 1982 to a few thousand by 1988. The collapse of Communism only quickened the revival, and now some 30,000 participants annually process 150 kilometers in a period of 6 days.[31] Other processions can last months and traverse great expanses of the Russian countryside. In the words of a nineteenth century Russian priest, these processions are "immortal chronicles," a much better means of preserving important events than "memorials of marble or metal."[32] And while not everyone who participates in these processions is a believer, many are seekers whose participation nevertheless deepens their spirituality. And quite often, participation in a procession leads to a conversion experience.

Devout Orthodox and Cultural Christians

With so many Russians identifying themselves as Orthodox believers, it is difficult to speak generally about a group that is so diverse. Alongside those who live out their Orthodox faith on a daily basis there are those whose connection to the church is more cultural, and perhaps related more to the identity of being "Orthodox" than it is in any way associated with the church life of a particular parish or with participation in pilgrimages. Then, of course, there are those who come somewhere in the middle. One way we can distinguish between the more devout believers, on the one hand, and those whose connection to Orthodoxy is more cultural, on the other, is by separating self-identified Orthodox believers into two groups, based upon their degree of piety.[33] In previous studies using such a dichotomy, I have shown that there are several distinctive trends, with the more devout Orthodox being more predominantly female and slightly older, though the younger generation appears to be finding the church earlier in their lives as well.[34] Devout Orthodox also tend to be more supportive of democracy than cultural Orthodox, though both are supportive of government intervention in the economy.[35]

Looking at Orthodox Russians through their membership in these two groups also sheds light on how they view the church and religion. Surveys regularly find that the church is the most trusted institution in Russian society, with around 60 percent of all Russians expressing their confidence in it. Using these categories, however, we can see that there is in fact great variation in these levels of trust (see Table 4.1). The more devout Orthodox have the highest levels of trust in the church, with over 92 percent saying that they have either a great deal of trust in the church (73.3 percent), or quite a lot of trust (19.3 percent). The cultural Orthodox still have a high

Table 4.1 Orthodox Christians on Church and Religion

	Devout Orthodox	Cultural Orthodox	Non-religious Russians
Trust in churches: great deal (quite a lot)	73.3 (19.3)	32.6 (43.9)	5.7 (30)
The church gives answers to people's spiritual problems	89.6	75.6	36.3
The church gives answers to moral problems	87.4	71.7	36
The church gives answers to problems of family life	78.5	57.7	24
The church gives answers to social problems	41.5	23.7	9.6

level of trust in the church, with a total of over 76 percent for both positive responses, but more have quite a lot of trust in the church (43.9 percent) than a great deal of trust (32.6 percent). Interestingly, and something that has remained overlooked by those who look at trust in institutions, is the fact that only very few non-religious Russians have a great deal of trust in the church.

In addition to trusting the church, Orthodox Christians in Russia also believe that the church provides answers to people's spiritual, moral, and family problems. While these numbers are significantly higher for devout Orthodox (89.6, 87.4, and 78.5 percent) than for cultural Orthodox (75.6, 71.7, and 57.7), the disparity in responses is not as great as those for trust. As a matter of fact, more than one-third of non-religious Russians still felt that the church provides answers to people's spiritual and moral problems. Finally, although the church is seen as having a significant role to play in people's spiritual, moral, and family life, there was less faith in the church as an institution that could provide answers to social problems. The evidence suggests that as the topic shifts away from the spiritual realm, the church is seen as having less relevance. Some might interpret this to mean that, although trusted and even endeared by many, the church is not looked to for answers of a more secular nature. Unfortunately, the situation is not quite so simple as that.

A Secular Russian State

The roots of Russia's religious renaissance rest in the jubilee celebration of 1988 and the rapid liberalization of Soviet religion policy. Once religion had been *de facto* liberalized, however, other more pressing events occupied Soviet authorities in the ensuing months, including the momentous events of 1989. While it would take until 1991 for the USSR to issue its new law on religion, the Russian Republic issued its own law in 1990, the law on "Freedom of Conscience and Religious Belief." This very liberal law introduced legal religious equality for the first time in Russian history, including the establishment of a secular state and a true separation of church and state. As with all new policies, however, its exact effects could not be determined in advance. One consequence of the law, which might have been predictable but was certainly unintended, was the flourishing of an open market of religious competition, one which prompted a dramatic increase in evangelism, proselytism, and the emergence of indigenous New Religious Movements (NRMs).

As Western religious organizations began to operate in Russia and new religious movements began to emerge, they were met with resistance not only by many of their intended converts, but also by government officials and the Russian Orthodox Church as well, as presenting a threat to Orthodoxy and even to Russian national identity. Metropolitan Kirill, describing the situation between the ROC and missionizing groups from the West, declared: "We were like a boxer who walks around for months with his arm in a cast and is then abruptly shoved into the ring, accompanied by shouts of encouragement. But there we encountered a well-trained opponent, in the form of a wide variety of missionaries..."[36] These missionaries, the argument goes, came with money and promises of trips to the West, enticements used to lure Russians away from the mother church. As many in the ROC saw it, the West had sympathized with the plight of the Russian church for decades as it was persecuted under Soviet rule, but as soon the church found itself in a position to rebuild and serve the people, the "sympathizers" then arrived in droves not to help but to try and lure these very same people away and over to their denomination.[37]

Such resentment and resistance would build up substantially over the next few years and culminate in the scrapping of that law and eventually the development of a de facto relationship of establishment between church and state in Russia. This relationship is progressing beyond mere *symphonia* and developing into perhaps the clearest example of an established Christian church in the world today. Getting to that point would not be a quick and simple journey, however, and while dissenting voices could do little to stop it, other religious traditions were even enlisted to take a back seat in this ride, while the rest have had to watch from the curb.

Orthodoxy's Return to Primacy

The first move toward ROC primacy was the 1993 attempt to change the 1990 law with the amendment "Introducing Changes and Additions to the RSFSR Law on Freedom of Religion." This amendment, which was passed by the Supreme Soviet but rejected by President Yeltsin, proposed to alter religious freedom in Russia fundamentally by restricting sharply the rights of foreign religious associations and by rendering state support to Russia's "traditional confessions" (Orthodoxy, Islam, Judaism, and Buddhism).[38] The introduction of the idea that certain traditions were "traditional" to Russia was certainly not due to any great sympathy on the part of the Russian state for these religions. Rather, it was simply necessary in order to give "equal treatment" to numerous ethnic groups, which have historically followed their traditions,[39] to give semblance of tolerance and ecumenicity to all of the country's citizens, and to present the impression to the outside world that Russia was permitting religious pluralism. But of course, this gesture was totally disingenuous. Two of those traditions—Islam and Judaism—have a very troubled past in Russia. Anti-Semitism has a particularly dark history in the Russian Empire, with pogroms rising up many times, in addition to the issues of discrimination and intolerance that still take place on a daily basis today. Islam has not fared much better. Though it is so closely connected to many of Russia's ethnic minorities that it is difficult or impossible to determine if acts of discrimination and/or violence against Muslims are religiously or racially inspired, more recent incidents—including the murder of Muslims on the streets of Moscow—are much more clearly religiously-motivated.

While the draft legislation that introduced the "four traditional confessions" concept never made it into law, as Yeltsin dissolved the parliament that October, it would raise its head again before long. Still, the president's battle with the parliament gave him the opportunity to rush through a modern and liberal constitution, one that included provisions on religious freedom and the separation of church and state. Article 28 of the 1993 Constitution stated:

Everyone is guaranteed the freedom of conscience, freedom of religious worship, including the right to profess, individually or jointly with others, any religion, or to profess no religion, to freely choose, possess and disseminate religious or other beliefs, and to act in conformity with them.[40]

Furthermore, Article 14 of the Constitution proclaimed:

1. The Russian Federation is a secular state. No religion may be instituted as state-sponsored or mandatory.
2. Religious associations are separated from the [S]tate, and are equal before the law.[41]

The passing of the new Constitution seemingly spelled the end of the opportunity to seek to change religious regulation at the federal level, and many regions began to take it upon themselves to draft and enact more restrictive regional laws on religion. The first region to do so was Tartarstan, which moved to ban "totalitarian charismatic religious sects" throughout the republic.[42] Another early region to do so was Tula, which passed a restrictive law in November 1994. This law was quickly used as a model by other regions, and in a brief period of time many regions had placed on the books laws that violated the federal law and constitutional guarantees. Moreover, the Constitutional Court was reluctant to intervene into the situation, either because it was too weak or sympathized with them.

This was just one more sign that Russian society was not prepared to live up to the ideals of religious liberty and church-state separation that had been promulgated in the heady days of Russia's turn toward democracy. The culmination of this backsliding was President Boris Yeltsin's signing of a new law on religion on September 26, 1997, which sharply curtailed the liberal spirit of the previous decade and narrowed the basic rights of freedom of conscience, freedom of religious association, and freedom of thought that Russia's nascent democratic government had earlier guaranteed.

Witte has described the conflict over religious rights in Russia as both a "theological war" and a "legal war."[43] The theological war, he suggests, represents the Russian Orthodox Church's efforts to recreate the country's spiritual and moral heritage and rebuild its moral consciousness after nearly 70 years of Soviet assault on these traditional centers of identity; in such endeavors, the Russian Orthodox Church faced competition from other religious faiths and organizations. The legal war defined the struggle over legal norms and measures in the effort to create a balance between religious freedom for all faiths and religious groups and the award of certain privileges for some of them. Additionally, the legal issue posed the question of whether the state, in light of the moral confusion and the spiritual crisis Russia faced in the 1990s, should moderate the full expression of religious liberty, as the international community understood that term.

While many in the Russian Orthodox Church officially favored these legal restrictions, political and religious leaders in Russia were sharply divided. This was most clearly seen outside Moscow where, almost immediately, regional courts and governments began trespassing over the law by restricting religious liberty to those groups they found distasteful. The unfolding picture of religious life in Russia was not what most had expected when the principles of democracy and liberty were first being touted by politicians such as Yeltsin, Yavlinsky, and Gaidar. Many of the nation's intended converts were put off by proselytizing groups taking advantage of Russia's new-found religious liberty to proclaim the Gospel and other faith traditions. The presence of Hare Krishnas, Jehovah's Witnesses, and Mormons along the streets of major Russian cities was not what people had expected when they voted in support of the 1993 Constitution. Local and regional courts, therefore, had few qualms about violating these constitutionally-guaranteed liberties when they were seen as causing harm to Russia's cultural environment. From a legal standpoint, such trespassing clearly violated the religion clauses of the Russian Constitution, presenting a constitutional dilemma. The passing of the 1997 law, however, resolved the battle between federal law and regional police and court action, but did so by nullifying the Constitutional guarantees and replacing them with a religion law that seemingly permitted religious discrimination and preferential treatment, complete with the "four traditional confessions" model attempted earlier.

President Yeltsin himself understood that these legal restrictions were an infringement on the constitutional rights of Russian citizens. In his July 23, 1997 veto of a draft bill passed by the State Duma, Yeltsin wrote that the law "contradicts the foundation of the constitutional structure of the Russian Federation and generally recognized principles and norms of international law."[44] Then in September, however, he publicly took a different view.[45] Signing into law the bill he had previously rejected, he supported Patriarch Aleksii II's position that "freedom does not mean general license."[46] Unless the government affirmed Russia's traditional faiths against the aggressive actions of other religious groups and sects, the Patriarch maintained, the renewal of Russia's own spiritual traditions stood little chance.

After 4 years of intense pressure brought by the Orthodox Church and by nationalist groups protesting the activities of outside missionary organizations, the game was over and liberty was the loser. Hastily pushed through the working groups of the parliament by Viktor Zerkaltsev, the Communist Party chairman of the committee on organizations and religious associations, who limited discussion and debate on the topic, the new law imposed much stricter regulation on religious organizations than had existed—on paper if not in practice—since 1990.

In contrast to the 1990 RSFSR law that prohibited religious discrimination, the 1997 law now distinguished between Russia's "traditional" and "non-traditional religions and sects," affording special privileges to the former. Amid this elite group were only four: Orthodoxy, Islam, Judaism, and Buddhism. Recognizing in its preamble, "the special contribution of Orthodoxy to the history of Russia and to the establishment and development of Russia's spirituality and culture," the 1997 law gave the Orthodox Church full legal privileges, and awarded it certain financial and material benefits, in many ways tantamount to establishment.[47] The preamble also acknowledged respect for "Christianity, Islam, Buddhism, and Judaism, and other religions and creeds which constitute an inseparable part of the historical heritage of Russia's peoples." They too would have full legal rights, but fewer advantages. Other religious organizations, especially those operating in Russia less than 15 years, would theoretically have freedom of worship and conscience, but would not receive material and financial benefits from the state and would be required to register each year.

The 1997 law also made the Russian Orthodox Church the only religious organization eligible to receive state aid for "the restoration, maintenance, and protection of buildings and objects which are monuments of history and culture."[48] The implications of this legal designation went much beyond material benefits. The law explicitly identified Orthodox Christianity with Russia's national memory and heritage, which had to be recovered and strengthened, and the church as an institution stood at the center of these efforts. The Council of Bishops proclaimed this identity in March 1997: "The Orthodox Church has for a thousand years of Russian history formed the spiritual and moral outlook of the Russian people, and...the overwhelming majority of religious believers belong to the Russian Orthodox Church."[49]

Being relegated to a subordinate status under the law, many religious organizations—including Catholics, Pentecostals, Baptists, and others— had to face an annual registration process that required them to pay a hefty fee and engage in a cumbersome, difficult, and time-consuming process, which, incidentally, was a forerunner of things to come, as a similar law was passed in 2006 regarding the registration of NGOs in Russia, and which applies to some religious organizations as well. Additional complex

issues concerned groups existing in Russia before 1917, but who nearly suffered eradication during the Communist period, including Pentecostals,
Orthodox Jews, and Lutherans. Whether their earlier presence would
be considered adequate proof of their long-standing existence remained
uncertain.[50] Should groups who arrived in Russia after 1982 fail to register themselves, they could conduct worship services, but would be prohibited from owning property and from creating and maintaining their
own schools and seminaries. Neither could they conduct religious rites in
hospitals, children's homes, and homes for the elderly, produce, import,
and distribute religious literature, print liturgical literature for religious
services, nor invite foreign guests to conduct these services. They faced
other discriminatory restrictions as well, limitations that contradicted
principles of religious liberty and freedom of conscience set forth earlier
and accepted by the international community.

By not placing all religious communities on an equal legal footing, the
1997 law violated principles of international human rights law and other
legal standards to which the Russian government had committed itself.[51]
The law contravened rights guaranteed in the 1993 Russian Constitution,
which incorporated international human rights conventions. These conventions prohibited discrimination on the basis of religion and protected
rights of freedom of religion, expression, and association. By violating such
principles, critics pointed out, the 1997 law undermined the fundamental
rights on which a democratic political order might be built. "Freedom of
conscience," wrote A. P. Pchelintsev, director of Russia's Institute of Religion
and Law, incorporated the "central principle" on which "rights, freedoms,
and respect for the individual rest."[52] Freedom of conscience offered the legal
and philosophical foundation that "protected the individual from the power
of monarchs and the tyranny of crowds."[53] Undermining this foundation,
the 1997 law challenged the constitutional norms the new Russian state created and to which it claimed to be devoted.

Proponents of the new law, however, remained strongly convinced of
its necessity. They worried about the declining influence of the Orthodox
Church, which they hoped would provide a bulwark for the building of
a post-Communist moral order, and they perceived the effects of non-
traditional religions as detrimental to Russia's moral fabric. They wanted
the Church to speak convincingly and quickly to many of Russia's difficult social problems—its alcoholism, crisis of values, family distresses,
and attraction to the material culture of the West. The rapid influx of
foreign missionaries, with their impressive organizational skills and well-
financed campaigns, and many with an ignorance of Russian language

and culture, offended Orthodox leaders and many Russians who saw their own culture threatened. Speaking in 1996, at the World Council of Churches, Metropolitan Kirill of Smolensk and Kaliningrad addressed the threat represented by the missionary crusade: "We expected that our fellow Christians would support and help our own missionary service. In reality, however, they have started fighting with our church, like boxers in a ring with pumped-up muscles, delivering blows."[54] Lumping together people of various confessions, Metropolitan Kirill stressed their mortal danger to the state's well being, especially at the present time of Russia's spiritual vulnerability: "For many of Russia today, 'non-Orthodox' means those who have come to destroy the spiritual unity of the people and the Orthodox faith—spiritual colonizers who by fair means and foul try to tear the people away from their church."[55]

Passage of the 1997 Law on Freedom of Conscience and on Religious Associations brought to the forefront additional issues concerning church and state. The new law exposed the tension between the development of a pluralistic society and state order, between religious and political liberty and the fear of anarchy characterizing the 1990s in Russia. The public's support for the 1997 law also showed its own lack of commitment to religious liberty and freedom of conscience, or even an understanding of such concepts. According to Mikhail Mchedlov, a Russian specialist on the sociology of religion, "Our research shows that approximately 83 percent of the population has little knowledge about laws on freedom of conscience."[56] To Mchedlov, this widespread ignorance defined the future agenda for religious believers: to be more active in propagandizing the laws protecting religious rights and to educate the Russian public about them, regardless of "whether these people are secular or religious."

In its conception, the 1997 law reverted to a "traditional" relationship between the Orthodox Church and the Russian state, a symphonic relationship, in which the church and state worked together harmoniously to manage worldly affairs and prepare inhabitants for entrance into the world to come. This "traditional" relationship was certainly imagined in the sense that Hobsbawm uses the term, since Russia's history is replete with as many instances of the state subverting and controlling the church as it is of acting according to *symphonia*.

Return to the Status Quo Ante?

Perhaps the most-feared component of the 1997 law was the legal requirement that all religious organizations had to re-register by March 1999 in order to continue legal operation in the country or face forced dissolution by the court. The trepidation associated with this requirement was not unfounded; 2,095 religious groups were found to be subject to dissolution by the Ministry of Justice after completion of the re-registration process. Those who failed to successfully re-register found themselves in that position for a variety of reasons; many simply did not attempt re-registration, others sought re-registration but were rejected for such reasons as incomplete or inaccurate registration forms. Some were not re-registered for unknown reasons.

Contrary to the suspicions of many observers of the cozy relationship between the Kremlin and the Patriarchate, the majority of the churches that failed to re-register were in fact Orthodox. Somewhat predictably, however, it was the non-Orthodox churches failing to make re-registration that were targeted for dissolution. As Vladimir Riakhovskii put it in an article in *Religiia i pravo*, "the *chinovniks* [sic], of course, did not have the courage to lay their hands on the most traditional confession [of Russia], and that is why several non-Orthodox organizations became the 'guinea pigs' for the legal procedures for court dissolution."[57]

When March 2000 rolled around, the deadline for dissolution of the churches that had failed to re-register, the Constitutional Court issued a reprieve in the form of an extension, postponing the deadline until the end of the year. According to Riakhovskii, state agencies requested to enforce the dissolution order in a minimal number of instances, and the court found no single petition to have sufficient grounds for dissolution. On the contrary, he points out that "in several such cases the court issued individual statements to the procurator's office and justice agencies about *their* trespassing of the law" (emphasis added).[58]

In a series of proclamations and decisions following the implementation of the 1997 law, the Constitutional Court decided that religious organizations that had been registered prior to the passage of the 1997 law, and which had not completed re-registration, could not be liquidated on that basis alone. In other words, they should be grandfathered in and continue to function on the legal basis of the pre-1997 law and according to their original charters. The only bases for dissolution would be violation of their charter or if they had ceased to exist, and in the latter case they would have to re-organize in accord with the 1997 law.

Not all religious organizations emerged unscathed. In several instances, the Constitutional Court, though rejecting an agency's request to forcibly dissolve a religious organization, did order a church that had failed to re-register to voluntarily liquidate itself. Many in fact did follow this course of action, and several quickly turned around and re-registered as new organizations, even under the same name and confessional affiliation. Still many others faced the real threat of liquidation by the court. By May 2002, 980 religious organizations in Russia had been dissolved.[59] The Ministry of Justice asserted that these religious organizations were in fact defunct, but religious minorities and the local NGO community often contended otherwise.

Whatever the true nature of the re-registration process and the dissolution of certain religious organizations in Russia under the 1997 law, the registration of new religious organizations has continued apace. By the end of 2006, 22,513 religious organizations operated legally in Russia, approximately 1,500 more than in 2002, and 5,500 more than when the law was passed in 1997. This number includes nearly 1,000 Baptist churches, more than 400 Kingdom Halls of Jehovah's Witnesses, and 53 churches of the Church of Jesus Christ of Latter Day Saints.[60] That being said, according to Forum 18, 39 of Stavropol's 49 mosques have been denied registration on arbitrary grounds, even though Islam is designated one of the four "traditional" religions of Russia.[61]

In the early 2000s, it was difficult to make sense of the seemingly incoherent actions of various Russian agencies regarding the implementation of the 1997 law on religious associations. As the legal situation regarding religious freedom evolved, some segments of civil society were working to stem the tide of a return to some pre-Soviet church-state arrangement, including Moscow's SOVA Center, which publishes news and analysis on religious extremism, violations of religious freedom, and even racism. Nevertheless, momentum in the direction of curtailing religious freedom and maintaining a secular state proved quite strong and popular.

In previous work, Wallace Daniel and I have suggested that the Constitutional Court was more committed to religious liberty than the legislative branch that passed the law in the first place and the justice organs that tried to enforce it according to their interpretation of the letter of the law. We concluded that such was not necessarily bad news, for it mirrored our own American development of religious liberty and separation of church and state. The extension of religious liberty in the United States evolved largely out of the Supreme Court's rulings on a large number of cases involving the violation of religious liberty and a breaching of the wall of separation by police agencies, state legislatures, and the U.S. Congress. It was through such landmark cases as *Cantwell v. Connecticut*, *Sherbert v. Verner*, and *Wisconsin v. Yoder*, that the U.S. Supreme Court guaranteed religious liberty to groups that average Americans may have found distasteful or strange, and in so doing secured religious liberty for us all. In Russia, we concluded, it would be a similar "fight for religious liberty by groups such as the Jehovah's Witnesses, the Church of Jesus Christ of Latter Day Saints, and the Salvation Army that will secure religious liberty for all of Russian society."[62]

By the end of 2009, it had become clear that religious liberty had lost this fight, however, and that the Russian Constitutional Court had given up its resistance to the more general shift apparent throughout Russian society toward intolerance and legal restrictions on the activities of "non-traditional" religious groups. For instance, in 2009, Medvedev created the "Presidential Commission of the Russian Federation to Counter Attempts to Falsify History to the Detriment of Russia's Interests," an organ used to sequester negative accounts of Russian history, including church-state collusion during the Soviet era. In May 2007 a Moscow District Court banned Koranic commentaries by Turkish theologian Said Nursi, judging them to be "extremist literature." Based on this ruling, the FSB has conducted raids on homes and detained Nursi followers as recently as February 2010.[63] The Jehovah's Witnesses found themselves under attack as well, with 34 of their publications—including their flagship publication *The Watchtower*—being banned as "extremist literature," while their property was also confiscated.[64]

These and other events had finally signaled to even the most optimistic Russia-watcher that an all-too-brief era in Russian church-state relations had come to an end. In its place stands a system in which Russian Orthodoxy enjoys primacy of place, if not outright establishment. The ROC involves itself in reviewing draft legislation, and the politicians vie with each other for the blessing of the patriarch and the church. Meanwhile, the country's youth look upon the situation as quite normal, and even positive. After all, in the versions of history and religion they receive in the public schools, all is as it should be. This is an easy position to hold, that is, unless you are *not* Orthodox, or even worse, actually a member of a *different* religious tradition.

Pluralism and (In)Tolerance

Much of Western scholarship on pluralism and democracy stems from the thought of James Madison and his belief that the greatest danger to democracy is the aggression "of interested majorities on the rights of minorities."[65] This theoretical literature assumes that pluralism goes together with democracy, and that the more pluralistic a polity is, the more democratic it is likely to be. Much democratic theorizing—as well as Western policy advising—is based upon theories that have their root in this assumption, from the

"Washington consensus" on post-Soviet democratization to America's Iraq and Afghanistan strategies as well.

The assumption undergirding the supposed effect of pluralism on democracy is that diversity will create an environment in which political groups will find it necessary to develop a *modus vivendi*, further assuming that the arrived-at arrangement will prove amenable to democratic politics. Recent scholarship, however, has problematized these assumptions. As this author has long argued and as Berger and Zijderveld have recently explained, plurality is not synonymous with pluralism. While the former merely designates a fact of diversity, the latter entails mutual recognition and acceptance of this diversity, with its various expressions being seen as equally valid. As Berger and Zijderveld describe the distinction, "If 'plurality' refers to a social reality (a reality that one may welcome or deplore), 'pluralism' is the attitude, possibly expanded into a full-blown philosophy, that *welcomes* the reality" (emphasis in original).[66]

Such a distinction is useful when viewing Russia. It is certainly a country characterized by "plurality," with its peoples representing over 128 ethnic groups, professing belief in every major world religion, and speaking dozens of native languages. But when it comes to pluralism, or the embrace of this diversity, the picture darkens quickly. Indeed, the legal battle discussed above is an excellent example of how intolerance can be legally-sanctioned by a ruling majority. Russia is not a monolith, however, and in addition to ethnic, religious, and linguistic diversity there exists a wide range of opinions on how to deal with this fact of plurality and what it means for the future of Russia.

Tolerance and Otherness

A recent study on religiosity, tolerance, and human rights in the Orthodox World suggests that tolerance and respect for others is a value embraced rather strongly in the Orthodox world, including Russia.[67] Nearly 70 percent of respondents in the most recent wave of the World Values Survey (2006) stated that they regarded raising their children to have respect and tolerance for others as important. This is nearly the same as in Germany, and only slightly less than in the United States and Canada (79 percent and 83.6 percent, respectively). Evidence abounds, however, indicating that levels of tolerance are actually low in Russia.[68] One immediately calls to mind the incident at the Sakharov Museum in January 2003, when several "Orthodox" hooligans smashed and destroyed the art exhibit *"Ostorozhno—Religiya"* (*Danger*—Religion). When brought before the Russian court, the charges against the culprits were not only dismissed by the judge, but the museum curator himself was subsequently brought up on charges and eventually found guilty of "inciting religious and ethnic hatred."[69]

Other artists have been the victims of lesser attacks, including pop-singer Madonna, whose concert in Moscow in the fall of 2006 was the cause for protests among so-called "Orthodox" Russians who considered her an "advocate of the Kabbalah" and vowed to prevent her from performing.[70] Those who participate in such activities, and the myriad other groups that exist, all demonstrate a serious lack of tolerance for "non-traditional" values and beliefs. These people whose racial and religious hatred rests upon a volatile mix of (non-canonical) Orthodox Christianity and Russian nationalism can be labeled with several different terms, including political Orthodox[71], radical Orthodox, or, perhaps the best description, the "Orthodox nationalists," an appropriate term coined by Verkhovsky (the director of the SOVA Center, mentioned above).[72] This phenomenon is clearly a reaction to the pluralizing effects of modernity, and is potentially a major obstacle to Russia's development into a modern society characterized by tolerance, respect for human rights, and the separation of church and state.

The most recent wave of the World Values Survey, completed in 2007 and now available for analysis is not a perfect measure by any means, but it does offer researchers some insight into the problem. The survey asks respondents, is it "important to Raise Children with Tolerance and Respect for others?" As Payne and I have pointed out elsewhere, 67.6 percent in Russia agreed— the highest of all Orthodox countries in the survey except for Georgia (n.b. Greece was not included in this survey).[73]

The importance attached to raising one's children to be tolerant and respectful of others is not only theoretically related to respect for human rights—in the countries that have the highest levels of respect for human rights (by a range of measures) citizens strongly value tolerance. For example, in the United States and Canada, approximately 80 percent of respondents to the World Values Survey answered positively to the above question (79 percent and 83.6 percent, respectively), while in Switzerland and Sweden agreement exceeds 90 percent (90.7 percent and 93.6 percent respectively). In Germany this level is significantly lower, however, with only 73.2 percent mentioning tolerance as important.

These data suggest that the discrepancy between Russia and the West is not as vast as one might suspect. This is a significant finding, since in many ways the embracing of tolerance and respect for others is a necessary prerequisite to embracing human rights. Moreover, since one's perception of the level of respect for human rights in his or her nation is necessarily related to the actual respect for human rights that exists there—and given the fact that some of these regimes are repressive by whatever conceptual apparatus one utilizes, Orthodox or otherwise—together these data may suggest that a necessary foundation for human rights is being laid, but that the regimes themselves are the obstacle, not necessarily the society or its culture, whether secular or religious. This is clearly seen by the fact that "raising children with religious belief" varied greatly from one Orthodox society to the next (with a clear bi-polar skew, with Romania, Georgia, and Moldova scoring high, while Bulgaria, Ukraine, and Russia scored very low) while the responses for "tolerance and respect" did not. This suggests that the embrace of tolerance is not closely tied to religious belief, and that a basis exists in Russian society for a true pluralism one that respects others despite their religious conviction or lack thereof.

One imaginative way of getting around the difficulty in determining the degree to which Russian citizens are actually tolerant toward others is by looking at the question in the survey, "Whom would you not like to have as your neighbor?" We can again use the method employed above to distinguish between the "devout Orthodox" and the "cultural Orthodox." The results yield great insight into this important dimension of tolerance (see Table 4.2). When it comes to one's neighbors, the highest levels of intolerance are for homosexuals, with 58 percent of all Russians responding that they would not like to have homosexuals as neighbors. The picture is only slightly better for Gypsies, with 45 percent of all Russians not wishing to have them as neighbors. Interestingly, this number was significantly lower for devout Orthodox, with only 40 percent feeling the same way. In general, Russians surveyed exhibited moderate levels of intolerance toward ethnic and religious minorities, with an average of around 10–15 percent indicating that they would not wish to have immigrants, Muslims, Jews, or members of a different race as neighbors. From the perspective of Orthodoxy and

Table 4.2 People You Would Not Like to Have as Neighbors

	Devout Orthodox	Cultural Orthodox	Non-orthodox Russians
Homosexuals	56.3	57.8	58.2
Gypsies	40.7	48.3	45.4
Immigrants	14.8	11.3	11.2
Muslims	14.1	14.5	13.7
Jews	12.6	12.1	11.5
People of different nationalities	11.1	9.3	8.2

tolerance, what is most interesting is that the devout Orthodox exhibited significantly higher levels of intolerance on several variables, including anti-Semitism and negative attitudes toward immigrants, while when it came to Islamophobia and negative attitudes toward Gypsies, they were surpassed here by the cultural Orthodox.

The evidence seems to suggest that citizens are not quite as tolerant as they present themselves to be. Though the exact translation of the World Values Survey into Russian is not available, it is most likely that the word used for "tolerance" in the survey was *terpimost'*, which is a somewhat distinct concept from that of *tolerantnost'*. Though both can be translated as "tolerance," *terpimost'* more accurately describes one's willingness to tolerate something, to put up with something, even unpleasant, and even something clearly harmful or in error. This is, of course, distinct from the Western human rights notion of tolerance, which is what is implied by the word *tolerantnost'*, but which is a more sophisticated word and concept, and unlikely to have been used in the translation for the survey questionnaire.

This distinction is precisely what Berger and Zijderveld have in mind when they distinguish between positive and negative tolerance. "Positive tolerance," they point out, "is characterized by genuine respect and openness in the encounter with individuals and groups that hold values different from one's own." On the contrary, negative tolerance "is an expression of indifference: 'Let them do their own thing'—'them' being those who believe or practice different things."[74] They further point out that it is the latter form of tolerance that has been growing in most of the developing world. Regardless of how the word "tolerance" was translated in the survey, it is most likely that respondents interpreted the word in a negative sense. The fact that only ten percent of attempted surveys were actually completed, due to refusals to participate in the survey—or even open their door—further indicates that levels of tolerance, no matter how translated, are still very low in societies recovering from more than half a century of authoritarian rule. In fact, the so-called East-West divide is probably more attributable to this past than it is to Orthodoxy, either as a theology or a lived religious tradition.

Political Extremism and Ethno-Religious Violence

While Russians surveyed responded quite positively regarding tolerance as a value, a small but sizable segment of Russian society has been increasingly turning to extremism and ethno-religious violence.[75] Perhaps the most startling case is that of Artur Ryno, a young Russian student at an Orthodox icon-painting school who was arrested in June 2007 on 37 counts of homicide.[76]

It turns out that he had spent more than a year targeting and killing members of minority ethnic groups in Moscow, mostly migrant workers from the traditionally-Muslim regions of Central Asia and the Caucasus. For people such as Ryno—including members of some quasi-fascist groups associated with Russia's "skinheads"—the combination of Russian nationalism and a perverted form of Orthodox Christianity is proving lethal.[77] The data in Table 4.3 illustrates that the case of Ryno is not an isolated one, although it is certainly one of the most horrific and extreme. Isolated cases of murder and beatings are increasingly pervasive in Russia today, with the number of murders rising sharply between the years 2006 and 2008 (see Table 4.3).

By far, Moscow is the primary locus of not only political extremism but also the violence that too often goes along with it. Between 2006 and 2008, official statistics record 146 murders and 649 beatings as being attributed to racist and neo-Nazi groups. For Russia as a whole, the respective numbers are 248 and 1,561. Furthermore, minorities in Russia are unlikely to turn to the police for assistance in such situations due to bias and abuse within the police force itself,[78] such that these numbers likely are underestimations. We must also bear in mind that Artur Ryno's victims are not counted here, since he is considered a serial murderer and not a racist or neo-Nazi extremist.

The picture across the rest of Russia is less extreme, but not at all comforting. St. Petersburg ranks second in terms of murders and racism-inspired beatings, with official statistics reporting 32 murders and 205 beatings. The figures drop dramatically once we turn our attention outside of the nation's two historic capitals, but certain cities and urban areas are clearly more violent than others. This includes Nizhnii Novgorod, Sverdlovsk Oblast', Irkutsk, and Voronezh. It is the last city which has been gaining increasing notoriety as a city of xenophobia and racist violence. While in Moscow and St. Petersburg much of this type of violence can be traced to the presence of migrant workers from Central Asia, this is not the case in Voronezh, where the violence has been directed primarily against university students from Africa and Asia. In one example, a student from Kenya told this author that he was approached almost daily and harassed by Russian youth, who incidentally were not students at the local university. The situation became increasingly bleak throughout 2005, until finally one of his friends, a student also from Kenya, was murdered by one of these groups. The student then transferred to a Canadian university, as did many of his friends.[79]

There are a few things we can conclude based upon this brief look into race-motivated violence in Russia. The first is that it is largely a phenomenon limited to Moscow and St. Petersburg. Even after we adjust for population, the number of such incidents is dramatically higher in these two cities

Table 4.3 Ethno-religious Violence in Russian Cities and Urban Areas

		Moscow	St. Petersburg	Belgorod	Vladivostok	Voronezh	Irkutsk	Nizhnii Novgorod	Sverdlovsk
2008	Murdered	57	15	0	0	2	0	2	4
	Injured	199	38	2	4	18	1	12	16
	Total	256	53	2	4	20	1	14	20
2007	Murdered	49	11	0	1	0	1	1	3
	Injured	222	111	1	3	16	53	41	17
	Total	271	122	1	4	16	54	42	20
2006	Murdered	40	6	0	2	1	0	0	0
	Injured	228	56	18	18	6	8	36	6
	Total	268	62	18	20	7	8	36	6

Source: Table compiled by author using data found in Verkhovsky, 2009.

than in any other city in Russia by a factor of around five, that is, holding population constant, the chances are five times greater that an immigrant or foreigner from Asia or Africa will be the victim of such an attack in these cities. This is at least partially attributable to the prevalence of both of these groups in Moscow and St. Petersburg, but that alone cannot account for the higher incidence in the capital cities. One must suspect that the politicization of identity is also related in some way, including stronger identification with Orthodox Christianity and Russian nationalism, phenomena increasingly on the rise in the two historic capitals.[80] It is not difficult to draw a link between greater political activity and greater numbers of immigrants and foreign students, especially in times of economic hardship and uncertainty.

Orthodoxy *qua Primus inter Non-pares*

After the collapse of Communism, competing sources of legitimacy that had previously been repressed and forced underground promptly came to the surface, like, as they say in Russia, mushrooms after a rain. Orthodoxy reemerged as one of the strongest voices. Crippled by many years of state repression, hindered by the lack of funds and other material resources, and weakened also by shortages of well-trained clergy, it has faced the daunting task "of rebuilding itself, of recovering its identity, and of speaking effectively to a changing society."[81] Unfortunately, in the process it has looked toward the state for assistance, and the state has all too enthusiastically obliged.

While the 1993 Constitution clearly defines Russia as a secular state, whose political institutions and legal structures are to be devoid of ideological and religious influences, the events of the past decade have thrown that status into doubt. Putin himself even rejects the idea. When asked if he thought that bestowing privileges on the ROC violated Russia's status as a secular state, the then-president responded: "This is not the case [Russia is not a secular state]: The law states that Russia has four traditional religions."[82] Certainly Mr. Putin, himself trained as a lawyer, understands the implications of what he is saying. Legal scholar Robert Blitt has pointed out that the preamble to the 1997 law, where the reference to the four traditional religions resides, has no force of law as a preamble.[83] Nevertheless, in post-Soviet Russia the law means what leaders say it means, and distinctions between preambles and statutory sections are more or less meaningless in a society in which 40–50 percent of all cases brought before the court are complicated by procedural violations.

If the involvement of Patriarch Pimen or Aleksii II in the inaugural ceremonies of presidents Yeltsin, Putin, or Medvedev could be dismissed as mere ceremony and not an egregious violation of Russia's religion law, other events clearly signal a dangerously close collusion between secular and sacred authority. Chapels on the premises of Russian governmental agencies, patron saints for the Strategic Rocket Forces and individual tank battalions, and access to draft legislation prepared for the Duma are all acts that suggest that the Russian Orthodox Church is now well-entrenched and developing into a *de facto* established church.

Given its force in law, however, it was the passage of the 1997 law that was perhaps the most critical point in Russia's return to the *status quo ante*, that is, to a situation in which the Russian Orthodox Church is more than just first among equals in Russia, but actually stands next to the state as its own equal. This certainly complicates the religious freedom situation in Russia. Of course, full religious liberty had never materialized even before the passing of the 1997 law, but that fateful act symbolized an abandonment of the ideal itself. If religious liberties had been curtailed under a law and constitution that had guaranteed them, what chance was there for full religious equality under a law that developed a hierarchy of preferred religions and offered quasi-establishment to the Russian Orthodox Church? In the decade after the passage of the 1997 law, many of the trappings of establishment quickly found their way into Russian society, ranging from the funding of church reconstruction for historic Orthodox churches destroyed during the Soviet era, to the introduction, in 2002, of an 11-year core curriculum on "Fundamentals of Orthodox Culture" into the public schools.[84]

The issue of gravest concern, however, is the effects of this new arrangement on the freedom of religion and practice of other religions. Initially, despite their desire and several attempts, state organs were relatively unsuccessful at curtailing the rights and liberties of religious believers and organizations in Russia. This was due to a combination of lack of will by some government agencies to carry out the letter of the law to its fullest possible degree, and the unwillingness of some to allow that to happen. The result was that religious groups in Russia were not clamped down upon as harshly as many feared. Even in 2006 the U.S. State Department concluded that the Russian government generally respected the right of freedom of religion in practice, while recognizing the imposition of restrictions upon certain groups, primarily Jehovah's Witnesses, Scientologists, and the Unification Church. The State Department concluded at the time that "government policy continued to contribute to the generally free practice of religion for most of the population."[85] The international religious freedom NGO *Forum 18* also reached a similar conclusion, stating that "fluctuation in religious freedom policy" remains the distinguishing feature of the Russian state's dealings with religious organizations, with some confessions seeing "significant improvement in [their] relations with the state," while others are feeling increasingly adverse effects, particularly Muslims,"[86] who are one of the "four traditional" religions of Russia.

More recent estimates, however, are less sanguine. As SOVA Center concluded in its survey on freedom of conscience in 2009, there are still many cases of discrimination against certain religious minorities in Russia today.[87] Among them is the misuse of anti-extremist legislation to attack the Jehovah's Witnesses, attacks on Muslims for their alleged (though highly suspect) connections to terrorist groups, and even the repression of the Falun Gong, carried out for the sake of good relations with China. As for the "four traditional" religions of Russia, SOVA reports that for the first time they are now being "explicitly mentioned in the Presidential decrees and other regulations, effectively establishing different treatment of different religions." This "explicit acceptance" of the four traditional religions "as exclusive partners of the state," they observe, "is perhaps the most significant step away from secularity in the entire post-Soviet period."[88]

In reflecting upon the evolution of Russian church-state relations over the past 25 years, it is necessary to bear in mind that it took nearly 150 years of legal battles for religious freedom and separation of church and state to be established in the United States. While it is often alluring to think that our model of separation of church and state was secured with Thomas Jefferson's letter to the Danbury Baptist Association in 1802, we often forget that his letter only marked the beginning of a long road to reach the measure of religious liberty we enjoy today. In charting its own path to freedom of assembly, conscience, and belief, it will take some time for these values to take root in Russia, especially after seven decades of forced secularization.

Notes

1. Moscow Patriarchate, "Celebration of the Millennium of the Baptism of Russ [*sic*]," Press Release, no. 1 (May 11, 1988), p. 5.
2. Marsh, *Unparalleled Reforms*, pp. 47–53.
3. L. I. Yemelyakh and Ya. Ya. Kozhurin, *Sovetskaya Istoricheskaya Nauka o Kreshchenii Rusi* (Leningrad: Znanie, 1986), p. 5.
4. Ibid, pp. 5–6.
5. K. Kharchev, "Utverzhdaya svobodu sovesti," *Pravda* (January 27, 1988), p. 3.
6. Ibid.

7. Cf. Akademyia Nauk SSSR, *Khristianstvo i Rus'* (Moscow: Nauka, 1988).
8. Yemelyakh and Kozhurin, p. 6.
9. Ibid., p. 27.
10. G. L. Kurbatov, E. D. Frolov, and I. Ya. Froyanov, *Khristianstvo: Antichnost', Vizantiya, Drevnyaya Rus'* (Moscow: Lenizdat, 1988), p. 328. For more on *dvoeverie*, see Stella Rock, *Popular Religion in Russia: 'Double Belief' and the Making of an Academic Myth* (London: Routledge, 2007).
11. Lev Lebedev, *Kreshchenie* Rusi (Moscow: Moscow Patriarchate, 1988).
12. Moscow Patriarchate, "Celebration of the Millennium of the Baptism of Russ [*sic*]," Press Release, May 11, 1988, p. 2.
13. Ibid., p. 4.
14. Pospielovsky, 1998, p. 353.
15. This is meant to refer to both the Stalin and Khrushchev periods, as the latter was accused of carrying out his own "cult of personality." See Chapter 3.
16. Moscow Patriarchate, "Celebration of the Millennium of the Baptism of Russ [*sic*]," Press Release, no. 1 (May 11, 1988), p. 5.
17. "Possibilities for Dialogue," *Moscow News*, No. 12 (March 20, 1988), p. 13.
18. Moscow Patriarchate, "Celebration of the Millennium of the Baptism of Russ [*sic*]," Press Release, no. 3 (June 4, 1988), p. 2
19. Moscow Patriarchate, "Celebration of the Millennium of the Baptism of Russ [*sic*]," Press Release, no. 5 (June 7, 1988), p. 4.
20. Ibid.
21. "I za sud'bu svoego Otechestva," *Novoe Vremya* (June 17, 1988), p. 5–6.
22. Ibid.
23. Iu. Zuev, "Dinamika Religioznosti v Rossii v XX veke i ee sotsiologiches-koe izuchenie," in V. Garadzha, *Sotsiologiya Religii* (Moscow: 1995), pp. 187–210.
24. Sergei Filatov and Dmitri Furman, "Religiya i politika v massovom soz-nanii," *Sotsiologicheskie Issledovaniya*, no. 7 (1992), pp. 3–5.
25. Kimmo Kaariainen, *Religion in Russia after the Collapse of Communism* (Lewiston, NY: Edwin Mellen, 1998), p. 84.
26. Unless otherwise noted, all calculations were made by the author using the WVS data available at: http://www.worldvaluessurvey.com
27. Kaariainen, p. 61.
28. Alexander Agadjanian, "Religious Responses to Social Changes in Russia: Traditional and New Religions Compared," *Journal of Contemporary Religion*, Vol. 11, No. 1 (1996), pp. 69–70.

29. Christopher Marsh and Artyom Tonoyan, "The Civic, Economic, and Political Consequences of Pentecostalism in Russia and Ukraine," *Society*, Vol. 46, No. 6 (2009), pp. 510–16.

30. Inna Naletova, "Orthodoxy Beyond the Church Walls: a Sociological Inquiry into Orthodox Religious Experience in Contemporary Russian Society," unpublished doctoral dissertation, Boston University, 2007. See also, Inna Naletova, "Orthodox *Yarmarki* as a Form of Civic Engagement," in Christopher Marsh, ed., *Burden or Blessing? Russian Orthodoxy and the Construction of Civil Society and Democracy* (Boston, MA: Institute on Culture, Religion, and World Affairs, Boston University, 2004), pp. 77–82.

31. Stella Rock, "The Revival of Pilgrimage in Modern Russia," lecture presented at the J.M. Dawson Institute of Church-State Studies, Baylor University, October 15, 2009.

32. Vera Shevzov, *Russian Orthodoxy on the Eve of the Revolution* (New York: Oxford University Press, 2004), p. 147.

33. The category labeled devout Orthodox includes only those respondents who identified themselves as Orthodox Christians, believe in God, and attend church services at least once per month. These selection criteria result in 186 devout Orthodox Christians in the survey, or 13.4 percent of respondents. The remaining self-identifying Orthodox (1,001), are labeled the cultural Orthodox. The third category is comprised of those respondents who listed no religious affiliation (1,210).

34. Christopher Marsh, "Russian Orthodox Christians and their Orientation toward Church and State," *Journal of Church & State*, Vol. 47, No. 3 (2005), pp. 545–62.

35. Christopher Marsh, "Orthodox Christians and Market Transition in Russia," *Society*, Vol. 44, No. 1 (2006), pp. 36–41; and Christopher Marsh, "Orthodox Christianity, Civil Society, and Russian Democracy," *Demokratizatsiya*, Vol. 13, No. 3 (2005), pp. 449–62.

36. "Interview with Russian Orthodox Metropolitan Kyrill [*sic*]: The Bible Calls it a Sin," *Spiegel Online* (January 10, 2008). Available at: http://www.spiegel.de/international/world/0,1518,527618-2,00.html

37. Metropolitan Kirill of Smolensk, "Gospel and Culture," in *Proselytism and Orthodoxy in Russia: The New War for Souls, John Witte, Jr. and Michael Bourdeaux*, eds. (Maryknoll: Orbis, 1999), pp. 66–76.

38. Harold Berman, "Freedom of Religion in Russia: An Amicus Brief for the Defendant," in Witte and Bourdeaux, pp. 275–6.

39. Incidentally, this has resulted in a situation in which these religious traditions are able to establish themselves as "hegemonic" religions in

certain republics. The best example of this is that of Islam in places like Tatarstan, Bashkortostan, and Dagestan. See Christopher Marsh and Paul Froese, "The State of Freedom in Russia: A Regional Analysis of Freedom of Religion, Media, and Markets," *Religion, State & Society*, Vol. 32, No. 2 (2004), pp. 137–49.

40. *Osnovny Zakon Rossisskoi Federatsii* (1993).

41. Ibid.

42. Lauren Homer and Lawrence Uzzell, "Federal and Provincial Religious Freedom Laws in Russia: A Struggle for and against Federalism and the Rule of Law," in Witte and Bourdeaux, pp. 284–309.

43. John Witte, Jr., "Introduction," pp. 1–14.

44. Press Service of the President of the Russian Federation, "Yeltsin Threatens Not to Enforce Law if Veto Overriden," *Report of the Press Service of the President of the Russian Federation*, No. 1997-07-23-006.

45. Yeltsin's final acquiescence to demands to ratify the law followed years of intense lobbying by the ROC, including a personal meeting between Patriarch Aleksey II and Yeltsin during the final stages of the attempt to introduce an amendment to the 1993 Constitution that ultimately failed. Cf. W. Cole Durham, Jr. *et al.*, "The Future of Religious Liberty in Russia: Report of the De Burght Conference on Pending Russian Legislation Restricting Religious Liberty," *Emory International Law Review*, 8 (1994), pp. 1–2.

46. "Yeltsin's Radio Broadcast," July 25, 1997. Translated and archived at: http://www.stetson.edu/~psteeves/relnews/9707.html; accessed March 7, 2007.

47. "Russian Federation Federal Law on Freedom of Conscience and on Religious Associations," *Emory International Law Review* 12 (1998), p. 657.

48. Witte, "Introduction," p. 14.

49. *Pravoslavnaya Moskva*, Vol. 7, No. 103 (March 1997), p. 12.

50. W. Cole Durham, Jr. and Laurel B. Homer, "Russia's 1997 Law on Freedom of Conscience and Religious Associations: An Analytical Appraisal," *Emory International Law Review* 12 (1998), pp. 200–1.

51. T. Jeremy Gunn, "The Law of the Russian Federation on the Freedom of Conscience and Religious Associations from a Human Rights Perspective," in Witte and Bourdeaux, pp. 241–56.

52. Anatolii Pchelintsev, "Religiia i prava cheloveka," in *Religiia i prava cheloveka: Na puti k svobode sovesti*, Vol. 3, eds. L. M. Vorontsova, A. V. Pchelintsev, and S. B. Filatov (Moscow: "Nauka," 1996), pp. 7–11.

53. Ibid., p. 8.

54. Metropolitan Kirill of Smolensk, "Gospel and Culture," p. 73.

55. Ibid., pp. 73–4.

56. Mikhail Mchedlov, in "Svoboda, sovesti, religiia, pravo (materialy 'kru-glogo stola')," *Voprosy filosofii*, no. 12 (1994), p. 4.

57. Vladimir Riakhovskii, "Eshche odin vazhnyi shag na puti k verkhoven-stvu prava," *Religiia i pravo*, no. 1 (2002), p. 2.

58. Ibid.

59. Ibid.

60. Bureau of Democracy, Human Rights, and Labor, U.S. Department of State, *International Religious Freedom Report*, 2006.

61. Geraldine Fagan, "Russia: Unregistered Religious Groups," (Oslo, Norway: Forum 18 News Service, 2005).

62. Wallace Daniel and Christopher Marsh, "Russia's 1997 Law on Freedom of Conscience in Context and Retrospect," *Journal of Church & State*, Vol. 48, No. 1 (Winter 2007), pp. 5–17.

63. Geraldine Fagan, "Russia: Three More Readers of Muslim Theologian Detained," *Forum 18 News Service* (February 23, 2010).

64. Geraldine Fagan and Felix Corley, "34 Jehovah's Witness Publications and One Congregation Banned," *Forum 18 News Service* (December 8, 2009). See also, RosBiznesKonsalting, "Verkhovniy Sud RF Ostavil bez Izmeneniya Reshenie o Zaprete Taganrogskoi Sekty Svidetelei Iegovy," available at: http://www.top.rbc.ru/

65. *The Federalist Papers*, No. 10.

66. Peter Berger and Anton Zijderveld, *In Praise of Doubt: How to have Convictions without Becoming a Fanatic* (New York: HarperCollins, 2009), p. 7.

67. Christopher Marsh and Daniel Payne, "Religiosity, Tolerance, and Respect for Human Rights in the Orthodox World," in *Orthodox Churches and Human Rights Discourse*, Alfons Brüning, ed. (Nijmegen: Nijmegen University Press, 2010).

68. M. Rykpin, *Svastika, Krest, Zvezda: Proizvedenia iskusstva v epokhu upravlyaemoi demokratii* (Moscow: Logos, 2006); A. Verkhovskiy, *Ksenofobiya, svoboda sovesti, i antiekstremizm v Rossii v 2008 godu* (Moscow: Tsentr "Sova", 2009); A. Verkhovskiy, *Radikalizm: Gosudarstvo protiv radikal'nogo natsionalisma* (Moscow: Tsentr "Panorama", 2002).

69. Rykpin, 2006.

70. Mosnews.com, "Radical Christians against Madonna Concert in Moscow," [http://www.mosnews.com/images/g/s150.shtml]; May 9, 2006.

71. Anastasia Mitrofanova, *The Politicization of Russian Orthodoxy* (Stuttgart: ibidem-Verlag, 2005).
72. Verkhovskiy, *Radikalizm: Gosudarstvo protiv radikal'nogo natsionalisma*, 2002. See also Verkhovskiy, *Ksenofobiya, svoboda sovesti, i antiekstremizm*, 2009, and Marlene Laruelle, *In the Name of the Nation: Nationalism and Politics in Contemporary Russia* (New York: Palgrave Macmillan, 2009).
73. Marsh and Payne, "Religiosity, Tolerance, and Respect for Human Rights in the Orthodox World," 2010.
74. Berger and Zijderveld, p. 31.
75. Verkhovsky, 2002, 2009.
76. For a fuller discussion of this topic, see Christopher Marsh, "Pluralism, (Un)Civil Society, and Authoritarianism in Russia's Region," in *The Politics of Sub-National Authoritarianism in Russia*, Vladimir Gel'man and Cameron Ross, eds. (Aldershot: Ashgate, 2010). See also the discussion on the negative forms of Orthodox spiritual capital, in Christopher Marsh, "Orthodox Spiritual Capital and Russian Reform," in *The Hidden Form of Capital: Spiritual Influences in Societal Progress*, Peter L. Berger and Gordon Redding, eds. (New York: Anthem, 2010).
77. By far the best account of this phenomenon is that offered by Laruelle (2009), especially pp. 60–70; see also pp. 35–48.
78. Emil Pain, "Xenophobia and Ethnopolitical Extremism in Post-Soviet Russia: Dynamics and Growth Factors," *Nationalities Papers*, No. 35 (2007), pp. 895–912.
79. Interview with the author, March 12, 2005, Voronezh, Russia.
80. Mitrofanova, 2005.
81. Wallace Daniel, Peter Berger, and Christopher Marsh, "Introduction," in *Perspectives on Church-State Relations in Russia*, Wallace Daniel, Peter Berger, and Christopher Marsh, eds. (Waco, TX: J.M. Dawson Institute of Church-State Studies, Baylor University, 2008), p. 2.
82. Interview by *Time* Magazine with Vladimir Putin. Cited in Robert Blitt, "How to Entrench a De Facto State Church in Russia: A Guide in Progress," *Brigham Young University Law Review*, No. 3 (2008), p. 734, fn. 127.
83. Ibid., p. 734.
84. Elena Lisovskaya, "Orthodoxy, Islam, and the Desecularization of Russian State Schools," 2010 Hugh and Beverly Wamble Lecture, February 11, 2010, J. M. Dawson Institute for Church-State Studies, Baylor University; See also Elena Lisovskaya and Vyacheslav Karpov, "Orthodoxy, Islam, and Desecularization of Russia's State Schools,"

Politics and Religion, Vol. 3, No. 2 (2010), and John Basil, "Orthodoxy and Public Education in the Russian Federation: The First Fifteen Years," in Daniel, Berger, and Marsh, *Perspectives on Church-State Relations in Russia*, pp. 37–62.

85. Bureau of Democracy, Human Rights, and Labor, 2006.

86. Geraldine Fagan, "Russia: Religious Freedom Survey, February 2005," *Forum 18 News Service* (2005).

87. Alexander Verkhovsky and Olga Sibireva, "Problemy realizatsii svobody sovesti v Rossii v 2009 godu," (Moscow: SOVA Tsentr, 2010). Available at: http://religion.sova-center.ru/publications/E3EF1C0/E89CD46

88. Ibid.

CHAPTER FIVE

China's Third Opium War: The CCP's Struggle with Religion

So we are going to go on letting you teach, trying to convert the people...After all we both believe that the truth will prevail; we think your beliefs untrue and false, therefore if we are right, the people will reject them, and your church will decay. If you are right, then the people will believe you, but as we are sure that you are wrong, we are prepared for that risk.[1]

—*Zhou Enlai*

The capture of Beijing by the People's Liberation Army (PLA) in October 1949 brought to power the Chinese Communist Party (CCP) and its leader, Mao Zedong. The CCP had been formed back in July 1921 on a small lake in Shanghai, in order to evade the police. Among the dozen Chinese intellectuals were two foreign representatives of Lenin's Comintern, an organization designed to foment Communist revolution around the world. At that time, Marxism was still very new to China. In fact, only small sections of Marx's works had been translated, including the *Communist Manifesto*, which had been translated by Chen Duxiu, who was elected that day secretary of the party's central committee.

China's situation in the world had made it ripe for such a Marxist movement. From its history of being "carved up like a melon" throughout the nineteenth century, to being betrayed at the hands of the Allied powers at Versailles, when Germany's concession territories (including Shanghai) were handed over to Japan rather than being immediately returned to the Chinese people, many among China's intellectual class were increasingly finding answers to the nation's predicament in Marxism. By the time of the Washington Conference of 1922, which returned the concession territories back to China, the damage had already been done. The CCP had been established and Sun Yat-sen had entered into an agreement with Lenin to accept Soviet aid. It had been less than 5 years since Li Dazhao and Chen Duxiu had formed the first Marxist study society at Peking University, and now the Communist Party stood alongside the *Guomindang* (*Kuomintang*; Nationalist Party) as the two major contenders for political power in China. It would be two decades of warlordism, chaos, and Japanese aggression, however, before the two would vie for control of the Middle Kingdom.

Two aspects of China's past resonated sharply with the Marxist-Leninist critique of the world capitalist system. First and foremost was the critique of global capitalism, and of Lenin's specific contribution, that of "imperialism as the highest stage of capitalism." Indeed, the history of nineteenth-century China was a history of colonial encroachment, the theft of raw materials, and the forced drawing of China into the world capitalist system. But Marxism contained another central element, and this too would resonate with China's Communists, as well as many other Chinese intellectuals. That element was the Marxist-Leninist critique of religion. Here, too, China's unique past led to a particular interpretation of Communist doctrine and its subsequent strong embrace. Marx's equating of religion with opium perhaps nowhere on the planet resonated quite the same way as it did in China, a country where the Opium Wars of the 1840s symbolized the West's attempt to draw China—and the Chinese people—into an exploitative and parasitic economic relationship with the West. Every Chinese citizen was aware—often firsthand—of the detrimental effects of opium addiction, and how the British promoted the sale of this drug, produced in its colony of India, as a means of exchange by which to acquire Chinese wares such as silk, porcelain, and tea without depleting their reserves of precious metals. This effect persisted after the establishment of new China. As Bishop Ting explains, Chinese are taught from "childhood that religion is opium, and since they are quite familiar with China's disastrous experience with the Opium War, they find religion so abhorrent that they unconsciously substitute emotion for science."[2]

They also learn of the often-disastrous history of religious rebellion in their own country. From the Taiping Rebellion of 1850–1864, which was started by unsuccessful civil service examinee Hong Xiuquan who read the Bible only to conclude that he was the brother of Jesus, to the Muslim Uprisings following thereafter, many Chinese began to equate religion ("Western" religions in particular) with fanaticism and violence. Marxism-Leninism offered a comprehensive theoretical explanation for it all, and in a way that they could readily understand, especially once articulated by the charismatic Mao Zedong. It was at his hands that the Communist regime embarked upon an "opium war" of their own—the CCP campaign to eradicate religion from the Middle Kingdom. In the process the Communists waged war against a religious-philosophical tradition thousands of years in the making and deeply-rooted in Chinese culture and custom.

From Tao to Mao

When approaching the topic of religion in China, one is immediately faced with the problem of how to address what are very different types of belief systems than that to which the Western reader has traditionally been exposed. Indeed, there is great controversy of whether or not one of the most influential bodies of thought in China—that of Confucianism—can even be considered a religion.[3] One must keep an open mind, however, and understand "religion" in a very broad sense if one wishes to compare the effect of government policy in such different contexts as Russia and China. In this regard, Berger's concept of a "sacred canopy" or Tillich's idea of "ultimate concerns" are quite useful ways of understanding religion and its social function. One must also toss aside the difference between sacred and secular—it is of little use in the Middle Kingdom. And contrary to what one would expect, the sacred is more prevalent in Chinese thought and society than in the West—in the person of the emperor, in nature, in mountains, and within human beings ourselves.

The omnipresence of the sacred in Chinese thought and its unity with the world around it is immediately grasped when one considers the long development of the Chinese term for religion, *zongjiao* (revered teaching). This neologism appears to have been introduced around the sixth century CE, at which time it referred rather specifically to Buddhism, with Yu even suggesting that it was a synonym for the ascending religious tradition from India.[4] Throughout the centuries, the term eventually came to refer to the *sanjiao* collectively, that is, Taoism, Confucianism, and Buddhism (see below), but it was not until the modern period that the term was adopted as a term of reference for other religious traditions, including Christianity, and Islam. The Japanese faced a similar predicament in selecting a term that would describe religion broadly enough to incorporate both indigenous and foreign religious traditions, and after franticly searching for a term that would be the equivalent of the German *Religionsübung* (religious practice), they settled on the Chinese term *zongjiao*, the kanji for which rendered the term *shūkyō*.[5]

Hardacre's explanation for Japan's adoption of the term *shūkyō* is equally applicable to China. As she explains, there was "no equivalent concept or term, no idea of a distinct sphere of life that could be called religious, and no idea of a generic religion of which there might be local variants like Christianity, Buddhism, and so on."[6] In both cases, it wasn't that Japan and China were void of religious practice and belief at the time—quite the contrary. Religion was such a deep part of their culture that its distinctiveness had not yet been articulated and sufficiently distinguished from other aspects of culture, belief, and ethical teachings.

From a Weberian perspective, we may conclude that Chinese society had not evolved to the point yet when the concept of religion had been sufficiently "differentiated" from other aspects of culture, though Weber's own writings on religion in China do not explore this.[7] As such, elements of Confucianism, Buddhism, Taoism, and folk religion blended together and merged into endless combinations. As the eminent scholar of Chinese religion C. K. Yang noted, in "popular religious life it was the moral and magical functions of the cults, and not the delineation of the boundary of religious faiths, that dominated people's consciousness."[8] This blending was not limited to the average person, but was prevalent among the sacerdotium as well. As Yang further explains, even "priests in some country temples were unable to reveal the identity of the religion to which they belonged. Centuries of mixing gods from different faiths into a common pantheon had produced a functionally oriented religious view that relegated the question of religious identity to a secondary place."[9]

If Chinese priests cannot name the religion which they preach, how can the outside observer hope to distinguish between the country's religious traditions? The twentieth century saw a great amount of differentiation in this regard, although the lines between the traditions are still often fuzzy. Taken together, China's most prevalent intellectual traditions of Taoism, Confucianism, and Buddhism can be considered the *sanjiao*, or "three teachings". One of the earliest references to this tripartite conception of religion is attributed to Li Shiqian, a prominent scholar of the sixth century, who penned the famous phrase, "Buddhism is the sun, Daoism the moon, and Confucianism the five planets."[10] Teiser explains that this likening of the three traditions to heavenly bodies suggests "that although they remain separate, they also coexist as equally indispensable phenomena of the natural world."[11] As the following discussion will illustrate, each tradition has its own unique emphasis vis-à-vis the others, and therefore its own unique contribution to the Chinese *weltanschauung*.

The Sanjiao

Taoism is China's oldest religious tradition, and can trace its roots back to prehistoric folk religion.[12] It is more closely associated with the life and writings of Lao Tzu (the "old master"), the author of the *Tao Te Ching* (The Way and its Power), who lived sometime between the fifth and second centuries BC.

The central concern of Taoism is "the way" (*dao*, more commonly referred to as "tao"), which can be understood as the natural order of the universe. People are supposed to live in accord with the way, in harmony with the world around them, by living according to the precept of *wu wei*, or non-action. What is meant by this is not that people do nothing, but that action should be effortless and in harmony with the natural forces at work in the universe. It is therefore "effortless doing," or "acting without acting" (*wei wu wei*). By acting in accord with nature and maintaining a passive state of receptiveness (*pu*), one becomes a part of the harmony of the universe.

Kohn has suggested that "Taoism" can be more easily understood by dividing it into three distinct manifestations, philosophical Taoism, religious Taoism, and folk Taoism.[13] There is great heuristic value in this distinction, since the practices, beliefs, and degrees of commitment vary greatly from group to group. There are even two distinct concepts for this in Chinese, *daojia* (philosophy of the way) and *daojiao* (teaching or "religion" of the way). Others, however, disagree with this method of classification, arguing that Taoism, despite such distinctions and great variation among adherents, must be considered a single religious tradition.[14]

If Taoism is an ontology of the cosmos, then Confucianism is China's civil religion. Indeed, where Taoism focuses on man's relationship to the universe, Confucianism focuses on the relationship between man, the state, and heaven.[15] The primary concern of Confucius himself was that rulers govern in accord with the *dao* (hence the early reference to Confucianism as *rudao*), which in his time he felt they were not doing. Likewise, all subjects should behave in accordance with their station in life, and view themselves in a hierarchical relationship with those around them, with duties and responsibilities to both those above and below them. This moral code is conveniently translated as *junjun, chenchen, fufu, zizi*, which loosely translated means "a lord rules as a lord, a subject serves as a subject, a father acts as a father, and a son behaves as a son." Harmony is thus achieved by each acting in accord with his station. This idea is clearly expressed in the *Analects* through the story of how, when the Duke of Qi asked Confucius about how to govern properly so as to achieve social harmony, he replied, "There is government, when the prince is prince, and the minister is minister, when the father is father, and the son is son."[16]

If Lao Tzu was the "mystic" who spoke of the unseen and intangible, Confucius was the "realist" whose moral axioms focused on real-world concerns of governance, social harmony, family relations, and self-cultivation. Here is where the *tao*, which is also a very important aspect of Confucianism, can be seen as something like a moral law of the universe, not simply the natural order of Lao Tzu. Though with slightly different meanings, Confucianism and Taoism can be seen—and often have been—as having a dualistic and synergistic relationship with each other.[17] Indeed, legend even has it that Lao Tzu had been a teacher of Confucius. While almost certainly untrue, the idea itself illustrates the desire to find the traditions in accord with one another.

Unlike Taoism and Confucianism, which are traditions indigenous to China, Buddhism is a foreign import which made its way into the Middle Kingdom by crossing the Himalayas. And whereas Taoism and Confucianism have their respective specialized functions, Buddhism's is that of a largely aesthetic religion of devotion, compassion, and transcendence. Buddhism's arrival and influence in China supposedly dates back to the reign of Emperor Ming (58–75 AD) of the Han Dynasty, who in a dream saw a golden deity flying in front of his palace. His advisors explained that this was the Buddha, and the emperor immediately dispatched envoys abroad to bring back knowledge of his teachings.[18] It was the arrival of Bodhidharma, however, a monk from India who traveled to China with new teachings and sutras around the turn of the sixth century AD, that led to Buddhism's subsequent rapid ascent.

The core tenet of Buddhism, that craving is the root of all pain and suffering in this world, resonated well among a Chinese society that had grown accustomed to viewing the world through the lens of Taoism and Confucianism. The emphasis on the path to enlightenment resonated both with Taoism and its idea of the way and mastering of *wu wei* as well as Confucianism and its idea of *ren*, or the sage-like person. Despite the congruence between the two traditions, what can properly be called Buddhism's indigenization in the centuries following Bodhidharma's arrival was not without tumult, and the situation only worsened once this third tradition joined the fray. It would be a long road to a state of harmony and mutual acceptance among the *sanjiao*, as discussed below.

Throughout their more than a millennium of coexistence in China, relations between the *sanjiao* have ranged from syncretism and mutual support to all-out attacks. The most congruous relationship between the three is probably that between Taoism and Confucianism. As Ji Qianlin points out, both are indigenous traditions with a long history of coexistence, and thus they have faced tensions from time to time, but overall their relationship is very harmonious. He feels that Buddhism's abhorrence to all forms of authority and hierarchy, however, make it incompatible with Confucianism, where such relationships are central.[19]

Taoism, Ji Qianlin continues, does not oppose such Confucian ideals as *junjun, chenchen, fufu, zizi,* so at their essence the traditions are compatible and even mutually supportive. Lu Guolong offers a similar perspective, suggesting that the Chinese cultural system has at its core the unity of heaven and man (*tianre heyi*), and that this unity rests on two pillars—Taoism and Confucianism. As he explains, Confucianism attempts to build an ethical system from man to heaven. This system begins with social reality and progresses to the ultimate end of a harmonious existence with the law of heaven. Taoism, on the other hand, is a logic which proceeds from heaven to man, and is a system based on the law of nature in order to ensure that social institutions do not violate the *tao* of heaven.[20]

There is a great deal of syncretism between the *sanjiao*, especially between Taoism and Buddhism. Both have borrowed concepts, symbols, and structures from the other, to the point where in the modern period the *yin-yang* is worn by Buddhists and the Taoists have a temple structure similar to the Buddhists. While Taoism and Confucianism seem to be a match made in heaven, the two have been in conflict with each other at various times in Chinese history, with each gaining the advantage during different periods. Initially, Confucianism was rejected as being a perversion of the *tao*, while later Confucianism ascended and Taoism was rejected as ancient superstition. In the middle, the two joined hands against their main competitor, Buddhism. By the time of late-imperial China, the *sanjiao* had come to enjoy a relatively harmonious existence, with specialized functions among them, although under the Qing (1644–1911) Confucianism (here specifically *Rujia*) reigned supreme. Since they were not exclusivistic traditions, there was a place for each, and a practitioner of one tradition would frequently participate in activities associated with the others. For example, someone well-versed in the Confucian classics would have found it natural to draw upon Taoism when contemplating one's existence, and to turn to Buddhism if he was seeking a more aesthetic religious experience.

Wise Men from the West

Only two other religious traditions have a significant presence in China, that of Christianity and Islam, both of which arrived in China via the Silk Road during the Tang dynasty (618–907). Most likely, Christians had visited China as early as the fifth century, but it was in 635 that a formal delegation arrived in the Tang capital of Chang'an (modern-day Xi'an) carrying icons of Christ, Mary, and the saints. These Nestorian Christians, "monks who came from the West and believed in one God,"[21] established a small community of Taoist Christians at Da Qin monastery, outside present-day Xi'an. Over the next two centuries, Nestorian communities established themselves in trading centers across the empire and enjoyed relative success until 845, when the emperor issued an edict proscribing Buddhism and ordering monks to return to private life. Apparently the Nestorians fell under this edict, since some 3,000 foreign monks were referred to in it. By the end of the Tang dynasty the Nestorians had almost completely disappeared.

The Mongol conquest of the thirteenth century brought a second opportunity for Christianity in China. Shortly after Marco Polo's visit to the Orient aroused the interest of Europeans, the Franciscan John of Montecorvino arrived in modern-day Beijing in 1294 with a letter of introduction from the pope and began work setting up churches in the capital, eventually baptizing some 6,000 converts. The Franciscan mission fell into decline by the late fourteenth century, however, and it would be another 200 years until the next attempt was made to establish a Christian foothold in China. The Jesuits arrived via the Silk Road, as did the Nestorians and Franciscans before them, and set up residence in 1583 not far from Canton. Among the group was a brilliant young monk named Matteo Ricci, who through his patience and respect for Chinese culture did more to bring Christianity to China than perhaps anyone else. Having won the confidence of China's rulers, Ricci established a residence in the capital in 1601, where he offered services to the emperor's court and attempted to adapt Christianity to blend more easily with Chinese culture, a strategy which eventually erupted into the Chinese Rites Controversy and a papal bull establishing strict parameters on just how far such accommodations could go.

Christianity survived the tumultuous Ming-Qing transition of 1644, and continued to flourish throughout the seventeenth century. Other Catholic orders entered China with the Spanish and the French, and the first native Chinese bishop was installed in 1685.[22] By the end of the century there were Christian centers in every province of China (except for Muslim Gansu), with about 75 foreign priests serving some 300,000 Christians.[23] The Christian foothold thus planted, the Protestant missionaries of the nineteenth century added to and eventually expanded the Christian missionary efforts in China, though in their first 25 years of mission work (1807–1832) only ten Chinese were baptized.[24]

Islam's arrival in China followed the same path as had Christianity, arriving only a few years later. According to Chinese Muslim tradition, the birth of Islam in China can be traced back to the arrival of Saad ibn Abi Waqqas, a companion of Muhammad, in the Tang capital in the year 650. The Chinese emperor Yung-Wei reportedly "respected" the teachings of Islam and considered them to be compatible with those of Confucius, and thus gave Muslims the freedom to worship and propagate their faith. The emperor even approved the construction of China's first mosque, which stands in Xi'an to this day.

Archaeological evidence suggests that China's first Muslims descended from Arab, Persian, Turkic, and Mongol merchants, militia, and officials who settled during the seventh to tenth centuries. During the Mongol rule of the Yuan dynasty (1279–1368), Turkic immigration from Central Asia into China and Chinese westward expansion greatly increased the size of the Muslim population, as did intermarrying among Chinese and Muslim peoples. The Ming period (1368–1644) is considered the golden age of Islam in China. While China's Muslims lived relatively isolated from ethnic Chinese in early centuries, the end of Mongol rule saw Muslims more fully integrated into Han society under the Ming, including through the adoption of Chinese names and customs, while still retaining their Islamic mode of dress and dietary practices.

These processes led to the formation of two rather distinct groups of Muslims in China, the first being comprised of non-Han ethnicities that have remained relatively homogeneous to this day, such as the Uyghurs of Xinjiang, and the second being ethnic Han who have evolved into the *Hui*, the only "ethnic" group (*minzu*) in China to have religion as its sole distinguishing characteristic of identity.[25] This categorization is kept despite the fact that many are not even practicing Muslims, and as a group they are closer to the Han in terms of demographic proximity and cultural accommodation, having adapted many Islamic practices to Han ways of life.

When one considers the fact that Kashgar is closer to Baghdad than Beijing—not to mention Islamabad or Tehran—one immediately senses the connection of China's Muslims with the greater Muslim world. While over the past few centuries Xinjiang has interacted with and been influenced by Han culture from the east, this is primarily a modern phenomenon.[26] Prior to the nineteenth and twentieth centuries, the Turkic-speaking and Islamic cultures of Xinjiang were influenced far more profoundly by the Muslim world of Central Asia, Persia, and Mughal India. The late nineteenth and early twentieth centuries, however, saw greater concern for such interactions, especially as Uyghur nationalism began to result in violent attempts at establishing an independent East Turkistan.[27] Beijing responded by attempting to draw Xinjiang closer to the rest of China and isolating China's Muslims from the rest of the Muslim world. Such would remain the strategy of the Chinese government after 1949 as well.

State Control of Religion in China

State control of religion in China does not begin only with the victory of the CCP in the Chinese Civil War in October 1949. In fact, archeological evidence suggests that religion and the state were closely intertwined with each other from the earliest periods of Chinese civilization. One only need take a brief look at China's history to see that a relationship between divination and political control was evident as far back as one can trace the history of the world's oldest continuous civilization. In his *Lord of the Four Quarters*, Perry characterized the ruler's role as that of the sacred representative of a religiously-viewed universe, representing divine power that metes out rewards and punishments and judges the behavior of humans.[28] In ancient China, the ruler clearly functioned as the central axis connecting heaven and earth, a role visually illustrated in the character for ruler (王), the centerline of which connects heaven (天) with earth (土).

With a 5,000-year history unpunctuated by the sort of sharp ruptures seen in the West and other parts of Asia, religious aspects of Chinese culture—such as divination bones and meteorological rites—were integrally related to political power. Perhaps no better example exists than the "mandate of heaven" (*tianming*), by which "heaven," a divine and quasi-personified agent, appointed a human ruler to govern the Middle Kingdom.[29] The "mandate of heaven," along with many other politico-religious practices, continued long into the modern era, even if only as symbolic acts carried out as components of China's civil religion. So, too, did the state's desire to control and regulate religious activity, both officially-sanctioned, and private, autonomous religious behavior, which in more than a few episodes eventually grew to challenge the former. Yu expresses it well when he says that such a relationship between religion and the state in ancient China allows one to "perceive readily both the seeds and flowering of competition and rivalry, leading to unavoidable tension and sporadic conflict between the Chinese state and any deviant figure or form of socio-religious movement" that may present itself.[30]

Prior to the nineteenth century, the most significant such episodes relate to the three dominant traditions themselves, the *sanjiao*, and their sometimes antagonistic behavior toward each other, as discussed above. Taoism is the oldest of the three teachings, and therefore has the deepest roots with state power. Not only was there a short-lived "Taoist theocracy" from 365–448, but under the Tang dynasty the rulers claimed descent from Lao Tzu himself and used religion to promote political and social harmony. As other religious traditions emerged, however, sharp battles eventually erupted with the state often finding itself in the middle. For example, from the start the teachings of Confucius were seen as contradictory to those of Taoism, and the latter's works were thus burned and outlawed for centuries. Once a Taoism-Confucianism relationship became relatively harmonious, the two had to contend with the newcomer from the West, Buddhism. Although its arrival was very early, it was the increased popularity and presence of Buddhism in China beginning in the sixth century that led to the confrontation, which began with a series of debates in which representatives from each side presented the strong points of their teachings regarding political and social stability, while criticizing the shortcomings of their opponent's tradition.[31] Debates led to outright battles, however, with the arrival of the Mongol rulers, who played one off against the other as they established political control. The seemingly accommodating arrangement of the *sanjiao* and its position in Chinese social and political life, therefore, was not arrived at without its share of battles and state involvement.

Of course, the next wave of competing religious traditions also came from the West, this time from farther afield. Neither Christianity nor Islam was very popular when they first entered China, however, and their lack of a strong presence prevented any strong negative response from their would-be rivals and the state that could be called upon to do their reckoning. In more recent Chinese history, however, both became increasingly popular, especially among minority ethnic groups, a fact which raised the ire of the more well-established traditions. It was not the response of China's traditional religions to this growth that brought the issue to a head, however, but rather the political nature of Christianity and Islam proper, especially once the two became linked up with political movements. Both the cases of the Taiping Rebellion and the Muslim Uprisings of the late-nineteenth century proved to the Chinese imperial regime that these religions were indeed dangerous, not just to the dominant religious position of the *sanjiao*, but to the stability of the Middle Kingdom itself.

That kingdom would come tumbling down in 1911, with two Chinese Christians playing important roles in subsequent developments. The first was Dr. Sun Yat-sen, who became the architect of the new, post-imperial Chinese state and its first president. After the former's death, General Chiang Kai-shek seized control of the *Guomindang*, and eventually came to control militarily large swathes of territory across Southern China. Only the Japanese invasion into the Chinese mainland prevented the Kuomintang's expansion of military control into the rest of the country, while also giving crucial time to the newly-formed and still fledgling Communist Party of China to form and expand.

While the *Guomindang* carried out a rather relaxed religion policy in the territories it governed, the CCP was already experimenting with ways of dealing with religious groups operating in the areas under their control. The geographic distribution of the two groups' strongholds, with the

Guomindang more established along the coastal areas and the CCP controlling areas farther inland, meant that most Protestants were enjoying the more relaxed KMT environment while many Catholics were facing the Communists' early restrictions on religion. Their story is one of imprisonment, torture, and even execution at the hands of the CCP, with some 40 Catholic missionaries and 15–20 Protestant missionaries losing their lives even before 1949.[32] It was because of this experience that the Catholics shared little of the Protestants' optimism about continuing their work under the CCP once they came to power.

A Soviet Model for Chinese Religion?

As with most every other policy area,[33] upon the victory of the Chinese Communist Party in the Civil War, Beijing looked to Moscow for guidance in formulating its initial religion policy. Both the existing state of church-state relations in the Soviet Union in 1949 as well as the Soviet experience between 1917 and that period, therefore, provided the model for Chinese policy architects as they sought legal, institutional, and policy options aimed at eradicating religion from China. While it is significant that Mao was receiving advice (as he understood it) and instructions (as Stalin intended it) at a time when the Soviet state was more open to religion, the Chinese were well aware that the then-current policy in the Soviet Union was only arrived at after earlier and severe crackdowns. The model that was adopted by the CCP in its early years in power, therefore, reflects the changes that took place in the Soviet Union between its founding and the model as it existed in 1949–1951.

It would be a fundamental error, however, to assume that China simply adopted a Soviet-style religion policy, even though we know that they modeled so many of their policies in the early years on the Soviet example. Very early on it was evident to some observers that the Chinese were not simply borrowing from the Soviet Union's religion policy in developing their own, but rather were drawing upon other sources, including their own reading of Marx and experiences offered by China's imperial history. Indeed, as Yu cogently argues, the regulation of religion in China is a millennia-old tradition.[34] That experience is probably just as significant as the example of their Communist friends in Moscow.

One must be careful not to dismiss the influence of the Soviet system of regulating religion, however, for such things as Marxist ideology, atheist propaganda, and religion policies had been worked out by the Soviets during their first few decades in power, and provided ready-made models to be followed, adapted, or rejected. But even the experience of the Soviet Union illustrated clearly to the Chinese that religion could not be wiped out overnight. "If in the Soviet Union, more than thirty years after the Socialist Revolution, the remnants of old thinking and consciousness have still not been overcome and religion has still not been eliminated, then the fact that here in China we cannot eliminate religion in the immediate future is entirely comprehensible."[35] At the outset of Communist rule, therefore, the CCP was much less naïve about the struggle they faced in combating religion, as the Soviet example made them acutely aware of how little had been achieved in the face of so much repression.

It is this fact that most likely accounts for a substantial amount of the divergence in the Soviet and Chinese approaches to controlling religion. As Renseelear Lee, one of the early scholars to consider the issue, commented back in 1964, "The Chinese and Russian Communists, as Marxist-Leninists, are fundamentally hostile towards religion, and are committed to its ultimate eradication. Although their attitudes towards religion are similar, their prescriptions for dealing with it are different."[36] Lee's explanation for the divergence in policies was rooted in their different conceptions of religion, "one optimistic, the other pessimistic," he suggested. While, given their policies, the Chinese apparently believed, according to Lee, that religion would progress along the road to extinction naturally, in accordance with the laws of Marxism-Leninism and with a minimum of overt anti-religious force, Lee concluded that "the Russians evidently do not believe in any 'law of development of religion,' and regard atheist propaganda as an essential factor in religion's ultimate disappearance."[37] As we will see, this is probably one of the areas of greatest divergence between Soviet and Chinese religion policy, with the Chinese virtually ignoring atheist propaganda, while the Soviets expended considerable efforts in this regard.

While Lee certainly reads his sources with a naïve eye, and is often misled by CCP rhetoric touting religious freedom under Party rule and attacking the Soviets for the severely restrictive policy recently carried out by Khrushchev, in at least one other important regard Lee is right. As he summarizes his findings,

"Chinese Communist religious policy, like Soviet religious policy, has been dictated by circumstance. The Chinese have not had to cope with strong institutional religion in their country and therefore, unlike the Russians, have never regarded religion as an ideological rival. The Russians feel that religion will not disappear without conscious antireligious efforts on their part. The Chinese, by contrast, feel that religion will disappear in accordance with a natural law of growth, development and extinction, and in response to the exigencies of socialist construction."[38]

Lee thus accurately concludes that, in regard to religion policy, "the Chinese have not imitated the Soviet model."[39] Despite the shortcomings of the sources he relies upon and his inability to actually conduct fieldwork due to the circumstances of the time, Lee's early assessment has stood the test of time. He identified the most significant ways in which Chinese religion policy deviated from that of their Soviet big brother, primarily the significance of China's lack of a single, highly-centralized church such as the Russian Orthodox Church, and the failure of the Chinese to zealously promote atheism.

In addition to the reasons he gives, referenced above, it should be added that the Chinese regarded the Russian and Soviet-era religious situation as completely different and utterly irrelevant to the formation of the CCP's religion policy. As Lü Daji, a leading Chinese religion scholar of the early Deng era, phrased it at the time, "religions in China have different characteristics from religion in Europe. There is no single religion that can obtain dominance as Christianity did in Europe or Islam has in the Arab world."[40] As we explored briefly above, there was no single religion that ever really played such a role in China, the only close approximation being the *sanjiao*, which still differs remarkably from exclusivistic and salvific religions such as Christianity and Islam.[41] While in some ways this should have made the task of eradicating religion easier, it also meant that the Chinese Communists would have to develop a system of controlling religion that could be used on some very diverse systems of religious belief.

Mao on Zongjiao

It is evident from China's initial actions regarding religion that, even if they wished to adopt a Soviet-style system of religious regulation, the CCP knew that they could not just jump into the then-current Stalin-era *concordat* system, but rather they would have to first "catch up". Catching up in the area of church-state relations meant destroying church infrastructure, nationalizing property, and greatly reducing the number of religious organizations in the country and the clergy who served them, to say nothing of dealing with individual believers themselves.

The CCP's official line on religion sounded remarkably like that of Lenin's 1918 decree on separation of church and state.[42] The first official pronouncement of a CCP policy was contained in the Common Program, passed by the Chinese People's Political Consultative Conference in September 1949. Article 3 nationalized all rural land belonging to "ancestral shrines, temples, monasteries, churches, schools, and organizations," while Article 5 guaranteed to citizens "freedom of thought, speech, publication, assembly, association...religious belief, and the freedom of holding processions and demonstrations."[43] The CCP's policy in this area can be traced back to the Constitution of the [Kiangsi] Soviet Republic of 1931, in which the government,

> guarantees true religious freedom to the workers, peasants, and the toiling population. Adhering to the principle of the complete separation of church and state, the Soviet state neither favors nor grants any financial assistance to any religion whatsoever. All Soviet citizens shall enjoy the right to engage in anti-religious propaganda. No religious institution of the imperialists shall be allowed to exist unless it shall comply with Soviet law.[44]

Similar ideas are present in Mao's statement to a delegation from Tibet shortly after its "liberation" by the PLA, "The Communist Party adopts the policy of protecting religion. Whether you believe in religion or not, and whether you believe in this religion or that religion, all of you will be respected. The Party respects religious belief. This policy, as presently adopted, will continue to be adopted in the future."[45] Once the CCP had consolidated its hold on power, however, such long lists of rights were no longer necessary. The 1954 PRC Constitution therefore simply guarantees every citizen "freedom of religious belief."[46] Rather than interpreting this simplification as a limitation of rights, Welch explains that the earlier promulgations were necessary to curtail the random actions of overzealous cadres who assumed the CCP would take a tough stance on religion. Once a policy had been formulated and disseminated, however, such specifics were no longer needed.[47] Several of the stories examined in Chapter 6, however, suggest the contrary, particularly the case of Xu Yun.

Many other statements by Mao, both before and after the CCP's ascension to power, indicate a comparatively soft stance on religion, especially in comparison with Stalin or Khrushchev. A case in point is one of Mao's earliest references to religion, from his *Report of an Investigation into the Peasant Movement in Hunan* from 1927. In this treatise on Communist organizing among the peasantry, Mao explained that it was "the peasants who made the idols, and when the time comes they will cast the idols aside with their own hands; there is no need for anyone else to do it for them prematurely."[48]

Mao continued by saying that the "Communist Party's propaganda policy in such matters should be, 'Draw the bow without shooting, just indicate the motions'."[49] Mao was here referring to a quote from Mencius, in which an archer may have to teach a dim-witted student how to shoot an arrow. In such a case, it is better to simply go through the motions, or simply illustrate the posture (*junzi yin er bufa, yueru ye*), without ever actually having the pupil shoot an arrow.[50]

A proper interpretation of Mao's remarks, therefore, would be that the CCP need not get too directly involved in curtailing religion, but they should lead by example and not be believers themselves. One of the most important texts on religion in Communist China, however, that by Bush, uses an early—and imprecise—translation of Mao's words and comes to a significantly more negative impression of his intent. This translation, which came across with Mao saying "Draw the bow full without letting go the arrow, and be on the alert," suggests more than just going through the motions in order illustrate the posture to a pupil. As Bush reads it, the "metaphor suggests a controlling power which is alert and ready to act, but only remains in readiness so long as no one steps out of line."[51] The accompanying footnote to the text, however, which Bush also refers to, is quite clear on Mao's intended meaning: "The point is that while Communists should guide the peasants in attaining a full measure of political consciousness, they should leave it to the peasants' own initiative to abolish superstitious and other bad practices." While not included in the 1954 edition which Bush used, subsequent editions added the text "and should not give them orders or do it for them."[52] Either way, there is no mention or insinuation at all in the footnote about taking action if the peasants fail to act, or if believers "step out of line."[53] Nevertheless, Bush's reading gives the misleading impression that Mao was really arguing that force could be used to overthrow religion.

This minor excursus is not to imply that Mao was sympathetic to religion. Such is not accurate at all. But he certainly was less hostile to religion than some have made him out to be. As Snow recorded after one of his interviews with Mao, the young Mao was raised by a rather devout Buddhist.

My father was in his early days, and in middle age, a skeptic, but my mother devoutly worshipped Buddha. She gave her children religious instruction, and we were all saddened that our father was an unbeliever. When I was nine years old I seriously discussed the problem of my father's lack of piety with my mother. We made many attempts then and later on to convert him, but without success. He only cursed us, and overwhelmed by his attacks, we withdrew to devise new plans. But he would have nothing to do with the gods.[54]

Mao's own abandonment of his faith was apparently gradual and steady, with no sharp rupture, and was related to a skepticism that developed as he became more educated. He was also significantly influenced by a primary school teacher who was strongly opposed to Buddhism and "wanted to get rid of the gods."[55] Rather than any strong animus against religion *per se*, Mao's disinclination toward religion was rather doctrinaire from a Marxist standpoint, seeing religion as rooted in man's inability to comprehend the world around him that eventually developed into a false consciousness used by the ruling classes to keep the masses docile and compliant. One of the most discouraging aspects of religion for Mao seems to have been the failure and reluctance of the peasantry to throw off religious superstition. As he apparently said to a group of peasants while conducting some propaganda against religion in the countryside of Hunan, "The gods and goddesses are indeed miserable objects. You have worshipped them for centuries, and they have not overthrown a single one of your local tyrants or evil gentry for you! Now you want to have your rent reduced. Let me ask, how will you go about it? Will you believe in the gods or in the peasant association?" Mao recalled that his "words made the peasants roar with laughter."[56]

Unlike Lenin, whose staunch anti-religious rhetoric calmed somewhat once faced with the exigencies of political power, Mao was much more consistent. While Lenin had early on equated the Bolshevik religion policy to a "war" against religion, Mao's mocking of religion or references to peasants pulling down their idols paled in comparison to the words of the Soviet Union's founder. Mao's words, however, would later prove prescient when the Red Guards wreaked havoc against religious believers, artifacts, and structures during the Cultural Revolution.

The Liberation of China and the Suppression of Religion

All indications are that Mao's metaphor was more than fanciful rhetoric. Indeed, as recently as 2007, leading China scholar Richard Madsen was describing China's religion policy as wanting to control religion—"until such time as religion can be completely strangled."[57] While much has changed over the past 60 years of CCP rule, including how much religion can be tolerated in China, a common feature has been the more or less consistent view that religion is a false consciousness that will eventually die of its own. From such a Marxist perspective (incidentally, based upon a more authentic reading of Marx and Engels than that which formed the basis of Soviet religion policy), religion is the residue of a bygone era, a socially backward practice, and doomed to extinction. As Chang phrased it in an early article, "religion is a necessary product of a certain stage of human development," whose "roots are class oppression and fear of natural forces."[58] The policy of the CCP should be, therefore, to regulate religion until such time as religion dies a natural death. As Bush nicely phrased it many years ago, while the "theorists repeatedly asserted that religion eventually would wither away...the question remained: How might good Communists contribute to that withering?"[59]

Three extenuating factors would greatly influence how the country's Communist leaders would put such Marxist thought into practice. The first such factor was the foreign composition of the Christian churches functioning in China at the time. While the first Chinese Catholic bishop had been consecrated back in 1685, not even one other had been installed during the next 200 years. In 1949, four-fifths of the bishops and two-fifths of all priests in China were foreigners.[60] The situation among the Protestant churches was not much better, with the massive infrastructure of the Protestants—which included hospitals, seminaries, colleges, and publishing houses—dominated by non-Chinese, especially at the level of senior administration. Regardless of any ideological commitment against religion, the situation was ripe for nativist reactions to such a powerful foreign presence, especially in a country committed to putting the preceding "one hundred years of humiliation" behind it. The anti-Christianity Movement of the 1920s was only the precursor to a much more significant and militant attack against Christianity that would be launched at the hands of the CCP once they took power.

Although the membership of the Christian Church in China at the time of the Revolution accounted for only a slight fraction of the population as a whole (less than 3.5 million out of a population of approximately 550 million),[61] its influence greatly exceeded its size. In addition to its leading role in medical science, hospitals, and education, China's Protestant and Catholic churches had relationships with more than 100 foreign mission boards, societies, orders, and international councils. In the past, these had been a source of the Church's strength. Now, in the new China, they were a liability.

In addition, this foreign presence and influence also meant vast amounts of wealth were in the hands of non-Chinese operating on Chinese soil, making them a potential threat against the fledgling Communist regime. Indeed, given both the Soviet experience with persecuting religion and the CCP's own early actions prior to the revolution, the Christian Church in China would have undoubtedly organized itself in resistance to Communist attempts to control it, as it had briefly tried to do throughout 1949 and into early 1950.

Finally, there was Christianity's connection to imperialism, a third factor which was able to be drawn upon to justify action against the church that would simultaneously address the other two factors. In fact, Christianity's connection to imperialism was the weakest of the three to prove. Christianity had been making slow inroads in China for centuries, long before China began to be effected by imperialism. And in response to charges of Western cultural imperialism, in earlier periods it was Chinese culture itself which seemed to be gaining converts among the Christian missionaries, many of whom, such as Matteo Ricci, dressed like Chinese and spoke Chinese. He was not, of course, a religious convert, however, as Ricci looked toward China's religious past as a precursor to the Gospel of Jesus Christ, not as an alternative and equally legitimate religion.[62]

In the end, however, Marx's reference to "religion as the opium of the people" was sufficient in China to establish a connection between religion and imperialism. After all, the Opium Wars were one of the greatest symbols of Western imperialism's encroachment upon China, and the drastic rise in the number of missionaries in China following thereafter left little doubt in the average Chinese's mind that the connection between imperialism and Christianity was anything less than nearly complete. Mao himself seemed convinced of the inextricable link between Christian missionary efforts and cultural imperialism. In 1939 while camped out at Yenan, Mao, and some others wrote, "The Imperialist Powers have never slackened their efforts to poison the minds of the Chinese people. This is their policy of cultural aggression. And it is carried out through missionary work, through establishing hospitals and schools, publishing newspapers and inducing Chinese students to study abroad." The aim of missionary efforts, rather than saving souls, was simply "to train intellectuals who will serve their interests and to dupe the people."[63]

This connection provided a useful scapegoat, too, for the CCP to attack Christianity for the other two factors of foreignness and financial power and influence. Brown explains the situation well. The idea was to strike at Christianity's foreignness. Around them they saw a considerable number of missionaries, particularly in the Catholic Church, and a host of Protestant and Catholic institutions which were dependent on foreign subsidies or which nevertheless still had connections that could be used to get financial resources. These foreign Christian connections were now regarded as instances of imperialist aggression.[64] As Brown points out, "Whenever the Communist government moved against the church or any other religious group, the announced purpose was always to purge the church of imperialistic elements, or to single out those who stood in the way of the people's progress, or to punish the unpatriotic."[65]

This approach was popularized among the masses by a whole range of fabricated and greatly-exaggerated stories. Not only do Christians "spread reactionary views which are hostile to new China, oppose the Communist Party, and slander the socialist system," they would argue, but they also "exploit religion to obtain money under false pretenses, rape women, cause loss and injury of life, and upset the social order and productive forces."[66] The whole movement became one "spies in our midst" episode, with the CCP mobilizing people against Christians in order to purge dangerous elements. "Imperialist elements and other reactionary elements hiding under the cover of religion often collect intelligence for imperialism," they warned. They also "fabricate rumors, and even organize insurrections and carry out other current counterrevolutionary activities," so one must be ever diligent.[67]

Reeling in Religion

Such propaganda stirred up patriotic and revolutionary zeal and bolstered the CCP's popular support. This meant that they could then rather easily go about reorganizing religious groups operating in the country in such a way that they could better control them, remold them, and ultimately contribute to their "withering." The method chosen was the three-self formula of self-governance, self-propagation, and self-support. Though seized upon by the CCP, this was actually an old idea dating back to nineteenth-century Protestant mission strategy, devised by Henry Venn and Rufus Anderson and later brought to China by the Presbyterian missionary John Nevius in the late 1800s.[68] The idea as originally articulated was that the best method of planting churches and having them prosper was to rapidly indigenize them and help them become self-sufficient. Indeed, there was a growing movement among Chinese Protestants in the early 1900s to do just that.

In the hands of Party bureaucrats, however, the three-self formula became a useful means of eliminating foreign dominance and justifying purges of the ranks of the churches. An illustration of this can be gleaned from Luo, whose presentation of the emergence of the Three-Self Movement is little more than a diatribe against Western imperialism. To Luo, the Three-Self Movement was a "patriotic anti-imperialist movement" aimed at uprooting "corrupt and evil traditions inside religion" and breaking the "connection between imperialism and religion."[69] Those who resisted were "counterrevolutionaries," including Ni Tuosheng (Watchman Nee), an "unprincipled and mean person" who had "raped numerous women."[70] While Watchman Nee would make an excellent case to examine in Chapter 6 for these and other reasons, his story is so controversial that there is no way to know the truth about the allegations leveled against him.[71] What is important to point out, however, is the irony that Watchman Nee had been one of the most active proponents of indigenizing the Christian Church in China along the lines of the three-self formula *before* the CCP came to power.

In comparison with the Soviet Union, which took nearly 20 years to develop a system of regulating, monitoring, and controlling religion, the Chinese accomplished similar tasks rather briskly. Between March 1950, when the first national conference of the United Front was convened to develop a strategy for dealing with Christianity, and 1957, the Chinese government had organized all major religious groups into indigenous and centralized associations. These were the China Islamic Association, the China Buddhist Association, the Chinese Taoist Association, the Chinese Catholic Patriotic Association, and the Three-Self Patriotic Movement (henceforth, TSPM). Additionally, a Bureau of Religious Affairs (*Guowuyuan zongjiao shiwu ju*) had been established, having evolved out of the Research Committee on Religion Issues (*Zongjiao wenti yanjiu xiaozu*) and the Division of Religious Affairs (*Zongjiao shiwu chu*). As Luo proudly assessed such "accomplishments" in the span of a mere 7 years, the CCP had "basically eliminated the exploiting classes and established a socialist system."[72]

Making Patriotic Believers

In order to establish such a system, the churches would have to be made patriotic, which not only meant loyal to the CCP, but led by Chinese, not for-eigners. One of the first developments in this area was a series of directives promulgated by the new government in 1950. Overall, they seemed quite even-handed and accommodating to religion. As *Renmin ribao* reported, officials were ordered "to permit freedom of religious activity," to protect religious buildings and property, to consult with religious leaders first if it was absolutely necessary to requisition certain buildings, and to "fully restore to their rightful owners" such buildings as were used by the government.[73] While these directives were often violated on the group, the real problem for religious liberty was that they pertained almost exclusively to religious insti-tutions. Religion, of course, encompassed more than simply the buildings in which they gathered to worship. To be "patriotic," believers would have to be corralled into newly-established religious organizations.

Religious leaders and lay believers were instructed in the new Marxist understanding of religion, and those who less than enthusiastically embraced such new knowledge found themselves the center of "struggle sessions." Before an audience of party functionaries, neighbors, and co-workers, believers stood (often handcuffed or held in wooden shoulder locks) and confessed their crimes against the motherland and promised to change their ways. Such actions were carried out as part of the "Three-Anti" and "Five-Anti" campaigns as well as the first anti-religion campaign of 1953. At the conclusion of the latter, Beijing mayor Peng Zhen proudly reported to the Governing Council that "4,000,000 duped members had withdrawn" from Buddhist sects, and that the battle with religion was essentially won.[74] Similar "victories" were claimed in regard to the other religions present in China at the time.

Worse than those who believed in religion were the foreigners who had come to China's shores spreading the dangerous Christian message. Despite all they had done for China and its people for hundreds of years, Christian missionaries became public enemy number one almost overnight. At a meeting between the leaders of seven Protestant denominations and Premier Zhou Enlai in May 1950, Zhou stated clearly that no new missionaries could enter China, no furloughed missionaries could return, and that, of those already in China, only those who beyond any shadow of a doubt had not engaged in any sort of political activity could remain. By the end of 1950, incidents contrived to embarrass or incriminate missionaries had become so commonplace that the Protestant mission boards launched a wholesale evacuation of China. In 1950 there had been an estimated 1,800–1,900 Protestant missionaries remaining in China. By early 1952, only 20 out of 637 missionaries from the China Inland Mission, 7 out of 571 Lutheran missionaries, and 3 out of 350 American Methodist missionaries remained in China. Others were not as lucky; the Rev. Olin Stockwell was by that time in prison, and Bishop Gene Carleton Lacy was dead.[75]

The exodus of the Roman Catholic Church's missionaries was considerably slower. At the eve of the Revolution, there were nearly 6,000 Catholic foreign missionaries in China. That number had dropped to just over 3,000 by January 1951, and almost in half again by the same time in 1952. The January 1956 issue of *Mission Bulletin* reported brusquely that only 16 priests and 11 sisters remained at the time, and that 13 of the priests, including one bishop, were in prison.[76] Additionally, the Catholic Church estimated that already by the end of 1951, 90 percent of their facilities had been either destroyed or confiscated by the PRC government, a flagrant violation of the 1950 directives published in *Renmin ribao*.

Even before the CCP launched its attack against religion, Buddhism was already in a greatly weakened state in comparison with earlier eras. Many temples and monasteries were practically in ruins, while others had been confiscated, reverted to local ownership, or simply abandoned. Already by February 1950, the story of the tremendous changes taking place was beginning to unfold. News of the situation in Shanghai told of how 500 of the 2,000 monks and nuns in Shanghai's 300 temples had already left and gone back to their ancestral villages to work, or had "volunteered" to join the South Expedition Corps or the East China Military and Political Academy. Those who remained found themselves no longer autonomous, but under the guidance of the newly organized "Association of Shanghai Buddhist Youth," the purpose of which was "to unite all the progressive elements among the Buddhist monks to study the New Democracy and to become useful members of society."[77]

The phrase "become useful members of society" was not added to the attack on the Buddhists arbitrarily. Unlike the Christians, who were resented and feared for their wealth and power, the Buddhists were considered weak, lazy, and as parasites. These parasites (abbots had it worse, as they were classified as "landowners") would have to become workers in the new China, and no longer live off the backs of the peasants. The story of such Buddhists as Xu Yun, discussed in the following chapter, tells a quite different story, however. As Xu Yun's Yunhua monastery, almost all of the monks worked the land owned by the monastery in order to provide for their own food, while only small parcels were leased out to local peasants. Even this economic relationship was far from exploitative, as it allowed peasants who could not afford to buy land to make a living while also providing the monastery with a source of money for the things they could not make themselves.[78]

Once the CCP came to power, however, Buddhist property and landholdings were largely broken up, primarily through the Land Reform Act of 1950. Land was confiscated from the monasteries and redistributed to the people, and while the monks and nuns might qualify for a small plot of land, they were unaccustomed to managing small plots on their own. These difficulties led many monks to eventually form mutual aid teams, only later to be driven into communes as the Great Leap Forward got underway. Other monasteries were less lucky; many were simply confiscated and turned into military barracks, army hospitals, and prisons.

In 1949 Buddhists were the largest single religious tradition in China, able to claim nearly 4 million monks and nuns and probably 100 million lay followers.[79] They were also in possession of more than 500,000 temples and monasteries. While Peng Zhen's claim that "4 million duped" Buddhists had abandoned their faith thus seems like a very insignificant impact, by 1957 the CCP had been quite effective at curtailing and controlling Buddhism in other ways. By that time, the number of temples and monasteries had been reduced to only 50,000, while the number of monks had declined to 1.2 million.[80] They had also effectively organized the country's Buddhists—Han Buddhists and Tibetan Buddhists alike—into a centralized, state-controlled body, the Chinese Buddhist Association.

As Welch summarized the situation and our estimates of it, "the number of monks is difficult to determine; the number of laymen is impossible to even estimate. The extent to which the association represented any of them is also a matter of conjecture."[81] The purpose of the CBA, rather, was to serve as an instrument for remolding Buddhism to suit the needs of the government. Additionally, it could serve to revise Buddhist doctrine and practice, to purge anti-Party elements, and to mobilize Buddhists to participate in national campaigns.[82] Doctrinally, the CBA was tasked with condemning superstitious beliefs, such as belief in spirits and the practice of divination and healing. They were also to condemn and discourage burning paper money, making sacrifices to gods and spirits, and accepting money for the conduct of religious ceremonies, which was seen as "cheating the masses".

As for Taoism, a tradition closely connected to Buddhism and entirely indigenous, the Communists put it on an even lower level than religion. Although they were still classified as "religious practitioners", they were more closely associated with "superstitious practitioners" such as geomancers, fortune-tellers, and diviners. Taoism was regarded by the CCP as a superstition without a moral foundation and a barrier to elevating the cultural level of the masses. It was also considered a political danger because Taoists secret societies had been the source of revolts in the past, and because the nature of the religion itself did not lend itself to state control. As Welch points out, the state could take over Taoist monasteries and round up groups of Taoist priests, but how could the government control a religion that, "when forbidden in one place, pops up again in another? How does a government control a priesthood which can take off its robes for a few years, seemingly forget about the rituals which priests are forbidden to exercise, and thus to all intents and purposes comply with regulations," only to rise once again at "any time, whenever it is convenient...?"[83]

Flowers, Weeds, and Ghosts

Perhaps because China's process of "reeling in religion" was carried out so quickly, reform and liberalization came almost as quickly. The first sign of a relaxation of religious practice was the Hundred Flowers Campaign of 1956–1957. As Mao said, the policy of the CCP would be "to let a hundred flowers blossom and a hundred schools of thought contend," suggesting that open dialogue and discussion among members of society and the government were to be permitted. This included religious believers and the atheist government. As Mao wrote in his essay *On the Correct Handling of Contradictions*, "We cannot abolish religion by administrative decree or force people not to believe in it. We cannot compel people to give up idealism, any more than we can force them to believe in Marxism."[84]

As intellectuals began to question the wisdom of Maoist policies such as land reform, the educational system, and restrictions on the media, Christians, and other believers also responded to the call to "bloom and contend." They spoke out openly about the discrimination they were facing, including in the workplace and, in regard to their children, in the schools. They also spoke out against the seizure of church buildings and property, the abusive language used against them by officials, and the overall denial of their constitutionally-guaranteed religious freedoms. Those Christians who served on consultative conferences also voiced their complaints at provincial and municipal meetings.

This period of "blooming and contending" was short-lived. The opposition to CCP rule was stronger than leaders had anticipated, and the response to the campaign was more than they could permit. The government's response was to announce that "weeds were growing in the garden of the hundred flowers and had to be cut down!"[85] The result was the Anti-Rightist campaign, when many of those who dared to speak out were sent to work camps or publicly denounced and humiliated. For Protestant Christians this campaign began in late 1957 when 130 Christian leaders were called to Beijing by the standing committee of the Three-Self Movement. At the meeting, six prominent church leaders were attacked for having criticized CCP policy during the campaign. Some of the others denounced were dismissed from their church positions and forced to join the ranks of the factory workers. Taking their cue from the Beijing accusation meeting, extremists in other parts of the country pursued Christians who had resisted the TSPM or were uncommitted to the socialist cause. They were denounced and sent off to the work camps.

As it turned out, the Anti-Rightist campaign was just the prelude for the Great Leap Forward. As with all other citizens, Christians were caught up in the great upheavals caused by Mao's disastrous policies. The massive public works projects, the strict regimentation of life in the communes, and the near round-the-clock work schedule made church worship or any religious activity very difficult. According to one visitor's account, it was at this point that Sunday schools and youth activities had entirely disappeared, and the only religious activity that remained was one-weekly worship services, and these, too, were in steady decline.[86]

Curbing Religion, Making Atheists

Despite the great efforts spent on curbing and controlling religious activity, the Communists seem to have recognized that coercion alone would not bring about a mass abandonment of faith among believers. As Mao had also written in *On the Correct Handling of Contradictions*, not only could they not simply abolish belief by decree or compel people to place their faith in Marxism, "The only way to settle questions of an ideological nature or controversial issues among the people is by the democratic method, the method of discussion, of criticism, of persuasion and education, and not by the method of coercion or repression."[87]

Zhou Enlai held a similar, though perhaps more certain, view. In a remark to a group of Chinese Christian leaders, the premier stated: "So we are going to go on letting you teach, trying to convert the people…After all we both believe that the truth will prevail; we think your beliefs untrue and false, therefore if we are right, the people will reject them, and your church will decay. If you are right, then the people will believe you, but as we are sure that you are wrong, we are prepared for that risk."[88]

Despite, or perhaps because of, the confidence each had in the truth of Marxism and its destiny to prevail over religion, the CCP never carried out a comprehensive and intensive program to promote atheism. In comparison with the Soviet Union, when it came to atheist propaganda efforts, the Chinese fell far short of their comrades in the USSR. While the Soviets had gone to great lengths to promote atheism, including mass publishing, adult educational programs, required college-level courses, even cinema, China's Communists never ran any atheist promotion campaign or put into place a comprehensive program to promote atheism among the masses.

Of course the CCP had implemented a sweeping program of ideological education. In the early years of the PRC, participation in study groups and attendance at lectures was required for all, while those who were resisted or whose loyalty was suspect faced stronger measures, including reeducation, reform through labor, and perhaps death for those who never gave in or who continued to openly criticize the regime. These efforts were mostly ideological in nature, however, and focused more on historical materialism, class struggle, and imperialism than on religion as the opium of the people. This seems rather contradictory on the part of the CCP leadership, for if they were going to allow religion to continue at all and face off religious belief with Marxism, they would have needed to promote atheism more aggressively if they had any hope of winning the people's "hearts and souls."

The CCP seemed to begin to recognize by the early 1960s that they would need to focus more attention on promoting atheism if they ever hoped to eradicate religion. The first major effort in this regard was the publication in 1962 of the book *Bu Pa Gui de Gushi* (Don't be Afraid of Ghosts). This book was published under the editorial direction of Mao Zedong himself, who played an important role in editing and publishing the book. In fact, he once even debated the chief editor, insisting that "we should belittle ghosts in general through strategy, but we also should treat them seriously through the use of tactics."[89]

That strategy was not well conceived, though there were a few tactical successes. For many years Renmin University of China Press has published compilations of articles about how belief in ghosts and spirits has been disproven by some scientific explanation. And while there was no journal on atheism during the Mao era, shortly after the Falun Gong crackdown the Institute of World Religion began publishing *Kexue yu wushenlun* (Science and Atheism). China's first atheism journal began publication in 2002 and is a rather objective social science journal. It was soon followed by *Wushenlun zazhi* (Atheism Magazine), which is a more popular publication in the sense of being "light reading" along the lines of something like *Readers' Digest*. But *Kexue yu wushenlun* is a serious publication and is aimed toward a well-educated audience, including academics, and Party members. It contains original articles on atheism of a theoretical nature as well as translations of Western scholars, including proponents of the New Atheism such as Dawkins. Its purpose is to promote research on issues of atheism and belief, rather than to promote atheistic views directly. In that regard it is quite similar to the post-Soviet version of *Nauka i Religiya*.

Ironically, it appears that more efforts in the area of atheist propaganda are being expended today in order to counter "cults" such as Falun Gong than during earlier periods of CCP rule. Not only was the introduction of *Kexue yu wushenlun* directly related to the rise in power of the Falun Gong and such groups as *Dongfang shandian* (Lightning from the East), another group that has been banned in China, but so was a fourth reprinting of *Bu Pa Gui de Gushi*. Its reprinting in 1999, however, was directly related to the

Party's attempt to dissuade people from what they consider dangerous cults. This is made clear in its preface:

> It has been 38 years since the book *Don't be afraid of Ghosts* was published...On the threshold of the new century, some types of pseudo-qi gong and pseudoscience revived, which had been slashed by cultural pioneers including Chen Duxiu and Lu Xun in the years of the "May Fourth" movement. They have attempted to gain fame by deceiving the public cloaked in the excuses of "promoting traditional culture" and "exercising to heal." At the same time, extensive worship/sacrifice ceremonies, superstition, and disturbing heresies are re-emerging, too. For example, its development and spread in some areas disturbed people's thoughts, shook people's beliefs, and therefore jeopardized the construction of socialism with Chinese characteristics.[90]

Along with the 1978 and 1982 reprintings, the total number of copies of China's main instrument of atheist propaganda reached 235,000. Publication efforts of this magnitude pale in comparison to those of the Soviet's, which could literally fill libraries. But there is a more telling difference between most of the examples of Chinese atheist efforts and those of the Soviets. *Bu Pa Gui de Gushi* and other similar works did not directly seek to disprove the existence of God, as the Soviet texts did, but rather they sought to counteract superstition among the masses and to promote a scientific worldview. Indeed, most atheist promotion efforts in China were against superstition more than they were about promoting scientific atheism. For some reason, when it came to countering religion, the Chinese placed much more emphasis on man's inability to control the forces of nature as an explanation for religion (an idea more prominent in the works of Freud and Nietzsche than in Marx) than they did on Marx's sinister "opium of the people" explanation or Engels' diatribes against the churches and their co-optation by the state. Perhaps the fact that Chinese religion is replete with beliefs and practices more often categorized as "superstition" rather than religion explains this response, including the attribution of illness or natural disasters to evil spirits. Whatever the cause, China's paltry efforts in promoting atheism has left the Chinese people more open to religious belief than if they had been indoctrinated in scientific atheism for decades.

Another, and perhaps related, explanation for the different approaches to the promotion of atheism may be the nature of Chinese religion as compared to Western religions, such as Christianity, with which the Russians were confronted.[91] According to Wei Dedong, a Chinese sociologist of religion who specializes in Buddhism, Chinese scholars at the time (and many today) viewed atheism as a reaction to Western religion, and not very relevant to the Chinese religious situation. Without the dominance of a Western religion such as Christianity in China, atheism was not a necessary response.[92] In many ways, the strength of Orthodox Christianity in Russia was countered with a strong atheistic response, while the weaker religious life of China only elicited a mild atheistic response. In addition to the logic of such a position, the evidence here from the comparative analysis of the Soviet Union and China seems to confirm such an explanation.

Tearing Down the Idols

The strict regulation of religion in China is certainly nothing new or unique to the Communist Party. As Yu points out, it has been going on for millennia.[93] Bays agrees, and even suggests that the Qing Dynasty's "Board of Rites supervised a religious bureaucracy much like today's RAB."[94] The CCP did not overtly attempt to abolish religion, Bays maintains, but rather their efforts in constructing a complex and comprehensive apparatus to control religious groups and organizations were aimed at monitoring them and isolating them from broader society. It is this apparatus that is very similar to those used by dynastic governments of the past.[95] But Beijing's new leaders not only registered and monitored religious believers as the dynasties of the past had done, but also systematically reduced their influence in society. Moreover, in terms of intensity, CCP religion policy surpassed most any other similar system of control concocted by regimes of the past.

By the early 1960s, however, a shift in CCP religion policy seemed to be on the horizon. While the Party was increasing its efforts on the atheist propaganda front, it was also simultaneously preparing to relax religion policy. One of the first signs of this was a debate on religion as "opium" that played itself out in the Party's ideological journal *Hongqi*[96] (Red Flag), as well as in the pages of *Wenhui Bao* and *Xin Chienshe*.[97] Soft-liners began to advocate for greater freedom for institutionalized religions, while superstition could still be targeted for elimination. They also argued for a reassessment of the concept of "opium of the people," even going so far as to suggest that, in a classless society like China, religion could function as something other than an opiate. The hard-liners, on the other hand, responded that religion was always an opiate, and that its substance could not change. They continued, therefore, to push for the elimination of religion along with superstition.

As we will see in subsequent chapters, debates like these often preceded important policy shifts. In this case, however, the "shift" that occurred was not so much a policy initiative from Zhongnanhai but rather the chaos of the Cultural Revolution. Chao even suggests that "the persecution of religion during the Cultural Revolution was a natural outcome of that theoretical debate."[98] Whereas religious activity had been allowed although greatly circumscribed up to this point, when the Cultural Revolution was launched in August of 1966, the Red Guards quickly went to work to achieve what the state had failed to accomplish—the complete annihilation of religion from the Middle Kingdom. All churches, temples, mosques, monasteries, road-side shrines—all religious venues of any kind—were shut down during the darkest hour in China's history. Even Confucius was not spared; his writings, knowledge of which for more than a millennium formed the basis for professional promotion, were condemned and destroyed. He was labeled "the number one criminal of feudal thinking" and his portrait, so venerated in Chinese art for centuries, was now carried through the streets with the label "I am an ox, a demon, a snake, and a devil."[99] As believers the world over lamented this devastation and destruction, *World Buddhism* declared, "the revolutionary action of the Red Guards in pulling down those dead wooden idols is most pleasing."[100] Mao was right—the state would not be necessary to eradicate religion, except that it was the urban youth tearing down the idols.

Notes

1. MacInnis, doc. 23, "Chou En-lai Speaking to Chinese Christians on the Christian Share in the Revolution" [1950], p. 24.
2. K. H. Ting, "Foreword," in Zhufeng Lou, *Religion Under Socialism in China*, Translated by Donald E. MacInnis and Zheng Xi'an (Armonk N.Y.: M.E. Sharpe, 1991), p. viii.
3. Anna Xiao Dong Sun, "The Fate of Confucianism as a Religion in Socialist China: Controversies and Paradoxes," in Fenggang Yang and Joseph B. Tawney, eds., *State, Market and Religions in Chinese Societies* (Leiden: E.J. Brill, 2005).
4. Anthony C. Yu, *State and Religion in China: Historical and Textual Perspectives* (Chicago: Open Court, 2005), p. 12.
5. Takashi Koizumi, et al. *Ningen to shūkyō: kindsi nihonjin no shūkyōkan* (Tokyo: Toyo bunka, 1982), 17–25. See also Yu's comment on the issue in Ibid., fn 10, pp. 152–3.
6. Helen Hardacre, *Shinto and the State, 1868–1988* (Princeton: Princeton University Press, 1989), p. 63.

7. Max Weber, *The Religion of China* (New York: Free Press, 1964).

8. C. K. Yang, *Religion in Chinese Society: A Study of Contemporary social functions of religion and some of their historical factors* (Prospect Heights, IL: Waveland Press, 1961), p. 25.

9. Ibid.

10. Cited in Stephen Teiser, "The Spirits of Chinese Religion," in *Religions of China in Practice*, edited by Donald S. Lopez (Princeton University Press, 1996).

11. Ibid.

12. Though in pinyin rendered as Daoism, I am following here the established convention of rendering it as Taoism.

13. Livia Kohn, *Daoism and Chinese Culture* (New Mexico: Three Pines Press, 2001).

14. Russel Kirkland, *Taoism: The Enduring Tradition* (New York: Routledge, 2004).

15. Lu Guolong. "Manifest the Tao of Heaven to Build the Ethics of Human Being: Taoism as the Theoretical Foundation of Chinese Culture," *Philosophical Studies*, Vol. 6 (1994).

16. *Analects* XII, 11, trans. Legge.

17. Lu, 1994.

18. Kenneth Ch'en, *Buddhism in China: A Historical Survey* (Princeton: Princeton University Press, 1964), pp. 29–30.

19. Ji Qianlin, "On Buddhism, Confucianism and Taoism," *Selected Papers of Ji Qianlin* (Beijing: Beijing Normal University Press, 1991).

20. Lu, 1994.

21. Martin Palmer, *The Jesus Sutras: Rediscovering the Lost Scrolls of Taoist Christianity* (New York: Random House, 2001), pp. 39–40.

22. Kenneth Latourette, *A History of Christian Missions in China* (London: Society for Promoting Christian Knowledge, 1929), pp. 122–4.

23. Ibid., pp. 128–9.

24. George Thompson Brown, *Christianity in the Peoples Republic of China* (Atlanta: John Knox, 1983), pp. 22–3.

25. Dru Gladney, "Islam in China: State Policing and Identity Politics," in *Making Religion, Making the State: The Politics of Religion in Modern China* (Berkely: University of California Press, 2009), pp. 153–5.

26. Graham Fuller and Jonathan Lipman, "Islam in Xinjiang," in S. Frederick Starr, ed., *Xinjiang: China's Muslim Borderland* (Armonk, N.Y.: M.E. Sharpe, 2004), pp. 326–7.

27. Justin Jon Rudelson, *Oasis Identities: Uyghur Nationalism along China's Silk Road* (New York: Columbia University Press, 1997).

28. John W. Perry, *Lord of the Four Quarters: Myths of the Royal Father* (New York: G. Braziller, 1966).

29. Kohn, p. 65.

30. Yu, 2005, p. 53.

31. Kohn, p. 106.

32. Richard Bush, Jr., *Religion in Communist China* (New York: Abingdon, 1970), fn. 35, p. 50. See also *God's Underground in Asia* (New York: Appleton-Century-Crofts, 1953).

33. My previous book explores this phenomenon in detail. See Marsh, *Unparalleled Reforms*.

34. Yu, 2005, p. 145.

35. Wang Tzu-yeh, "Basic Attitude of Marxist-Leninists Towards the Problem of Religion," *Xuexi* 3, no. 2 (March 16, 1951), 9–10; Cited in Holmes Welch, p. 5, fn. 12.

36. Rensselaer W. Lee, "General Aspects of Chinese Communist Religious Policy, with Soviet Comparisons," *The China Quarterly*, No. 19 (July-September 1964), p. 161.

37. Ibid., p. 165.

38. Ibid., p. 167.

39. Ibid.

40. Lü Daji, "Zhengque renshi zongjiao wenti de kexue zhinan—chongdu makesi 'heige'er fazhexue pipan' daoyan," *Shijie Zongjiao Yanjiu*, Vol. 2 (1981), p. 4.

41. For more on the impact such monotheistic beliefs can have on political and social outcomes, see Rodney Stark, *One True God* (Princeton: Princeton University, 2001).

42. There was no need at this time to separate the schools from the church, since that had been accomplished in November 1925 when the Beijing Interim Government released the *Method on Founding schools by Foreigners* (*Waiguoren Juanzi Sheli Xuexiao Qingqiu Renke Banfa*).

43. MacInnis, doc. 16, "The Common Program" [1949], p. 21.

44. MacInnis, doc. 13, "Constitution of the [Chinese] Soviet Republic" [1931], p. 19.

45. MacInnis, doc. 9, "To the Tibetan Goodwill Mission" [1952], p. 14.

46. MacInnis, doc. 17, "Constitution of the People's Republic of China" [1954], p. 21.

47. Holmes Welch, *Buddhism Under Mao* (Cambridge: Harvard University, 1972), p. 2.

48. "Report of an Investigation into the Peasant Movement in Hunan," *Selected Works of Mao Tse-Tung*, Vol. 1 (Beijing: Foreign Language Press, 1975), p. 46.

49. Ibid.
50. Mencius, *Jinxin Shang*.
51. Bush, pp. 30–1. Cf. Mao Tse-tung, *Report of an Investigation into the Peasant Movement in Hunan* [1927] (Peking: FLP, 1953), p. 45.
52. "Report of an Investigation," fn. 22, p. 58.
53. Bush quotes the 1954 edition, which uses this somewhat different translation. All subsequent editions I have found (1961, 1966, and 1975) are all perfectly in agreement with their translation of this text and the accompanying footnote.
54. Edgar Snow, *Red Star Over China* (New York, Grove, 1968), p. 134.
55. Ibid., p. 136.
56. "Report of an Investigation..." p. 47.
57. Richard Madsen, "China's Confounding Religious Revival," *Current History* (September 2007), pp. 288–95.
58. Chang Chiyi, *Minzu Tuanjie* (April 1962), pp. 2–5.
59. Bush, p. 38.
60. Brown, p. 87.
61. Figure for Catholic and Protestant believers in 1949 from Fenggang Yang, "The Red, Black, and Gray Markets of Religion in China," *Sociological Quarterly*, 47 (2006), p. 103.
62. The most recent articulation of such an idea is that offered by the Eastern Orthodox Church, particularly as expressed by Seraphim Rose in his, *Orthodoxy and the Religion of the Future* (Platina, CA: St. Herman of Alaska Brotherhood, 1975).
63. MacInnis, doc. 4, "The Chinese Revolution and the Chinese Communist Party: On Religious Cultural Aggression" [1939], p. 12.
64. Brown, p. 39.
65. Ibid., p. 36.
66. Liu Qunwang and Yu Xiang, *Hongqi* (February 26, 1964).
67. Ibid.
68. See, John Nevius, *The Planting and Development of Missionary Churches* [1886]; reprinted, (Hancock, NH: Monadnock Press, 2003). See also, Rufus Anderson, *To Advance the Gospel; Selections from the Writings of Rufus Anderson*, R. Pierce Beaver, ed. (Grand Rapids, Mich.: Eerdmans, 1967), and Henry Venn, *To Apply the Gospel; Selections from the Writings of Henry Venn*. Max Warren, ed. (Grand Rapids, Mich: Eerdmans, 1971). For a discussion of how African churches faced similar struggle to end their "ecclesiastical externality," see Paul Gifford, *African Christianity: Its Public Role* (Indiana: Indiana University, 1998), pp. 44–7.
69. Lou, p. 56.

70. Ibid., p. 59.

71. See, for example, Joseph Tse-Hei Lee, "Watchman Nee and the Little Flock Movement in Maoist China," *Church History* Vol. 74, no. 1 (March 2005), pp. 68–96; and Ka-Lun Leung, *Ni Tuoshen de rongru shengchu* (Hong Kong: Alliance Bible Seminary, 2003).

72. Luo, p. 59.

73. Bush, p. 104.

74. Welch, p. 297.

75. Bush, p. 44.

76. *China Missionary Bulletin,* No. VIII (January 1956) p. 85.

77. Welch, pp. 298–9.

78. Jy Din Sakya, *Empty Cloud: The Teachings of Xu Yun and a Remembrance of the Great Chinese Zen Master* (Taipei: Corporate Body of the Buddha Educational Foundation, 2004), p. 8.

79. We have no figure for the number of lay believers in 1949, but *Modern Buddhism* reported in 1957 that there were 100,000,000 at that time. There is no reason to believe that that number increased during that time, so this should be seen as a conservative estimate when applied to 1949. *Modern Buddhism* (August, 1957), p. 4.

80. Shi Dongchu, *Zhongguo Fojiao Jindai Shi* (Taibei: Zhongguo Fojiao Wenhua Guan, 1974), p. 1022.

81. Welch, p. 305.

82. Ibid., pp. 305–06.

83. Ibid., p. 392.

84. MacInnis, doc. 7, "On the Correct Handling of Contradictions" [1957], p. 13.

85. Brown, p. 103.

86. Ibid., p. 112.

87. MacInnis, doc. 7, "On the Correct Handling of Contradictions" [1957], p. 13.

88. Ibid., doc. 23, "Chou En-lai Speaking to Chinese Christians on the Christian Share in the Revolution" [1950], p. 24.

89. Tian Chunming, "Mao Zedong yu bu pa gui de gushi," *Wenxue Bao,* (December 11, 2003).

90. *Bu pa gui de gushi* (Beijing, 1999).

91. Incidentally, when it came to Islam, the Soviets dealt with it quite differently than with Orthodox Christianity, further supporting Wei Dedong's thesis. See Paul Froese, "'I am an Atheist and a Muslim': Islam, Communism, and Ideological Competition," *Journal of Church & State,* vol. 47. No. 3 (2005), pp. 473–501.

92. Interview with the author, Renmin University, May 2, 2008.
93. Yu, p. 145.
94. Bays, pp. 26–7.
95. Ibid., pp. 34–5.
96. Jonathan Chao, "China's Religious Policy," *China and the Church Today*, May-June 1979, pp. 1–3.
97. See, among others: You Xiang and Liu Junwang, "Ma Kesi Lie Ning zhuyi zongjiaoguan de jige wenti," *Xin Chienshe* (September 20, 1963); Bing Quan, Xiao Fu, and Yu He, "Zhengque lijie 'zongjiao shi renmin de yapian'—yu Ya Hanzhang tongzhi shangque," *Wenhui Bao* (June 23, 1964); and Liang Hao and Yang Zhen, "Zongjiao conglai jiushi renmin de yapian—yu Ya Hanzhang tongzhi shangque," *Xin Chienshe* (December 20, 1965).
98. Chao, "China's Religious Policy."
99. Welch, p. 377, fn. 72.
100. Welch, p. 344, fn. 130.

CHAPTER SIX

Keeping the Faith: The Persistence of Religious Life in Communist China

I am a Roman Catholic Bishop. If I denounce the Holy Father, not only would I not be a Bishop, I would not even be a Catholic. You can cut off my head, but you can never take away my duty.[1]

—*Cardinal Kung*

Despite the great "achievements" made in the Soviet Union in curtailing religion, no other country had ever come as close to wiping out religion as did China during the Cultural Revolution. The only other close contender is Albania under Enver Hoxha, which in 1967 declared itself the world's first atheist state after having shut down 2,169 Mosques, churches, and monasteries in a Red Guard-style crackdown.[2] Still, in terms of scale, speed, and method, Albania's "attainment of atheism" pales in comparison. While in Albania these religious institutions were "handed over to the youth," in China the seizure, forceful closing, burning, looting, and wanton destruction of religious buildings and property unfolded virtually without warning, without direction, and without remorse. As Mao had said nearly 40 years earlier, it was "the peasants who made the idols, and when the time comes they will cast the idols aside with their own hands." He was right, except that it wasn't the peasants pulling down the idols, but urban youths high on revolutionary rhetoric and empowered by Mao's words, which they carried with them in his *Little Red Book*.

In the ensuing attack, all believers of whatever denomination, theological conviction, or political persuasion suffered. In the West it is often thought that it was the Christians who suffered most during the Cultural Revolution, but other religions suffered the same fate. No one was exempt—not Buddhist, not Confucian, not Taoist. In fact, the Taoists, who had not been the focus of any real crackdown since the revolution, since the Communists didn't really even consider Taoism a religion, ultimately suffered like any other "religion."[3] During the height of the Cultural Revolution, most Buddhist temples in China were closed, many were looted, and some priceless art treasures and ancient manuscripts were burned. Red Guards frequently set fire to images and statues of Buddha and used "axes, picks, and iron spikes to crush the sculptures to pieces."[4] Perhaps Buddhism's deep connection to Chinese culture made it a prime example of the four olds (si jiu), that is, old customs, old culture, old habits, and old ideas, which Mao had called upon the youth to "sweep away" in the early days of the Cultural Revolution.[5] Rallying cries such as "beat down the Jesus following" didn't make things much easier for Christians, either, whether Three-Self or House Church Christians—leaders from the latter, who had tried to cooperate with the CCP worked alongside those from the former in the work camps. The Religious Affairs Bureau even ceased to function.

If any group suffered less than others, it was probably China's Muslims. Their special ethnic minority status, their main presence in the peripheral areas, and the importance of maintaining good relations with Pakistan and other states of the Muslim world, afforded them some leniency. Nevertheless, most mosques were closed during the Cultural Revolution and some were destroyed, and it was reported that study of the Koran was forbidden in some places and that Muslim religious leaders were humiliated by being forced to eat pork and lick the heads of pigs.[6]

At the height of the Cultural Revolution each and every church in the People's Republic of China was closed. They were either padlocked or else used for some other purpose—as warehouses, factories, or schools. As Brown lamented, for "the first time in more than three hundred years there was no public Christian worship of God in that vast land."[7]

The key word here, however, is "public". As Enver Hoxha himself had explained to the fourth Congress of the Albanian Democratic Front where he first announced Albania's attainment of atheism, policy measures alone are "insufficient to eradicate religious feelings":

> It is wrong to maintain that religion means church, mosque, priest, imam, icons, etc., and that if these disappear then automatically religion and its influence on the people will also disappear. We must be realists. The struggle against habits, traditions, old norms and against religious viewpoints, which are deeply rooted in the course of centuries in the conscience of the people, have not yet come to an end. This is a long, complicated and difficult struggle.[8]

It is this "long, complicated and difficult struggle" that provides the theme for this chapter. Just as Chapter 3 focused on the resistance to the Soviet attempt to strangle faith and promote atheism, this chapter takes a similar look at Chinese believers who defied their government by refusing to abandon their religious convictions. Indeed, in the case of China, not only did people resist forced secularization, religious belief actually made significant inroads *during* CCP control, except perhaps during the Cultural Revolution. Whereas in the Soviet Union religious belief dropped only slightly from the Bolshevik Revolution until the abandonment of Marxist ideology, in China the number of Christians skyrocketed from only 3.5 million in 1949 (or ½ of 1 percent) to perhaps 66 million today (or 5 percent of the present population). Even if we attribute most of this growth to the post-liberalization period, figures suggest that the number of Catholics increased modestly between 1949 and 1982 while the number of Protestants nearly quadrupled.[9] Once one takes into account generational replacement, this means millions of people came to lives of faith during the height of China's Marxist religion policies. Once again, it is only through the life stories of some of these believers that one can see not only the effects of China's religion policy on the people, but how belief animated their lives as they sought to live out a life of faith in a society that not only severely restricted their religious freedom but also mocked their beliefs as "backward" and mere "superstition."

Protestantism: Patriotic or Parasitic?

As we saw in the previous chapter, "reeling" in religion was a difficult struggle, and many people suffered. Given the progress that has been made over the past half century, however, we can see in retrospect that efforts to indigenize Christianity in China were necessary. While the policy used to bring that change about might not have been the most wise, both sides of the modernist-fundamentalist debate actually agreed on the need to make Christianity in China "Chinese." The main point of contention was over the means of achieving this goal—a centralized institution run by the state, or autonomous religious communities. Indeed, most of the Protestants who resisted the Three-Self Movement did so, not because they wanted to maintain Western ties—they argued that they had none—but rather they did not want to be affiliated with other churches in China with which they had theological disagreements. The co-option of the mission strategy of the "three-selfs" was mostly a means of severing foreign ties between Christianity and Western missionaries.

As M. Searle Bates pointed out some time ago, however, the "foreign ties" argument used by the CCP was actually quite far from reality. In many cases, Christian churches were receiving little or no foreign aid and apparently could get along just fine without it. Moreover, some were indeed directed by Chinese, with missionary influence negligible and easily circumvented. Severing ties with foreign organizations meant that a few operations would have to cut back some of their programs significantly, primarily in the medical field, since the missions ran such a vast hospital network. In terms of Chinese leadership, only a small number of churches were actually not staffed adequately by well-trained Chinese. As he concluded, "Broadly speaking, local churches, many schools, and the simpler medical work" in the hospitals "were carried or largely carried by Chinese" themselves.[10]

The issue was more one of identity. As Bishop Ting commented in a 1990 interview, "As long as foreign missionaries led the advance in China," the then head of the TSPM commented, "our Christians were looked upon as foreigners. Becoming a Christian was becoming a foreigner to many Chinese." Bishop Ting continued, pointing out that "Christianity was therefore looked upon as something not really for the Chinese people." As he concluded, "This image had to be changed for there to be growth."[11] Indeed, this was a serious issue, as the slaughter of Chinese Christians during the Boxer Rebellion illustrates. And as the growth of Christianity over the past half century proves, the indigenization of Chinese Christianity has apparently helped its spread in China. But it was a process that came at a very high price for some, particularly those who resisted unification with the TSPM.

The Dean of the House Church: Wang Mingdao

Wang Mingdao's troubles didn't begin only when the CCP began to organize all of China's churches into the Three-Self Movement. They date back significantly farther than that. He was born in the midst of the Boxer Rebellion, and almost simultaneously his father, a doctor at a Methodist hospital, committed suicide as he feared the rebels would breach the wall of the compound where they were held up and kill everyone. In the end, the "boxers," as the kung fu practicing *Yihequan* (Righteous and Harmonious Fists) were called by the Westerners, proved no match for modern firearms. Wang Tie (or "Iron Wang" as he was affectionately known), his sister, and his recently-widowed mother found themselves quickly impoverished.

Already at the age of 20, Wang was fired from his teaching post at a Chinese Presbyterian school in Baoding for speaking out against the church's practice of simply sprinkling candidates for baptism. The young Wang, who had only been baptized in the Congregational Church at age 12, had been told by a colleague of his at the school that, unless he repented for his sins and received baptism by immersion his Christian transformation would remain incomplete. Wang, who already considered himself a Christian and was known for pointing out the sinful ways of others, initially scoffed at the idea. But upon some deep soul-searching he realized that he was still a sinner. "The more I prayed, the more conscious I became of my unworthiness. I was unclean, vicious, and hateful." The "illuminating light of the Holy Spirit," he later recalled, made him conscious of his "own utter depravity."[12] His colleague was soon dismissed from the school for criticizing the baptismal practices of the Presbyterian Church, and Wang, too, became convinced that full immersion was the only salvific method of baptism. He willingly sacrificed his job over the issue, as he was also asked to leave. After being given one day to pack his things, Wang and five of his students who agreed with him left the school for Beijing, being baptized on the way by a Chinese pastor who immersed them in a river so icy that the water on their clothes froze "hard and solid like thin boards."[13]

Now unemployed, Wang returned home to live with his sister and mother, and with his father deceased, Wang was expected to provide for the family. Instead, he fashioned the shed next to their house into "God's Bible School," preaching to whomever showed up. Soon, word of his charisma and Christian witness spread, and he had to abandon the backyard for rented space, eventually constructing a large building to house all of his flock. Only a week after the Christian Tabernacle, as the new church was called, was dedicated, the Japanese occupied the city. This brought Wang into his first episode of church-state tensions, as the Japanese sought to organize all Christian churches into a single umbrella organization that they could more easily control. Wang refused to participate on theological grounds, writing the Japanese authorities and insisting that, since the organization was comprised of "churches of different faiths," uniting with them would make it difficult "to preserve an unadulterated faith." He also refused to put the seal of the Japanese Army Bureau on his publication, *Spiritual Food Quarterly*, as required by the occupying forces. Amazingly, the Japanese—despite threats—never punished Wang or interfered with his activities. This he took as divine providence and confirmation of God's protection.[14]

During a meeting with the Japanese officer charged with uniting all the churches in China into a centralized organization, Wang had made it clear that he would not sacrifice his faith or cave in to threats. I will "pay any price, make any sacrifice," he said.[15] His opinion had not changed when the rulers of the country changed hands in 1949. Already at this early stage of Mao-era church-state relations, Wang Mingdao (he had by this point changed his name to *mingdao*, or "bright path") had refused to follow the crowd, refusing to sign a document being widely circulated that identified Christianity as a tool of imperialism.

Throughout his already more than 20 years of evangelism and preaching, he had never been connected with any foreign group, not to mention affiliated with a missionary society or denominational organization. Indeed, he had been one of the early supporters of the three-self formula developed by Venn and Anderson and brought to China by Nevius. While the idea was new to the Communists, it had been a central principle of Wang Mingdao's and other Chinese Christians from the start.[16] His experience with the Presbyterian school where he once worked, with the Congregational Church into which he had been first baptized, and his subsequent relations with denominational churches throughout his life attested to the fact that he believed firmly in the independence of churches on theological grounds, as they were better able to ensure doctrinal purity and uphold the behavior of the congregation. Pastor Wang even criticized the influence of foreign money on the church, arguing that "it attracted and rewarded parasites who fawned after Western missionaries in hope" of gaining financial benefits.[17] When it came to severing foreign ties, therefore, Wang's church had none to sever. In fact, an accusation meeting against him in July 1954 failed utterly, as only a quarter of those present supported sentencing him for any of the charges leveled against him, including not having sympathy for the government and having a "very individualistic style" to his preaching.[18] As Aikman points out, "no one outside of the Communist Party itself or its various toadies seriously considered Wang a tool of anybody."[19]

That didn't stop the CCP from arresting him in August 1955 for protesting against the Three-Self Patriotic Movement. Wang, his wife Debra, and 18 of his student followers were sent to prison for their defiance. After nearly 1 year in prison, Wang began to break. Two prisoners had been put in the same cell as Wang after being coached on how to frighten and demoralize Wang, with promises of benefits if they succeeded. Their horrifying tales of torture and relentless prodding had their intended effect, and Wang began to question his faith and convictions. He soon began to recant his position and eventually signed a confession, promised to join the TSPM, and to preach only permitted material, and he was subsequently released.

His freedom was bittersweet, however, and shortly afterwards his conscience began to plague him. In his mind, he had betrayed Christ, much like Peter had denied Christ three times. Wang Mingdao only did it once, however, and unlike Peter, he recanted. In 1958 he and his wife were arrested again, this time receiving life and 15-year sentences, respectively.

Wang ultimately spent 22 years in a prison labor camp, finally being released in 1980 as the CCP closed the book on the Cultural Revolution and pursued a new strategy in Chinese church-state relations. Upon his release, he immediately plunged himself back into evangelism, becoming involved in the house church movement in Beijing until his death. What earned Wang the title of the "dean of the house churches," however, was not his time in prison or simply his defiance. Others, including Watchman Nee, Allen Lamb, Moses Xie, and Samuel Lamb all defied the CCP and suffered similar fates. Rather, it was probably Wang's clearly articulated rejection of the TSPM on theological grounds.

Wang argued that his and his followers' main contention with the TSPM was not political, but rather theological, and that it was a debate that was 20 years in the making. The Three-Self Movement was simply modernism in a new guise, and as such it was a threat against the traditional core of Christian belief. To Wang, the TSPM was simply another attempt to force liberal modernist theology on the fundamentalist churches. By labeling them "unpatriotic" if they failed to join, the terms of debate were being obfuscated.

In Wang's pamphlet, "We, Because of Faith," the defiant pastor articulately argued that the contention between him and the three-self leadership was purely over the Christian faith itself. In good debating style, Wang quoted his opponents verbatim and at length, and then attacked their positions one point at a time. The targets of this approach were Y. T. Wu and K. H. Ting, particularly the former's book *Darkness and Light*. Ting was at this point dean of the Nanjing Union Theological Seminary, while Wu was the leading modernist intellectual and the leader and theological voice of the TSPM. Wu had been educated at Columbia University and Union Theological Seminary—where he had studied under Reinhold Niebuhr. Wang pointed out that in *Darkness and Light* (one can immediately sense the influence of Niebuhr even in the title), Wu had explicitly rejected all of the fundamental points of faith held dear by Wang and other fundamentalist Chinese Christians. As Harvey explains, Wu and other modernists "had dumped the gospel and now offered the faithful mere placebos that could never get at the root of human misery and social disorder."[20] The fundamentalists, Wang pointed out, held firm to the orthodox doctrines of Biblical inerrancy, the Virgin Birth of Christ, substitutionary atonement, Christ's bodily resurrection, and the Second Coming. These "are all serious theological differences," Wang stressed, and because of them he could not join any organization that espoused anything other than orthodox Christianity.

Indeed, this was what got him fired from his job back when he was 20 years old. Now, a senior pastor who had spent time in prison for his convictions, Wang Mingdao was willing to fight for his faith, no matter what the cost. "These people have no faith; they do not believe in Jesus; they are not Christians," Wang declared. "Masquerading as Christians, they mix with church people and spread some kind of ambiguous, false doctrine to lead astray true believers and corrupt their faith." In the "name of my Lord Jesus Christ I shall fight against them."[21] That fight would cost him more than 20 years of his life in this world, but to him, this was a pittance, for he was sure in his convictions. As he had remarked on another occasion, but which clearly illustrates his God-fearing attitude, "I prefer to be attacked by men than to call forth the wrath of God."[22]

Rendering Unto Caesar: Bishop K. H. Ting

One of the men who would attack him was Bishop K. H. Ting. Together, they represent the two contending sides of the three-self/house church debate. It has even been said, to understand Chinese Christianity you only need to understand two men—Wang Mingdao and K. H. Ting.[23] A former Anglican bishop, Ting was the head of the Nanjing Union Theological Seminary during the time of the formation of the TSPM, and along with Wu, one of the organ's chief apologists, came out against Wang Mingdao. Upon the death of Wu in 1979, Ting became the head of both the TSPM and the newly-formed China Christian Council, posts he would hold until his retirement in 1997.

Bishop Ting (Ding Guangxun) was born in Shanghai in 1915, making him significantly younger than Pastor Wang. This also meant they he did not experience the collapse of imperial China and that he was very young during the formative events of the May Fourth Movement and the settlement after World War I. He received his education at St. John's University in Shanghai, and later received graduate degrees from Columbia University and Union Theological Seminary. Upon graduation he moved to Switzerland to take a position with the World Student Christian Federation in Geneva. Shortly after the CCP gained control of the country, Ting returned to Shanghai and quickly rose through the ranks. In 1953 he was named the first dean of the newly-established (by uniting several existing seminaries) Nanjing Union Theological Seminary, and the following year he became a member of the standing committee of the TSPM, where he would work closely with Wu, who served in many ways as his mentor.

Unlike Wu, however, whose theology was strongly influenced by Western theologians such as Karl Barth and Reinhold Niebuhr, Ting's theology is an amalgamation of 1930s Anglican theology and his own unique Christological viewpoint, which he calls the "Cosmic Christ." The former is rooted in his St. John's education, while the latter seems to have deep Taoist influences, though to his mind these are simply elements of traditional Chinese culture. Indeed, as he said in one of his more well-known sermons, "these two points about Christ—the cosmic extent of his role and the Christlike love with which God runs the universe—are not entirely foreign to Chinese culture." He then proceeds to quote a long passage from the *Tao Te Ching*, only returning to Christian belief to conclude that "this passage prepares the Chinese soil for receiving a Christ whose dimensions are cosmic."[24]

Although Bishop Ting's theological viewpoints are interesting, they were mostly developed after his appointment as head of the TSPM and China Christian Council in 1980. Back in the 1950s, he was still very much the junior theologian to Wu, and joined the latter in his attacks against Wang Mingdao and other holdouts who refused to join the TSPM. These attacks were not theological masterpieces, but rather politically-motivated retorts drawing upon theological justifications. As he wrote, "Wang Mingdao has published many articles, most of them expressing his hatred toward New China and his irrational thinking. He has tried to develop hatred among the Chinese Christians toward New China and has compared China with the kingdom of Nebuchanezzar and Christians with Daniel and his three associates."

This theme, of allegiance to the "new China" (*xinhua*), as the CCP was calling the society they were building, was one of the main arguments Ting leveled against the intransigent Wang. Ting was adamant that duty to the nation was tantamount to duty to God, making his refusal to unite with the TSPM a betrayal of both God and country. As he explained, "Either as a Chinese who loves the nation or as a Christian who loves the church, he must realize the importance of unity." Not uniting was treasonous: The TSPM "seeks to unify all believers together to be against imperialism and to love the nation [literally, *aiguo*, or patriotism]. There is no excuse," Ting continued, "for a believer to not join the movement—unless one does not want to be against imperialism."[25] As Harvey explains, "once one accepts the narrative of the nation-state as the common ground of unity, rationality, and human identity, challenging that unity at any level is by nature counterrevolutionary."[26]

This was precisely how Ting went after Wang, who "mentions nothing of imperialism or of using religion to control people. He does everything to misconstrue our self-governing, self-propagating, and self-supporting principles," Ting charged, "and has distorted people's understanding of the

Three-Self Movement, even accusing its leaders of being false prophets and disciples of Judas."[27] Indeed, this last point was even listed among his crimes when Wang was arrested. As he concluded, Wang Mingdao's "use of the Bible is purely politically motivated."

One of Wang's greatest contentions against the unification efforts of the TSPM was that the theological differences between the fundamentalist and modernist churches were too vast for them to unite. To this, Ting countered that doctrinal unity was not necessary, and because all Christians believed "in the same Heavenly Father and the same Bible" they are "redeemed by the same Christ [and] are guided by the same Holy Spirit," they did not need to agree on specific matters that had traditionally divided modernists and fundamentalists. Wang considered Ting's position monistic and unorthodox. As he countered, "The modernists who explain away the fundamental doctrines about Christ and say they are not essential to faith, are they not dishonoring, despising, and denying the Son?" To Wang, the lack of focus on the Biblical Jesus was too great a difference to be overlooked. As he argued, "To say one believes in the Father is not enough; he must also believe in the Son as proof that he believes in the Father." Ever since their writings deemphasizing the doctrines of the Virgin Birth, physical resurrection, etc., Wang dismissed the modernists as unorthodox, arguing that they viewed Scripture as symbolic and even mythological. "Since the modernists do not honor the Son, since they despise Him and deny Him, since they transgress and abide not in His doctrine, how can we acknowledge that they believe with us in the same Father?"[28]

Wang's demand that the Father can only be known through the Son and the Son only through a proper understanding of Scripture illustrated just how vast a divide separated the two sides of the debate. With the state on his side—or perhaps more accurately with him on the state's side—Ting, Wu, and the TSPM would prevail. But for every thing there is a season, and that season came for Ting during the Cultural Revolution. Ting's life fell apart, as the TSPM was dismantled and the seminary he headed was shut down. He was even forced to move out of his apartment and into more modest quarters. Nevertheless, his treatment was certainly far better at that time than Wang's, who was physically tortured during the Cultural Revolution.

Both of their lives improved dramatically in 1980, however, as a new era in church-state relations was launched under Deng Xiaoping. Wang Mingdao was released from prison and took up his post as "dean of the house church," while Ting returned to his position as dean of the Nanjing Union Theological Seminary. And as the TSPM was reopened, Ting took over as its head, assuming the post of his long-time mentor, Y. T. Wu, who had passed away the year before. Also in 1980, the China Christian Council was formed, an organization which promotes the unity of churches both nationally and internationally, and Ting was chosen to be its first president, a position he would hold until his retirement in 1997.

During his nearly 20 years of TSPM leadership, Ting worked tirelessly to construct a uniquely Chinese Christian theology and to unify the Christian Church in China. He also sought to engage and dialogue with the international ecumenical movement, which the CCC joined in 1991. To some, Ting worked hard to promote religious freedom in China and advocate for greater reform. To others, he was a CCP stooge and hatchet-man, if not perhaps even a non-believer. While sharp disagreement continues on Ting's contribution to Christianity in China, all are in agreement that he left a considerable mark on religion in China.

Rome's Precious Jewel: The Catholic Church in China

While Wang Mingdao and Bishop Ting debated theology and Christology in arguing their positions on the independence vs. unity of the Protestant churches in China, no such theological debates were needed when it came to the Catholic Church. The three-self demand that the Roman Catholic Church in China sever its ties with the Vatican meant that it would no longer be a part of the Catholic Church. To the CCP, having Chinese Catholics answer to a foreign entity such as the Vatican was another form of imperialism and simply unacceptable. By definition (their definition), such an arrangement could not be patriotic. Indeed, unlike the Orthodox Church, which had for several centuries by this point been "nationalized" in different parts of the world under autocephalous patriarchs, the Catholic Church had been quite effective at keeping ethnicity and nationalism separate from church affairs. There were no "national" Catholic churches, as there were Orthodox or even Protestant churches, for example, the Presbyterian Church and its relationship to Scotland, the Anglican Church and its connection to England, the Reformed Church and its association with the Netherlands. In this regard, making a "patriotic' association of Chinese Protestants made good sense—if it were not carried out coercively. But for Catholicism, becoming a "national" church meant no longer being Catholic.

A Roman Catholic must accept the supreme authority of the pope as the leader of the universal Roman Catholic Church, no matter how unfavorable the circumstances are. A Roman Catholic cannot accept the authority of any other entity or church without breaking with the Church itself. This means that a Catholic in China could not join the Chinese Catholic

Patriotic Association, or at least do so and remain Catholic in the eyes of the Church. Remaining loyal to the Roman Pontiff meant that one could remain in full communion with the Holy Father and the universal Church, but it also meant that one was a member of an illegal association in China, a member in the "underground" Catholic Church. In 1996 Pope John Paul II sent a message to China's Catholics, proudly proclaiming the underground Catholic Church "a precious jewel" of the Catholic Church. "The Bishop must be the first witness of the faith which he professes and preaches," the Pontiff continued, even "to the point of 'shedding his blood' as the apostles did and as so many other Pastors have done down the centuries." The "bishop" to whom he was referring was probably none other than Cardinal Kung.

The Noble Son of China: Cardinal Kung

Just as Wang Mingdao was a symbol of Protestant resistance to CCP religion policies, Cardinal Ignatius Kung (Gong Pinmei) likewise symbolized the Catholic Church's resistance to Communist attempts to coerce them. Arrested 1 month after Wang Mingdao, in the same wave of crackdowns, Kung was the Bishop of Shanghai, a position he had been elevated to only days before the CCP took power in 1949. Bishop Kung's fate was unfolding before him. Soon this sixth generation Catholic and the first Chinese bishop of Shanghai would have his faith labeled "imperialist" and "unpatriotic." The battle that would consume his life from that day forward was taking shape, and it was a battle this pious Christian would not shy away from, not even under the harshest of treatment.

Ignatius Kung was born in 1901 in Shanghai to a Catholic family of at least five generations, and received an excellent education at home both in Chinese classics and religion. These were taught to him and his siblings by his aunt Martha, who also encouraged the young Ignatius to consider the priesthood. This he did, pursuing his seminary studies after high school. After ordination, Kung held a series of school directorships, including those run by the Jesuits. It was from this position that he was made a bishop in 1949.

In the short span of 5 years, Bishop Kung went from newly-appointed prelate to enemy of the Chinese state. He not only led the diocese of the three largest cities in China, but also served as the leader of the Legion of Mary, a lay group devoted to the veneration of Mary. This group proved to be a very effective movement for the strengthening of parish life and providing services when priests were under surveillance or otherwise unable to perform their duties. The government declared the Legion of Mary illegal, charging that it was engaged in espionage activities "under the cloak of religion." The fact that its name was rendered into Chinese as the "Army of the Holy Mother" certainly didn't help their cause. Communist Party officials demanded that all members of the movement register with the Public Security Bureau and acknowledge its counter-revolutionary nature, or face imprisonment. The bishop told his flock not to comply and that they must, under any circumstance, uphold their faith. The faithful trusted Bishop Kung, and nearly all of the members of the Legion of Mary obeyed. The punishment was swift and severe—hundreds of members were arrested and imprisoned. The group's leader did not go unpunished. First, they continued to try and persuade him to join the emerging China Patriotic Catholic Association. As he continued to refuse, he soon found himself in a public "struggle session" at Shanghai's dog racing stadium. Bishop Kung was shoved to the microphone to make his confession, with his hands bound behind his back, and wearing only his pajamas. Rather than offer up the sort of confession the Communists wanted, however, the faithful servant "confessed" his faith in the Church: "Long live Christ the King. Long live the Pope," he exclaimed.

Shanghai was a center of resistance at the time. As late as 1954, it was reported that 115 out of 143 dioceses were still resistant to the patriotic movement. By 1955 the percentage of Catholics who continued to refuse to cooperate with the patriotic movement had dropped to about 30 percent.[29] Shanghai's *Jiefang ribao* (*Liberation Daily*) began publishing a slew of readers' letters attacking "the criminal activities" of Kung's "antirevolutionary group." Attacks on the bishop were to be found in newspaper editorials, cartoons, and articles, although they were not as vicious as in previous barrages against the church. Government charges were amplified to make Bishop Kung the most fearsome spy and saboteur Shanghai had seen in years.[30]

At the same time, a highly respected missionary superior had been jailed. Once his jailers discovered that he was sick and on medication, they withheld his medicine and watched his health plummet. To get his medication back, he was coerced into accusing Bishop Kung in a taped confession.[31] With sufficient evidence and public support, they could now move against the popular Shanghai priest.

During the night of September 7, 1955, Bishop Kung, along with 21 priests, two Carmelite nuns, and from 200–300 lay Catholics were arrested in Shanghai. Between 15 and 20 additional priests and another 600–700 lay believers were then rounded up on the night of September 26. By the end of November, a total of some 1,500 people in Shanghai alone had been arrested.[32] This was part of a larger sweep being carried out across the country as part of an intensive campaign against the whole church. Once it was completed, this marked the end of any effective resistance by the church.

With Kung now under arrest, a group of Shanghai priests loyal to him and the church were then assembled and the taped confession denouncing him was played. "We do not accuse Bishop Kung," the authorities explained, "it is your own leader who has accused him." The priests, who either did not understand that the tape must have been made under duress, or simply feigned their surprise, immediately responded with a statement expressing their appreciation to the government for weeding out the pernicious prelate. "We thank God for His wise guidance in that the People's Government has taken proper measures to save our church in Shanghai from the road of death on which Kung Pinmei was leading it."[33] Auxiliary Bishop Li Debei, leader of the patriotic Catholic association in Tianjiin, responded to the news of Kung's conviction, "all of our patriotic Catholics understand clearly that the…Court of Shanghai has severely punished them," referring to not only Kung but Fr Walsh and some others who had been tried simultaneously. They were not signaled out "because they are Catholics, but because they are counterrevolutionaries and international spies. This is a problem of eliminating our enemies." The patriotic church leader then praised the PRC, "our government has consistently protected the freedom of religious beliefs."[34]

Though in public he had been charged with such acts as organizing acts of violence, encouraging the resistance movement, spreading rumors, poisoning the minds of youth, cruelly killing babies, and listening to Voice of America broadcasts, once formally charged in the courts the picture was less sinister. Bishop Kung had not participated in required patriotic movement activities and had prevented others from doing so, and he had denied the sacraments to patriotic Catholics and would not allow children to join Communist groups. These latter two charges were in regard to the Communist Party's demand that communion should be given to the Pioneers, a Communist version of the Boy Scouts. Bishop Kung had refused, arguing that only the bishop and his priests could judge someone's worthiness to receive the sacrament. He would not offer communion to boys who had sworn to fight for the atheistic and materialist doctrine of Communism.[35]

The arrest, of course, was simply a way of forcing Bishop Kung to comply. He was held in captivity without a trial for 5 years, during which time he was regularly asked to recant and join the CCPA, which he refused each time. Finally, at his 1960 trial at the Shanghai Intermediate People's Court, Bishop Kung was first accused of "sabotaging the anti-imperialist and patriotic movement of Catholics…and persecuting patriotic Catholics." But then the chief prosecutor once more asked him to recant, even telling him it was not necessary to say the words—a simply nod of his head would set him free. He replied to the court, "I am a Roman Catholic Bishop. If I denounce the Holy Father, not only would I not be a Bishop, I would not even be a Catholic. You can cut off my head, but you can never take away my duty."[36]

As he explained in a 1993 interview: "Jesus founded the Church upon the rock of Saint Peter. Anyone who claims to belong to the universal Roman Catholic Church, yet does not recognize the Supreme Pontiff as the head of the Church, actually does not belong to the universal Roman Catholic Church." This was clear to Bishop Kung, and he saw no other option but to choose "the road of imprisonment rather than belonging to the Patriotic Association and cutting off my allegiance to the Holy See." That decision meant that he would be sentenced to 25 years in prison, in addition to the time he had already served awaiting trial. For more than 30 years Bishop Kung rotted in a Chinese jail where he suffered horribly. He spent long periods in solitary confinement, was not allowed to receive visitors, letters, or money, or to buy essential items.

Bishop Kung was released under house arrest in 1985 at age 84. Shortly thereafter he was given an audience with Cardinal Sin of the Philippines, who had hoped to meet Bishop Kung during his visit to China. Arrangements were made for such a meeting, with Cardinal Sin and Bishop Kung seated on opposite ends of the table and separated by more than 20 Party members. The two were not permitted even to speak to each other, so after awhile Cardinal Sin suggested that each man sing a song to liven up the otherwise silent gathering. When the time came for Bishop Kung to sing, he began singing a hymn in Latin, "*Tu es Petrus et super hanc petram aedificabo Ecclesiam meam*" (You are Peter and upon this rock I will build my Church). A bishop of the Chinese Catholic Patriotic Association immediately informed his superiors of Kung's ruse. The octagenerian ex-con was told to be silent, but Kung refused; he sang every word while looking right at the visiting prelate. Cardinal Sin carried Bishop Kung's message to the world—here is a man of God who never faltered in his love for his church or his people despite unimaginable suffering, isolation and pain.[37]

In 1988 Bishop Kung was permitted to travel to the United States for medical treatment. Shortly thereafter, he was well enough to travel to Rome for a private audience with Pope John Paul II. It was at that meeting that

"Bishop" Kung found out that he was in fact "Cardinal" Kung. The Holy Father told Kung that he had elevated him to Cardinal, *in pectore*, back in 1979. The Pope asked Cardinal Kung to keep his position secret until he announced himself, if ever. Ever obedient, Kung did not even tell his own family. Pope John Paul II presented Cardinal Kung with his red cardinal's hat in a ceremony on June 28, 1991, at the Consistory in the Vatican. At the event, the wheelchair-bound, ailing Kung raised himself up from the wheelchair, tossed aside his cane and made his way to kneel at the foot of the Pontiff.[38]

Although he was never allowed to return to his homeland, Cardinal Kung spent the last years of his life celebrating public Masses and leading a media campaign to publicize the plight of the Catholic Church in China through the Cardinal Kung Foundation. When he passed in 2000 due to stomach cancer, then-Cardinal Ratzinger said, "In your decades of fidelity to the Church, you have followed the example of Christ the Good Shepherd, and even in the face of great suffering, have not ceased to proclaim the truth of the Gospel by your words and example." Pope John Paul II, who himself had lived under Communism and who had secretly elevated Kung to the position of cardinal almost immediately after his own election as Pontiff, called Kung "noble son of China and of the Church."[39]

Buddhism(s) in China

As religious traditions that emerged and developed in far off lands, the various forms of Christianity in China were tied up in many people's minds as "foreign" and, with the main missionary efforts corresponding in time with colonialism, as "imperialist" as well. As Bishop Ting commented in a 1990 interview, "Becoming a Christian was becoming a foreigner to many Chinese. Christianity therefore was looked upon as not really something for the Chinese people."[40]

Buddhism is a somewhat different case, however, for although it still retains many attributes that immediately attest to its foreignness, such as its theological language (e.g., dharma, bodhisattva, samsara, prajna, etc.), certain variants have become clearly indigenized. The prime example here is what is referred to as "Han Buddhism," or those forms of Buddhism in China *other* than Tibetan Buddhism. While all variants of Buddhism trace their origin to Siddhartha Gautama and India, Tibetan Buddhism is distinguished from other forms of Mahayana Buddhism in China, such as Chan (known in Japan as Zen) Buddhism. This distinction is not due to its association with Vajrayana and tantric teachings, however, but rather by its structure and the hierarchical system of lamas. In Chinese, it is even referred to as Lamaism (*Lamajiao*). The power of the lamas, in particular of the Dalai Lama and Panchen Lama, particularly raised the ire of the Communists, as they were seen as despotic and exploitative elements.

Of course, the origins of Chan Buddhism were just as foreign. Although Chan Buddhism had existed in China for nearly two millennia by the time the Communists took control, it had somehow effectively indigenized. While the image of its most important historical figure, Bodhidharma (or *Da Mo*), still attested to its foreign roots (in Chinese art he resembles a Japanese rendering of Commodore Perry more than a sage from India), to say that Chan Buddhism was somehow not authentically Chinese would be akin to arguing that Christianity was an alien religious tradition to Europe. While both statements are historically accurate, each religion had become so imbued in the greater culture—indeed formed an important component of that culture—that they were for all intents and purposes indigenous. Whether foreign or indigenous, however, mattered little to the Communists who took power in 1949, for whom all religion was a target.

Friend or Foe? The Case of Xu Yun

Although he was living in Hong Kong during the Civil War, Xu Yun returned to the mainland in 1949, just before the CCP victory. His disciples had warned him against this, explaining to the 110-year old monk that monastic life in China would be greatly disrupted by the Communists after they won the Civil War, which looked increasingly likely at the time. Nevertheless, Xu Yun explained that this was precisely why he needed to return, in order to do what he could to protect the *sangha*, or community of monks.

The Venerable Master Xu Yun was born with the name Xiao Deqing and became a monk at age 19 at Gushan monastery. He became renowned for his rare abilities in *samādhi*, a trance-like meditative state.[41] After a 3-week *samādhi* meditation at Zhongnan Shan he took the name "empty cloud," so named because he had come so close to nirvana during his *samādhi* that his earthly existence was very much like "one of those clouds that linger at the top of a mountain" which "a person can reach out and try to grab" but one's hand will always remain empty."[42]

When deciding to return to the mainland in 1949, Xu Yun perhaps figured that, as China's most revered monk, so renowned for his meditation practices, with so many disciples, and who had worked tirelessly to restore so many ancient monasteries, he was not in much danger personally. In terms of the Party leaders in Beijing he was probably right. After all, many years ago he had helped Zhu De—second in rank only to Mao himself—by giving the defeated army officer refuge in the monastery over which he was abbot.[43] Nor was this the only story of him helping people, including Communists, as he was a devout believer in the monastic tradition of providing compassionate shelter to all who needed it.[44] But Xu Yun never figured his fate would rest in the hands of some lower-ranking, overzealous local cadres.

Xu Yun's first 2 years as abbot of Yunmen Si in Northern Guangdong went by without incident. The venerable monk was even proactive in adjusting to the new circumstances, and the monks of the monastery began to recultivate fallow fields themselves and make great strides in becoming self-sufficient.[45] But in the spring of 1951 the regional land reform committee decided to accelerate land reform efforts in Guangdong and take a harsher line toward the "landlords" there. Soon over 100 cadres descended upon Yunmen si and forbade anyone from entering or leaving. Xu Yun was confined to the abbot's quarters, while the sangha was held separately in the meditation and dharma halls. The cadres then began to turn the monastery upside down as they searched every inch of the place. After failing to find what they were after, they arrested several officers of the monastery and packed up some of the monastery's possessions, including Xu Yun's commentaries, lectures, and correspondence, and then left.

Apparently, they were acting upon information that alleged that arms and radio transmitters had been hidden in the monastery, along with gold and silver. Though their search had turned up nothing, several days later they returned and arrested some 26 members of the sangha. They proceeded to torture and beat them, trying to force them to turn over the arms and hidden gold. Several monks disappeared, while others were brutally beaten. Miao Yun, Xu Yun's most promising disciple, was beaten to death after protesting his innocence. The episode continued for 10 days until finally their rage turned against the master himself.

Xu Yun was confined to a small room, with the windows and doors sealed. He was given no food or water, and was not permitted to leave even to use the toilet. After a week of internment ten large men came in and tried to force him to turn over the guns and gold. The master replied that there was none, and then the first of several beatings was begun. Over the course of several days, Xu Yun was beaten with wooden sticks, iron rods, and police truncheons. All the while, the venerable master sat in the lotus position in meditation. In order to protect himself, he had entered into *samādhi* once again and remained in this state for 8 days.[46] In the evenings, his acolytes would come in and tend to him, and each morning his interrogators would return, astonished that the centenarian was still alive. After several such episodes, the leader of the group asked one of the monks, "why is it that the old boy can't be beaten to death?" The monk replied to the perplexed thug, "The venerable master has accepted suffering in order to help all sentient beings. For you people he has averted natural disasters. He cannot be beaten to death. Some day you will understand these things yourself." Master Xu Yun was not beaten again.

By this time, word of the whole affair had leaked out of the monastery and made its way to the master's disciples, including those in Beijing. Almost immediately, the local authorities received a telegram from the capital ordering an investigation. A special commission soon followed, but when asked by central government authorities if he had been mistreated, Xu Yun only replied, "no," and simply requested that they conduct a thorough investigation into the affair. Xu Yun apologized to his disciples, saying "my heavy karma has dragged all of you down too. Now that things have turned out like this, you probably should go your separate ways and try to live out your lives."[47] None of his disciples left their master, however, and they began to rebuild the monastery once again.

As Welch accurately points out, the case of Xu Yun vividly illustrates the two sides of the CCP policy on religion at the time, and on Buddhism in particular. When regarded as hostile to the regime, Buddhists were vigorously repressed. When it appeared they could be used to rally support domestically and to win friends abroad, they were accorded favor and patronage.[48] This episode also illustrates, however, two other important facts. The first is the great ambiguity over religion policy during the early period of CCP rule, and secondly, that at this time a harder line was being unilaterally carried out in some provinces compared with the central government and Party leadership. In fact, the Xu Yun episode is an excellent example of the latter, for while he was being beaten in his own monastery by local cadres, back in Beijing his name was placed atop a list of 18 eminent Buddhist monks who were about to be convened to discuss the establishment of a national Buddhist association.

From that point on, Xu Yun's name was attached to the movement to form the Chinese Buddhist Association, though he largely remained aloof from its activities, only participating in some of its ceremonies. Xu Yun retired to the Zhenru Temple at Yunju shan in Jiangxi, where he spent the last years of his life restoring the famous Tang Dynasty monastery. Shortly before he died, however, he gave his acolytes a map of the location where

$28,000 in gold was buried beneath a tree at the Yunmen Temple with orders to hand it over the government with instructions to use it for the renovation of the Guangxiao Temple. Apparently, Xu Yun trusted the government of 1959, unlike the local authorities who had ransacked his monastery 7 years earlier, causing the death of his most promising disciple.

Beijing's Young Rival: The Dalai Lama

When the CBA was officially formed in May 1953, Xu Yun was the only Han Buddhist among the four honorary presidents of the association, with the others being the Mongolian Chagangegen, the Panchen Lama, and the Dalai Lama. In many ways Xu Yun and the Dalai Lama were opposites, especially in the eyes of Beijing bureaucrats and Party leaders. At 113 years old, Xu Yun was the oldest public figure in China at the time, while the Dalai Lama was still 2 months shy of his eighteenth birthday. He had already been in the public spotlight since he was two years old, however, at which point he had been identified as the *tulku*, or the reincarnation of the thirteenth Dalai Lama. It had only been 2 years, however, since he added the role of Tibet's political leader to that of the nation's spiritual leader, and that was upon the occasion of the imminent arrival of PLA forces in Lhasa. In an emergency meeting, an oracle was consulted and it was decided that the young Dalai Lama should immediately be elevated to political leader, a position held at the time by his regent until he reached the age of majority.

Xu Yun also represented a religious tradition that was seen as deeply rooted in Han culture, with Mao himself even confessing that he had been a Buddhist believer as a young man (which may explain why Mao, when presented with a case against Xu Yun before the April 1959 National People's Congress, responded, "Oh, what a mess! We are having an NPC meeting. Why bring up this stuff? Take it away, take it away").[49] On the contrary, however, in the eyes Party leaders the Dalai Lama represented a foreign, evil, and vile tradition. The "Lamaism" of Tibet was seen as not only an exploitative economic system worse than European feudalism, perhaps even more revolting was the alleged prevalence of pedophilia among the monks and the practice of scatophagy, which the Communists supposedly witnessed firsthand during the Dalai Lama's visit to Beijing in 1954–1955.[50] Though both Xu Yun and the Dalai Lama represented Buddhism in new China, the variants of this tradition must been seen as at least as distinct as Protestantism and Catholicism.[51]

Of all the contrasts one can draw between these two figures, perhaps none was more significant than the geo-political role of each. While Xu Yun was abbot of a small monastery in remote northern Guangdong, the most valuable possession of which was the gold he had stashed away from the Communists, the Dalai Lama was the religious and political leader of Tibet, encompassing a huge territory of great geo-strategic importance. At the center was a political controversy that has remained intractable to this day—the independence of the tiny nation.

The CCP dealt gently with Tibet during their early days in power. Indeed, the Dalai Lama considered the CCP victory in Beijing as a relatively irrelevant fact for Tibet, which he considered a firmly established independent nation-state, though he never used that term himself. In fact, as best as one can surmise from his use of terms, the Dalai Lama draws virtually no distinction between a nation as a people and a nation-state as an internationally-recognized and juridically-sovereign member of the international community of states. He attributes Tibet's lack of such recognition, rather, to their tradition of isolation, and the Chinese troops which were in Lhasa at the collapse of the Qing dynasty were "Manchu" troops, not Chinese troops resident in their own country, as the PRC contends.[52]

If these are the ideas of a very seasoned international leader, one can only imagine what was going through the mind of a 15-year-old boy who only days before had been more pre-occupied with his Buddhist studies, tinkering with old cars, and an upcoming opera upon news that PLA forces had entered Tibet. The young Dalai Lama thus found himself in the middle of geo-strategic calculations that were years in the making. Yet very quickly the Dalai Lama would have to mature, and this he did quite remarkably. In the area of Tibet that the PLA had occupied was the Kumbum monastery, the abbot of which turned out to be Thubten Jigme Norbu, the Dalai Lama's older brother. The CCP, apparently after some rather harsh treatment, convinced him to travel to Lhasa and convert his brother to a position favorable to the Communist's objective of bringing Tibet under PRC control. According to the Dalai Lama's account, Norbu was to assassinate his brother if he failed to change his mind, and it was only upon his acceptance of such a mission that he was released and sent on his way to Lhasa.[53] In his own words, Norbu wrote that the CCP indicated that, "should the Dalai Lama resist the march of progress…ways and means would have to be found to get rid of him. At this point they even let me see quite clearly that if necessary they would regard fratricide as justifiable in the circumstances if there remained no other way of advancing the cause of Communism."[54] While not quite as sinister as the version recounted by the Dalai Lama, the point is moot, because Norbu only agreed to the mission in order to warn his brother to flee for his life.

Upon the suggestion of his older brother, the Dalai Lama relocated to Southern Tibet, to the city of Dromo. He also sent delegations to the United States, the United Kingdom, Nepal, and Beijing. The former were to request military support to help defend Tibet against PRC aggression, while the latter was to negotiate a PLA withdrawal. Norbu himself headed to the United States, which he was sure would support Tibet, as they were fighting against Communist expansion. As far as the Dalai Lama knew at the time—or has admitted since—the first three delegations were refused an audience. In fact, the United States did work with Norbu and, although they did not want to get openly involved, they began training a group of Tibetans to return and carry out covert operations aimed at destabilizing the PRC.[55] In the end, the operation was a total failure, and eventually abandoned.

Of more immediate consequence, however, was the delegation sent to Beijing, which went completely awry. Though the delegation had been charged only with fact-finding, the Dalai Lama contends that he listened in amazement to Radio Peking as he heard news of a newly-signed "Seventeen Point Agreement" between the PRC and "local government" of Tibet, which—among other things—agreed to return to "the big family of the motherland—the People's Republic of China." The second clause stipulated that the "local government" of Tibet would "actively assist" the PLA in entering Tibet, while the final clause deprived Tibet of all authority over external relations. According to the Chinese account, the Dalai Lama had been consulted by members of his mission.[56]

For our purposes here, the issue of religious freedom is the central concern. Though his brother had explained to him that the Communists were not only "non-religious but were actually opposed to the practice of religion,"[57] the agreement declared a policy of freedom of religious belief. In subsequent meetings and negotiations, other concessions were made as well. Beijing promised not to get involved in the income of the monasteries, which they were doing with other religions, and Mao even held back land redistribution, saying it was for the Tibetans to decide whether or not land would be divided.[58] And as already mentioned in the previous chapter, Mao stated to the 1952 Tibetan mission to Beijing that "The Communist Party adopts the policy of protecting religion. Whether you believe in religion or not, and whether you believe in this religion or that religion, all of you will be respected." By most accounts, religion "was almost totally unaffected by Tibet's becoming part of socialist China."[59]

This did not mean that Mao had some affinity for Tibetan Buddhism. In fact, he expressed his personal feelings to the Dalai Lama himself. In his last meeting with Tibet's spiritual leader, he told him that "religion is poison."

"It has two great defects," Mao continued, "it undermines the race, and secondly, it retards the progress of the country. Tibet and Mongolia have both been poisoned by it."[60] The Dalai Lama was not only deeply offended, but horrified. He rightly suspected that Mao was no friend of Tibet, and that trouble was looming on the horizon, both figuratively and literally.

The assimilation of Tibet into the PRC was plagued with problems, not of a religious nature, but rather purely political. The Dalai Lama's prime ministers and the PLA leader resident in Lhasa, General Zhang Jingwu, were constantly arguing over such issues as troop command, placement, quartering, and even the flag flown. The arrival in Lhasa over a very brief period of so many PLA forces, effectively doubling the city's population, put a major strain on the food supply. As General Zhang pushed the Tibetans to provide grain that simply wasn't there, one of the Dalai Lama's prime ministers accurately pointed out that, if the troops were in Lhasa for the defense of the territory from foreign aggressors—as the PLA claimed—they should leave the city and secure the border region. Some others were more explicit: "PLA, get out of Tibet" they yelled as they marched past Chinese political and military offices.[61]

These and other politico-military disagreements resulted in a deterioration of relations between the two parties. Mao's promise of religious freedom for Tibet quickly turned around, and soon a pamphlet appeared that depicted lamas and monks as "more ferocious than wild animals," accused them of raping women and young boys. The pamphlet's author was purported to be a Tibetan calling to his people to throw off their "potentates," and who said that the god he believed in was Communism.[62] While Bush recounts this episode, he is not altogether convinced that such a person actually existed, and apparently suspects that authorship of this pamphlet was more likely attributable to some CCP ideologues. But the Dalai Lama himself knew the likely candidate for authorship—one Phuntsog Wangyal, a Tibetan who had been converted to Communism many years before while a school teacher in a Chinese Mission school in Lhasa. Wangyal served as the interpreter between Mao and the Dalai Lama during the latter's visit to Beijing in 1954, and the two became fast friends. Wangyal even used his access to try to explain to the Dalai Lama that "religion was not a reliable thing to base one's life on," and that astrology should not be used as a tool to govern Tibet.[63]

Although the Dalai Lama's first visit to Beijing was a pleasant one for him, affairs had quickly deteriorated after he returned to Lhasa. What happened next is still controversial to this day. Apparently the Dalai Lama was invited to a theatrical performance at a PLA camp outside Lhasa in March of

1959,[64] but he failed to respond to the invite, as he was busy preparing for his theological exams. Upon an inquiry into his planned presence at the event, the Dalai Lama became suspicious.[65] Soon word spread through Lhasa that this was all a ploy to take the Dalai Lama prisoner. The Tibetans revolted. During the confusion, the Dalai Lama was slipped out of Tibet and into India. From that point on he would live in exile and work for the independence of Tibet, functioning perhaps more as the political leader of his nation than the religious leader.

Meanwhile, the revolt was put down violently and the Seventeen Point agreement was abandoned. The CCP then began a systematic attack on the religious and aristocratic elite, quickly confiscating all religious estates. Over 1,000 monasteries were destroyed, countless lamas and monks were killed and/or imprisoned, and a full-scale campaign to exterminate religion was carried out. Ancient art objects in the monasteries were confiscated, while those composed of rare alloys were melted down. Clay artifacts were simply thrown away, while sacred scriptures were burned. Monks suspected of having taken part in the revolt were shot, while others were sent to unknown destinations. While the Potala was preserved as a Potemkin Village of religious freedom, only 300 of the 20,000 remained in all of Lhasa, and even those were forced to do manual labor, a practice proscribed for most monks. With the Dalai Lama's flight, religious freedom in Tibet had suffered a huge blow.

The Blood of the Martyrs

Bishop Fulton Sheen once wrote that "the West has its Mindszenty, but the East has its Kung. God is glorified in his saints."[66] It is certainly true that Christians and other believers in both the East and the West suffered under Communist persecution, and it is probably impossible to determine if persecution was worse in the Soviet Union or Mao's China. But when it comes to the persistence of faith under persecution, the Chinese win hands down. Rather than curbing religion, the control and repression of religious organizations and believers in China actually led to a slow and prolonged climb in the number of religious adherents. In this respect, Tertullian's prophetic statement that the blood of the martyrs is the seed of the church was nowhere so accurate as in China. Indeed, some had suggested that this might happen. Ya Hanchang had argued in the early 1960s that "the use of administrative orders to compel people to discard theism will inevitably drive religion underground." This was the wrong approach, he argued, for it would only "make lawful things unlawful, and turn open activities into clandestine activities." Moreover, such tactics would "only strengthen the faith of the theists and religious disciples," who would "then become more unwilling than ever to give up their beliefs and more fanatical than ever to worship their gods and adhere to their religion."[67]

At approximately the same time, Liu Chunwang and Yu Xiang were arguing that the proper policy for the CCP should be to "eliminate religious roots and influences gradually among the masses by the spread of knowledge and education, as well as by the removal of the masses' fear of natural forces."[68] As we saw in the previous chapter, this shift in policy appeared evident on the eve of the Cultural Revolution, but instead the country took a different direction, one in which not only believers suffered, but all segments of society. Ironically, it is perhaps due to the wanton destructiveness and indiscriminate persecution of the Cultural Revolution that there was such a strong consensus to rethink so much of the Chinese socialist experiment following the death of Mao Zedong and Zhou Enlai. In that reassessment, a more liberal approach to religion under socialism would finally be taken.

Notes

1. Cardinal Kung Foundation, "Biography of Cardinal Kung." Available at: http://www.cardinalkungfoundation.org/. Accessed December 22, 2009.

2. "Albania Claims: 'First Atheist State in the World'," *Radio Free Europe Research Report* (October 9, 1967). See also "Albania Institutes Red Guard Type Movement," *Radio Free Europe Research Report* (February 13, 1967).

3. Bush, pp. 382–92.

4. Ibid., pp. 343–4.

5. Jonathan Spence, *The Search for Modern China* (New York: W.W. Norton, 1999), p. 575.

6. Robert Orr, *Religion in China* (New York: Friendship Press, 1980), pp. 123–4.

7. G. Thompson Brown, *Christianity in the Peoples Republic of China* (Atlanta: John Knox Press, 1983), pp. 125–6.

8. "Report to Fourth Congress of the Albanian Democratic Front," *Zeri i Popullit* (September 15, 1967). Cited in "Albania Claims," pp. 2–3.

9. Data from Table 1, Fenggang Yang, "The Red, Black, and Gray Markets of Religion in China," *Sociological Quarterly*, 47 (2006), p. 103.

10. M. Searle Bates, "The Church in China in the Twentieth Century," in William Richardson, ed., *China and Christian Responsibility* (New York: Maryknoll, 1968), p. 69.
11. Britt Towery, "Interview with Bishop K.H. Ting of China," *Journal of Church and State*, Vol. 32, No. 3 (1990), p. 721.
12. Thomas Harvey, *Acquainted with Grief: Wang Mingdao's Stand for the Persecuted Church in China* (Grand Rapids: Brazos Press, 2002), p. 19.
13. Ibid., p. 20.
14. Ibid., p. 45.
15. Ibid.
16. M. Searle Bates, 1968, p. 69.
17. Ibid., p. 33.
18. Bush, pp. 214–15.
19. David Aikman, *Jesus in Beijing: How Christianity is Transforming China and Changing the Global Balance of Power* (New York: Regnery, 2003), p. 54.
20. Harvey, p. 39.
21. Aikman, p. 158.
22. Cited in Ibid., fn. 2, p. 50.
23. Harvey, p. 7.
24. K.H. Ting, "The Cosmic Christ," in *A Chinese Contribution to Ecumenical Theology: Selected Writings of Bishop K. H. Ting*, eds. Janice and Philip Wickeri (Geneva: WCC Publications, 2002), p. 100.
25. K. H. Ting, "Zheng Gao Wang Mingdao," *Tian Feng* 477–8 (August 8, 1955), p. 608.
26. Harvey, p. 80.
27. Ting, "Zheng Gao Wang Mindao," p. 604.
28. Wang Mingdao, "We Because of Faith." Cited in Harvey, pp. 86–7.
29. Brown, pp. 88–9.
30. Ibid., p. 126.
31. Ibid., p. 125.
32. Ibid., p. 124.
33. Ibid., p. 125.
34. Ibid., p. 148.
35. Ibid., p. 129.
36. Cardinal Kung Foundation, "Biography of Cardinal Kung."
37. Ibid.
38. Ibid.
39. Joseph Kung, "A Rebuttal to 'Keeping the Faith' by Adam Minter," Available at: http://www.cardinalkungfoundation.org/. Accessed December 22, 2009.

40. Towery, p. 721.
41. Huimin Bhiksu, "An Inquiry into Master Xuyun's Experiences of Long-dwelling in *Samādhi*," *Chung-Hwa Buddhist Journal*, 22 (2009), pp. 45–68.
42. Jy Din Sakya, *Empty Cloud*, p. 3.
43. Holmes Welch, *Buddhism Under Mao* (Cambridge: Harvard University Press, 1972), fn. 64, p. 253.
44. Ibid., fn. 65, p. 253.
45. Jy Din Sakya, p. 9.
46. Bhiksu, 2009.
47. Welch, p. 251.
48. Welch, p. 257.
49. Ibid.
50. A. Tom Grunfeld, *The Making of Modern Tibet* (Armonk, NY: M. E. Sharpe, 1996).
51. Ch'en even explains that Chan Buddhism, due to its lack of emphasis on the tripitakas or formal status among clergy, along with its syncretism with Taoism, is sometimes not even considered a form of Buddhism by other Buddhists. Ch'en, 1964, pp. 357–64.
52. Dalai Lama, *Freedom in Exile: The Autobiography of the Dalai Lama* (New York: Harper Collins, 1990), pp. 49–81.
53. Ibid., p. 54.
54. Mary Craig, *Kundun: A Biography of the Family of the Dalai Lama* (Washington, D.C.: Counterpoint, 1997), p. 139.
55. Jetsun Pema, *Tibet: My Story* (Dorset, England: Element Books, 1997), p. 54. See also Grunfeld, 1996, p. 110–11.
56. Grunfeld, p. 111.
57. Dalai Lama, *Freedom in Exile*, p. 55
58. Union Research Institute, *Tibet 1950–1967* (Hong Kong: Union Research Institute, 1968), p. 308.
59. Melvyn Goldstein, "Introduction," in Melvyn Goldstein and Matthew Kapstein, eds., *Buddhism in Contemporary Tibet: Religious Revival and Cultural Identity* (Berkeley: University of California Press, 1998), p. 7.
60. Dalai Lama, *My Land and My People* (New York: McGraw, 1962), p. 88.
61. Grunfeld, p. 115.
62. *China Missionary Bulletin,* No. XII (May, 1960), pp. 494–5.
63. Dalai Lama, *Freedom in Exile*, pp. 86–7.
64. The Dalai Lama recounts in *Freedom in Exile* that he had been "ordered to appear before Communist officials in Beijing"; this is probably due to a lapse in his memory.

65. Grunfeld offers the strongest evidence here on the issue.

66. *Mission*, 1957.

67. "A Discussion on Translated Works on Atheism," *Renmin Ribao* (October 30, 1962). Cited in Bush, p. 33.

68. "The Correct Recognition," *Hongqi* (February 26, 1964). Cited in Bush, p. 35.

CHAPTER SEVEN

From Religious Anesthesia to Jesus Fever

Based on the statement 'religion is the opium of the people,' must we ban religion like drugs? This is no doubt unnecessary. From a Marxist perspective, spiritual opium and material opium are in principle different. To ban material opium is both necessary and possible; however, when dealing with spiritual opium, banning it by administrative orders is very absurd. Problems in the spiritual realm can only be solved by spiritual means.[1]

—*Lü Daji*

On March 16, 1979, the Beijing offices of China's Religious Affairs Bureau were reopened after having been shut down during the Cultural Revolution. While feared by many believers in China, and despised by believers outside the country praying for religious liberty for their Chinese brothers and sisters, the reopening of the RAB was a very good sign for religion in the Middle Kingdom. After the long dark winter of the Cultural Revolution, this administrative development heralded in a new era in Chinese church-state relations. Unlike some historical events which take years for their significance to be recognized, the reopening of the RAB and other related events were immediately recognized by those watching the Christian Church in China as indicative of a major shift in Chinese church-state policy. Jonathan Chao, perhaps the foremost among this group, devoted an entire issue of *China and the Church Today* to the topic, which even included a map of the RAB's facilities.

Today, the State Administration of Religious Affairs (SARA, as the RAB was renamed a few years ago) is still the primary organization charged with regulating religious affairs in China, and its policies and tone have changed even more over the past 30 years. During this period, China has gradually but steadily expanded religious liberty to the extent that today most believers in that country enjoy the basic rights of religious freedom. Although there certainly remain areas of religious expression that are highly regulated and even proscribed by the state—including unregistered "house" churches and politicized religious groups such as Falun Gong and Dongfeng Shandian—for the most part, the average Chinese citizen enjoys "the right to freedom of thought, conscience and religion...[including the] freedom to change his religion or belief, and freedom...to manifest his religion or belief in teaching, practice, worship and observance" (Article 18, Universal Declaration of Human Rights).

Millions of Chinese have taken advantage of these rights by embracing religion, often for the first time in their lives. While Buddhism remains a popular choice, as it has for more than a millennium, China is also turning to Christianity as never before and in numbers that would surprise even Matteo Ricci and Robert Morrison. This "Jesus fever," as the phenomenon is called in Chinese, probably would not have happened, however, if the Party had not pursued a theoretical reassessment of the nature of religion, superstition, and the meaning of Marx's fateful words, "religion is the opium of the people."

The Chinese Reassessment of Religion

The root of China's shift in religion policy rests squarely in the early months of 1979. Between that fateful spring and 1982, the CCP put into place a religion policy that not only reversed that of the Cultural Revolution era, but which was also more liberal than the policy which had preceded it. In many ways, the debate and resulting reforms of this period were a continuation of the debate that had played itself out in the pages of *Hongqi* during the 1963–1965 period. With the wounds of the Cultural Revolution still fresh, however, radical and repressive policy options were now off the agenda. As Chao pointed out at the time, this time around the soft-liners finally won the day.[2]

As with other realms of PRC policy,[3] the shift in managing religious affairs was integrally tied to a reassessment of relevant theoretical issues. The issues that were at the center of this reassessment were the nature of religion and superstition, the proper role of each in a socialist society, and the meaning of religious freedom. And given China's unique history, this reassessment included an important debate on the meaning of religion as "opium," with the topic being given much greater emphasis than Marx had ever intended, or could possibly have imagined.

Perhaps the first sign that change was on the horizon was the publication of an article in *Renmin Ribao* the day before the RAB opened its doors again. Published in the form of an editorial response to readers' questions, it was penned by Xiao Xianfa, the man who would be sitting in the director's chair the day the RAB resumed operations. As Jonathan Chao argued at the time, this editorial "may be taken as a statement on current Chinese Communist religious policy because of the definitive manner" in which the author addressed definitions of religion and religious freedom, and "also because it was written following the National Conference of Religious Studies" (held in Kunming, February 12–22, 1979).[4]

Published under the title *"Zongjiao he fengjian mixin"* ("Religion and Feudal Superstition"), this article would come to symbolize a new era of religious freedom in China.[5] Nevertheless, its author stated quite explicitly and up front that "all Marxists oppose religion in any form," and defined religion as "the vain and erroneous response of man to his feelings of impotence and fear in the face of natural and social forces." Xiao also repeated the standard mantra of the Marxist critique of religion, phrasing it thus: Marxism says that "religion is the opiate that lulls the spirits of people, and is the tool by which the exploiting class controls the people." *Zongjiao he fengjian mixin* was clearly no *apologia* for religion, but in critiquing religious belief, Xiao was also arguing for a more liberal policy toward believers. As he stated:

> …religion is a problem of worldview which has innumerable connections with idealism. If we want to solve this problem, we must rely on the elimination of classes and on the dissemination and development of culture and science, which are long-range tasks. Before people have thoroughly transformed their beliefs in this kind of idealism, we must recognize, permit, and respect the beliefs of the masses of people.[6]

All Chinese citizens, therefore, are "free to believe in religion, free not to believe, and free to propagate atheism," Xiao pointed out. This articulation of "freedom of religious belief" comes directly from the PRC Constitution. While the first two rights are straight out of Article 18 of the Universal Declaration on Human Rights, the last has its roots in Stalin's 1929 law on religion. Such had been the *de jure* situation since the 1954 PRC Constitution, but of course the *de facto* reality had deviated from that considerably—sometimes flagrantly.

The significance of the *Zongjiao he fengjian mixin* article is that Xiao was expanding and clarifying the vague religious freedom guarantees outlined in the PRC Constitution. Most significantly, he stated that all religions are equal, no matter how large or small, and that no religion can ever occupy a position of dominance in China. Religious believers, he stated, are "free to have friendly relations" with believers from other countries, something that had been highly suspect since the days when relations with foreign religious groups could get one labeled a "running dog of capitalism." Finally, Xiao also stated that everyone's political status was equal, no matter whether they were a believer or not. As evidence of this fact, Xiao pointed out that several Christians served on the Chinese People's Consultative Conference, including Y. T. Wu, K. H. Ting, and Zhao Fusan. Wu had been the head of the TSPM since its founding, but he would not live to see the institution reopened. Instead, it would be his protégé K. H. Ting who would take over its leadership when it opened later that year, along with that of the newly-created China Christian Council (CCC) the following year. As for Zhao, he would soon take the helm of the Institute of World Religion of the Chinese Academy of Social Science (CASS) which itself was preparing to reopen.

In commenting on Xiao's editorial, Jonathan Chao pointed out at the time that such proclamations of religious freedom were not based on any belief among the CCP that there was any "intrinsic value in religion" or that people held any "inalienable right" to religious freedom. Rather, these measures were little more than a "temporary leniency" in order to enlist the support of religious believers in the construction of Chinese socialism.[7] While that may have been the intention, these "temporary" measures have proved to be long-lived and their "leniency" has expanded greatly over the past three decades.

Xiao's article was the culmination of a very early stage of deliberations among Party leaders and religious affairs officials and can be taken as the articulation of its main conclusions. The first such meeting had been held in late December 1978 in Nanjing, while the second was the February 1979 Kunming conference mentioned above. The purpose of this second conference was to initiate a process of scholarly study on religion, thus providing an empirical basis upon which policy could be built. As such, it was very much in line with Deng's recently articulated formulation of "seeking truth from facts" (*shi shi qiu shi*), a phrase that meant that the Party should not blindly follow ideological formulations in the face of evidence that they do not work in practice. Many of those "facts" would be published in the journal of the newly-reopened Institute of World Religions, *Shijie zongjiao yanjiu* (World Religion Studies). The limits of just how far the reassessment of religion could be pushed would be tested on the pages of that journal.

Religious Opium: Narcotic or Anesthetic?

From a close reading of *Shijie zongjiao yanjiu*, particularly the years 1980–1984, one can clearly determine a few things. First, it took some time for more theoretical articles to see the light of day, most likely because, once the new era of openness had begun, it took some time for them to be researched and written. The first articles to appear, therefore, dealt mostly with religions well established in China, such as Taoism and Buddhism. A few articles began to appear pointing to religion's role in bolstering nationalism, including an interesting examination of the Ming period and Chinese nationalism. A 1984 article on Martin Luther even praised the father of the Protestant movement for breaking away from the Catholic Church and using the Bible as a tool in class struggle and national liberation.

The real debate of significance, however, was that over the meaning of religion as "the opium of the people." The hardliners of the 1963–1965 period, including Liang Hao, Yang Zhen, Bing Quan, and Xiao Fu, had argued that those who took a softer approach to religion, such Ya Hanzhang, had seriously deviated from true Marxist tenets of religion. Selected for particular attack was Ya's distinction between religion and superstition, which provided a means of distinguishing between them and thus could have allowed a sphere of greater freedom for religion.[8] While Ya and other soft-liners intended this and saw it as a positive development, hardliners recognized its implications and were intent of preventing any such "deviation." Religion is always opium, and all religions are opium, they argued.[9]

While the Cultural Revolution was now over, the debate began anew, and this time, the soft-liners pointed to that disastrous period as the outcome of an incorrect understanding of religion as opium. Lü Daji struck the first blow, arguing that Lin Biao and the Gang of Four had carried out a non-Marxist religion policy under the guise of Marxism: "They wholly denied our achievements in the area of religion over a period of 17 years, they dismissed religious organs, banned all normal religious activities, and even swept out all religious believers as demons." Through their misguided policies, they "attempted to eradicate religion overnight by totalitarian means." Such a policy was not only anti-Marxist, Lü argued, it was also counterproductive, and "provided excuses to religious reactionaries who are cloaking themselves in religion in order to provoke religious mania." While the perpetrators of the Cultural Revolution had carried out their "misconduct" under "the banner of Marxism, they are actually anti-Marxist in essence." When it came to his judgment of the events of the past and what must be done, Lü was explicit: "All facts prove that one of the disasters brought by their coercive feudal fascist political rule and fake Marxist ideological rule is that they blemished the purity of Marxism and Mao Zedong Thought," we cannot "deny their misdeed, [and] we must also protect the fundamentals of Marxism."[10]

Lü Daji was not alone in his critique and assessment. He was joined in the same issue by Zhang Ji'an, who elaborated on Marx's *Introduction to a Contribution to the Critique of Hegel's Philosophy of Right*, the ostensible topic of Lü Daji's article. In fact, however, neither article really dealt with the piece in which Marx had written the words "religion is the opium of the people." Apparently both sought to avoid scrutiny by titling their articles in such a way as to appear to be writing from an Orthodox Marxist perspective. Using a similar tactic, Zhang turned to Mao himself for his critique of the Gang of Four, pointing to his *On Coalition Government.* As Mao had argued prior to the CCP's victory,

> All religions are permitted in China's Liberated Area, in accordance with the principle of freedom of religious belief. All believers in Protestantism, Catholicism, Islam, Buddhism, and other faiths enjoy the protection of the people's government as long as they are abiding by its laws. Everyone is free to believe or not to believe; neither compulsion nor discrimination is permitted.[11]

Zhang pointed out that this policy was the basis of the CCP's religion policy after the liberation, and that "when our Party correctly carried out the policy of religious freedom, we got good results." It is, therefore, "an absolute misunderstanding to believe that the statement "religion is the opium of the people" was the theoretical basis for the extremist policies carried out during the Cultural Revolution. "The crime that the 'Gang of Four' committed," Zhang continued, was related to "their anti-revolutionary activities, and it is not necessarily related to Marxist theory on religion."[12]

Simply denouncing the Gang of Four, however, was not sufficient to form a basis for the future course of CCP policy on religion. While the Cultural Revolution had been a deviation, and early CCP policy had been correct, the issue of moving beyond even that period still needed to be addressed. The crux of the matter was over the meaning of "opium" in Marx's famous phrase. In the matter of a paragraph, Lü practically ended a debate that had been dragging on for two decades. Just because Marx said "religion is the opium of the people," Lü asked, "must we ban religion like drugs? This is no doubt unnecessary." Lü argued that "spiritual opium and material opium are principally different," and "to ban material opium is both necessary and possible; however, to deal with spiritual opium, banning it by administrative orders is very absurd." Rather, "problems in the spiritual realm can only be solved by spiritual means."[13]

Zhang went a step further, however, not only disassociating religious opium from narcotics, but classifying it as a different drug entirely: "Our ultimate goal in studying religion is to help the masses recognize the nature of religion and its function as an anesthetic." While narcotics have no medicinal value, of course, anesthetics are necessary to alleviate pain during difficult procedures. What could be more painful than the development of socialism? Zhang, therefore, was reframing the whole idea of what opium meant as expressed by Marx. Lü would carry this point a step further the following year in an article in which he quoted Lenin (probably based upon an incorrect translation) as referring to religion as an anesthetic.[14] With religion now classified as an anesthetic rather than a narcotic, Zhang called for it to be treated more leniently. If religion is a false consciousness, then treat it as such, he wrote. Policies should be aimed at "awakening the masses addicted to the 'dream of religion'," only then can the Party "can get rid of man's spiritual chains and build 'heaven' in the real world."[15] And while atheist propaganda is critical in order to carry out such work, "attempting to eradicate religion [by force] will only arouse people's interests toward religion, and is the best way to prevent religion from demise."[16]

Of course, China's closing of the case on the Cultural Revolution and taking a new direction in managing religious affairs was influenced by numerous factors, certainly including many closed-door meetings among the Party's senior cadre. But in these articles, Lü and Zhang had opened up a public discussion on the issue that would play itself out over several years, and they had established the main lines of argumentation: the Gang of Four policy had been wrong, their approach was not truly Marxist, and a more liberal approach was necessary and authentically in line with Marxism, Leninism, and Mao Zedong Thought.

China's Long March to Religious Liberty

In framing the debate, Lü and Zhang not only established a break with the past, they also provided a footing for a more liberal policy toward religion, a footing that could be seen as orthodox from a Marxist standpoint, and thus could deflect criticism from the left. That policy, however, remained to be written. It soon took shape, however, in the form of the 1982 PRC Constitution and the Party's Document 19. The Constitution's religious freedom provision was quite simple, stating in Article 36 that "citizens of the People's Republic of China enjoy freedom of religious belief."

The more specific articulation of Chinese religion policy was laid out by the Party in Document 19, issued by the Central Committee of the CCP on March 31, 1982. Throughout, freedom of religious belief is defined essentially in terms of freedom of conscience, and public religious expression is either limited or proscribed, including the freedom of propagation, a right atheists enjoy but believers do not. In general, the rights to freedom of religion expressed in the 1982 PRC Constitution and Document 19 do not include the right to express one's religious convictions in the public sphere. Religion is understood as a private matter and must remain as such, with the influence of believers on society something that should be prevented. Individuals are free to conduct religious activities so long as they do so under the supervision of the patriotic religious associations, and therefore under the state's watchful eye. Such religious activities are considered "normal," while all activities conducted by believers outside the patriotic associations are considered "abnormal" or "illegal" religious activities, and thus subject to restriction and proscription. This includes house churches, Bible study groups, itinerant preaching, and the unofficial publication of Bibles; these activities are violations of the law, and as such those who engage in them are subject to penalties under China's criminal law code.

As the Party's central document concerning religion, Document 19 was distributed to county-level Party secretaries, and the TSPM held an extended Executive Committee meeting in Beijing in September 1982 to study it.[17] Afterwards, the TSPM and the CCC, in conjunction with local RAB offices, began the implementation of its provisions, particularly the requirement that all religious activities take place within the patriotic associations. They urged the house churches to join the TSPM, and while a few did join, the majority preferred to retain their independence and face the consequences. These became somewhat severe during the period 1983–1984, but they soon relaxed again. This shift was probably due to the economic reforms that had been recently launched, which resulted in a general relaxation of social control, in the religious sphere as well as the economic arena. In fact, quite a few house church leaders who had been arrested during the 1983–1984 crackdown were released or found their sentences significantly reduced.[18] Ironically, it was during this phase of relaxation that several more house churches joined the TSPM, though now they did so by simply formally joining and paying their dues, but all the while retaining their autonomy and carrying on their activities just as before.

Overall, the 1980s were a period of revival for religious life in China. While many people who were taking advantage of the more open religious climate by professing a religious faith had been "atheists" during the Cultural Revolution, the only thing that had probably changed was their willingness to admit their faith. Others, however, particularly the younger generation, were coming to faith for the first time. Together, their numbers were swelling rapidly. Halfway through the decade, the TSPM had some 3 million members meeting in 4,000 registered churches.[19] By 1988 the number of open TSPM churches had grown to around 6,500, of which 2,700 were newly built, and that rate of expansion could not keep pace with the number of believers.[20] At same time, some 50 million believers with at least 200,000 meeting places remained outside the TSPM structure.[21] They would not prove to be the real threat to China's stability, however, a threat that almost toppled China's 50-year-old regime.

The Year of Miracles

The year 1989 has been described as *annus mirabilis*, a year of miracles, a time when even "the most quixotic optimists proved too cautious."[22] In April of that year, thousands of students began to gather in Tiananmen Square in Beijing to call upon the Chinese government to implement democratic reforms. By mid-May, their numbers had swelled to over a quarter of a million. Similar demonstrations were also underway throughout Eastern Europe, and by late August East Germans picnicking along the Austrian border began to cross over to freedom in the West. Within weeks, the Berlin Wall was pulled down, followed quickly by student demonstrations in Prague and culminating in the overthrow of Communist rule in Romania on Christmas Day. By the end of the year, the Communist regimes of Eastern Europe had fallen, and the winds of change were blowing east into the Soviet Union itself.

While the year 1989 may have appeared as a "year of miracles" to opposition forces in the Communist world and observers in the West, it was a year of fear for Communist leaders in Beijing. The thousands of demonstrators that had gathered in Tiananmen Square throughout April and May of that year were only dispersed through force, their demands remaining unmet, and their actions being labeled "counterrevolutionary." The troops that had stormed the city on June 4 to reestablish order did so at the cost of around 1,000 lives and another 10,000 persons injured.

We do not know how many of the demonstrators at Tiananmen were believers, but they certainly had the sympathy of many in the Church. As a matter of fact, many of the staff and students of the Nanjing Theological Seminary—headed by TSPM and CCC chairman K. H. Ting—had themselves marched in support of the democracy movement. We also know that Ting, who had taken a visibly pro-reformist stance prior to the demonstrations, himself had come out in support of the students and the demonstrators. On May 18 he issued a statement supporting the "patriotic activities" of the students, even calling on the State Council to enter into a dialogue with them. "I am glad that Christians are making their presence felt in these demonstrations," he said, "I am very glad that the students in the Nanjing Theological Seminary are taking an active part."[23] Though later this support would lead to an attempt to purge Ting, he was apparently too strong for his detractors and emerged unscathed.

The Tiananmen uprising lead the government to reconsider religion policy, just as it did with other policy realms at the time, including economics and politics. Between the fall of 1989 and the following summer, state organs concerned with religion held numerous meetings to discuss the policy implications of this social catastrophe. The most important of these were three conferences held in Beijing, including a seminar organized by the Chinese Academy of Social Science (CASS) and a meeting at Zhongnanhai between Jiang Zemin and the five leaders of China's national religious organizations. At the briefing, Jiang emphasized the balance between limited tolerance of religious activities that conformed to Party policy and the repression of those that did not.[24]

The fruit of these efforts was a new series of practical measures and policy directives, foremost among them being Document 6, "Notice on Further Tackling Certain Problems of Religious Work." Issued by the CCP Central Committee and State Council in February 1991, it is a policy reformulation that addresses many of the concerns expressed at the meetings over the two preceding years. It focused heavily on the need for "vigilance against hostile foreign forces" and warned officials and Party members to be "on the lookout" for illegal activities being carried out "under the cloak of religion."[25] The essential difference between Document 19 and the new Document 6 was the strong emphasis placed on control and management of religious groups. Whereas, when issued in 1982, Document 19 had clearly represented a shift toward increased tolerance of believers, Document 6 was a move in the other direction, imposing stricter controls on religious affairs, especially unregistered religious activities. Illegal religious organizations were targeted for eliminated, and those found to be in violation of the policy were to be penalized according to criminal law.[26]

Avoiding Peaceful Evolution

An underlying theme present in Document 6 are the "three-antis," that is, anti-infiltration, anti-subversion, and anti-peaceful evolution (*heping yanbian*). While clearly rooted in CCP interpretations of Marxist thought and Party policy over the previous 40 years, each was also seen as influential in the collapse of Communism in Eastern Europe, which was at this time increasingly worrying China's Communist leaders. In fact, infiltration and subversion are essentially tactical components of the strategy of "peaceful evolution." While the former two terms are commonplace, the latter is a code word in China for a purposeful strategy Western nations use to pressure socialist states to "evolve" (read: collapse), including the use of economic incentives and the promotion of human rights.[27] Peaceful evolution was seen by many in China as at the center of the collapse of Communism in Eastern Europe and later the Soviet Union.[28] In regard to Czechoslovakia and East Germany in particular, the social turmoil in these satellite states was seen as having its roots in "the West's peaceful evolution strategy" and the "antisocialist activities" of opposition forces and the Roman Catholic Church.[29]

This is how the events in Eastern Europe came to serve as a warning sign to China's leaders. The West's strategy of peaceful evolution was as much directed against China as it was against the Communist regimes of Europe. The role of the churches in tearing down Communist rule in Eastern Europe, therefore, put CCP leaders on alert. In that process, the Catholic Church had been identified—both in the West as well as in China—as a key player in the regime transitions there. In particular, Chinese leaders identified the Catholic Church as having played an important role in the overthrow of Poland's regime. As Ramet summarizes this line of thought, "the CCP concluded that religious organizations, particularly the Catholic Church, had played a role in destabilizing the communist systems of Eastern Europe, and it was determined to take the necessary steps to prevent the same thing from happening in China."[30]

Within weeks of the issuing of Document 6, another major event unfolded, the August 1991 attempted coup in the Soviet Union. If Chinese leaders could take solace in the fact that the regimes of Eastern Europe were "puppet" regimes and not legitimate Communist states like China, the impending collapse of the USSR quickly destroyed any such illusions. The CCP quickly began to think very seriously about what the collapse of Communism in the USSR would mean for China. In an internal document attributed to the Ideology and Theory Department of the *China Youth Daily*, entitled "Realistic Responses and Strategic Choices for China after the Soviet Coup," a group of party and government officials active in consulting for the post-Tiananmen leadership explored the changing situation and what it meant for China.[31] Four of the article's seven points focus explicitly on the implications of the collapse of Communism in the Soviet Union for the future of Communist rule in China. Unlike the role of the Catholic Church in Poland, however, only partial responsibility was placed on the Russian Orthodox Church, which they maintained was a "conservative religion that hinders reform," but no mention was made of the church's direct role in the coup, or the role of peaceful evolution (quite accurately, I might add).

But the coup was just a dress rehearsal for the collapse of the Soviet Union, and once it came tumbling down without a whimper in December of that year, the CCP had to face the fact that it was a dying breed. Taken together, the events in Eastern Europe and the Soviet Union between 1989 and 1991 had a tremendous impact on China, and its impact on religious affairs is perhaps the most clear example of this, with many internal policies and official reports stating explicitly that China must "manage" correctly religious affairs if it is to avoid the sort of collapse that occurred in Eastern Europe and the Soviet Union. One such document is from the RAB entitled "China's Current Religious Question: Once Again an Inquiry into the Five Characteristics of Religion."[32] In this internal (*neibu*) document, RAB director Ye Xiaowen examined the disintegrative role religion played in the Communist states of Eastern Europe:

> The disintegration of the Soviet Union and the dramatic change in Eastern Europe resulted from their domestic political and economic failures and the sharpening of social contradictions there, including the failure of their policy toward religion over the long term that resulted in the alienation of religious believers. Religion became a weapon in the hands of the dissidents for inciting the masses and creating political disturbances, thus hastening the collapse of the Soviet and East European communist parties.[33]

The role played by religion, according to Ye, was two-pronged. On the one hand, he argued that religious revival is often coupled with conflict and war: "When there is national oppression...religion plays the role of a sacred banner under which the nation fights national oppression and serves as an important tie for national unity."[34] Additionally, foreign religious organizations are seen as attempting to infiltrate the Chinese system and bring about a peaceful evolution. As Ye explained, "Today, with the support of the Vatican, the Catholic underground has few followers in China but considerable capabilities...The various departments must coordinate their efforts and fight a prolonged general defensive war against infiltration by hostile foreign religious forces."[35]

Luo Shuze, in an internal document published under the auspices of the theoretical journal of the CCP (*Qiushi*), elaborates on this threat. China must remain "vigilant against hostile international forces using religion to try to Westernize and divide" the country.[36] As Luo argues, since the 1980s, "one of their strategies for subverting socialist countries has been the cultivation of religious forces in those countries and the use of religion as their tie with the underground political forces." In employing such a strategy, Western forces hope "to divide" China and "to achieve pluralistic political beliefs through pluralistic religious beliefs."[37] In "the name of religion," Western forces "engage in activities designed to divide the nationalities" as they attempt "to achieve the objectives of undermining national unity, subverting the socialist system, and splitting the great motherland."[38]

The argument that the CCP tightened its religion policy at this time due to their understanding of the role religion played in the collapse of Communism in Eastern Europe and the Soviet Union is not a commonly-accepted position. Hardly any commentators on China's religious affairs make mention of it. Let me quote further from this same document, therefore, where Luo makes the effect explicit:

> We need to learn from the lessons of the disintegration of the Soviet Union and the precipitous changes in Eastern Europe. One of these lessons is the lowering of vigilance against Western infiltration by the use of religion. As a result of the errors of the former socialist countries in the Soviet Union and Eastern Europe in their handling of the religious question, religion became an instrument in the hands of the political dissidents for stirring up trouble when the domestic politics and economy became mired in trouble and all kinds of social contradictions sharpened. That hastened the downfall of the Soviet and East European communist parties.[39]

These policy prescriptions quickly made their way onto the desks of local level bureaucrats responsible for implementing religious policy. An excellent example of this is a secret memorandum from the Tongxiang Municipal Public Security Bureau which instructs RAB offices at the village and township levels about strategies for curbing illegal religious activities.[40] The justification for issuing this memorandum was that "infiltration and subversive activities on the part of outside hostile forces that use religion as a means to Westernize and divide our country have increased." These "outside forces" are "energetically fostering anti-government forces in an attempt to 'gospelize' China, trying vainly to bring about in China the kind of evolution [i.e., peaceful evolution] that is taking place in Eastern Europe and the former Soviet Union."[41] Such a view on the role of religion in the collapse of Communism helps explain China's tightening of control and regulation of religious activities during this era.

Chinese leaders learned from the East European example that the church and other civil society actors can play important roles in tearing down

Communism. They did more than identify this as a factor, however—they also sought to implement policies that they hoped would prevent a similar occurrence in China.[42] One of the most important results of this process was a retightening of the country's religious policy. This retightening was not to be overly severe, however, nor did it last long. While connections with foreigners had to cease or be hidden, and house churches faced increased pressure to register, as the 1990s progressed things more or less returned to "normal," meaning relatively free for most believers. In that environment, religion continued to make inroads among a population becoming increasingly disillusioned with Communism.

Qigong, Falun Gong, and China's Gray Market of Religion

The events in Eastern Europe were not the only thing that made the CCP uneasy in the early 1990s. They were also increasingly disturbed by the rapid growth of religion in their own country, including the rise of Islam in Xinjiang and Gansu, the flowering of indigenous sects in various parts of the country, and the unprecedented spread of Christianity in the southeastern provinces. It was, of course, the country's more liberal religion policy that had facilitated the rise and proliferation of these groups. Rather than peaceful evolution threatening China's stability, with the Catholic Church fomenting revolution or Tibetan separatists engaging in suicide bombing, the greatest threats to China's stability were probably indigenous forms of belief that had only recently organized and were, in the eyes of party leaders at least, quickly threatening the regime.

The foremost among them were *qigong* groups, hybrid spiritual-health groups that practice breathing exercises in an attempt to maintain health, relieve stress, and develop spiritual awareness.[43] Having their roots in Buddhist qigong practices and Taoist alchemy, many practitioners believe their exercises can not only heal them of diseases but also allow them to cultivate supernatural abilities, including the power to levitate. Top party ideologues such as Yu Guangyuan have voiced strong criticisms of these supposed paranormal abilities (*teyi gongneng*) and called for their restriction.[44]

Between 1979 and 1999, thousands of qigong groups emerged throughout China with an untold number of practitioners, though certainly numbering in the hundreds of thousands (Yang provides a list of 17 "widespread, major" qigong groups that emerged between 1979 and 1992).[45] Some of the large qigong groups established "cultivation and education bases" (*xiulian peixun jidi*) and "research centers" (*yanjiu zhongxin*) with magnificent buildings, and organized hundreds or thousands of "cultivation points" (*liangong dian*), most of which were in public parks or streets. As Yang points out, the largest and most effective of these became powerful economic enterprises with efficient organization and enthusiastic cadres.[46]

Many qigong groups also adopted scientific terminology, insisting that they were related to science instead of religion. Indeed, Taoist alchemy is an early form of science, and Traditional Chinese Medicine is increasingly recognized as a legitimate medical practice. In fact, it was some top-ranked scientists holding high-level political positions who helped qigong take off in the 1980s.[47] But their purpose in presenting themselves as scientific was to avoid falling under religious affair regulations, however, beginning in about 1990, some qigong masters began to face prosecution and even jail time for their illegal practices.[48] Some qigong groups then decided to seek registration as a religious group, such as Falun Gong, which tried unsuccessfully to join the Chinese Buddhist Association.

When they formed in 1992, Falun Gong looked like just another group of qigong practitioners. As they grew rapidly, however, Chinese authorities became concerned. By the mid-1990s, they had evolved into a well-organized religious group, certainly meeting the criteria of a new religious movement (NRM), though apparently many of its practitioners did not consider or perhaps realize that their activity was religious in any sense. Nevertheless, the group seemed to pose no threat to the powerful PRC. The government changed its opinion on April 25, 1999, however, when 10,000 Falun Gong members quietly and in an orderly fashion assembled outside Zhongnanhai. By late afternoon, the demonstrators had dispersed as quickly and quietly as they had assembled early that spring morning. The purpose of this assembly was to demand official legalization of their group. They carried no signs, shouted no slogans, only stood before the residence and offices of the senior CCP leadership and meditated. According to Li Hongzhi, the leader of Falun Gong, their purpose was not political. "We do not involve ourselves in politics and we abide by the laws of the country," Li said shortly afterwards.[49] According to members of the group, however, Li was prepared to use his supernatural abilities to levitate over the compound and ultimately assume control of the government. Their explanation for why that didn't happen is, according to his followers, that he changed his mind.[50]

For almost 2 months, China was ominously quiet about the whole incident. Then on June 20, 1999, an article appeared in *Renmin Ribao* which, although not mentioning Falun Gong by name, expressed the necessity of opposing superstition and pseudo-science.[51] In keeping with the Party line on religion, the article advocated promoting a scientific worldview in order to achieve development and modernization, and laid out the proper behavior for Party members and officials, that is, they should not be involved in any such "cults". The government was apparently concerned about widespread Falun Gong membership among officials and Party members.[52] Spokespersons for Falun Gong quickly protested the government's use of the label "cult," while Li further declared that he would "not take Falun Gong practitioners to confront" the government.[53] Mass protests then erupted in several cities against the media criticism of the group.

Then 2 months later, now nearly 3 months after the Falun Gong's demonstration of strength outside Zhongnanhai, public security officers quietly moved against the group and just after midnight on July 20, they rounded up key leaders and practitioners. The preceding period had been used to make all the necessary preparations, and now the government quickly confiscated and destroyed Falun Gong materials, tapes, and books, and issued a steady stream of invective against the group and its leader in the media. Meanwhile, massive demonstrations in some 30 cities followed; in cities such as Beijing and Shanghai the public security officers detained so many people that they had to be held in sports stadiums.

The CCP now declared Falun Gong an "evil cult" (*xie jiao*) and on July 23 stated that the April 25 Falun Gong demonstration had been "the most serious political incident" in China since the Tiananmen incident.[54] In quick succession, Zhong Gong, Xiang Gong, and other large qigong groups were also labeled "evil cults" and banned, their key leaders prosecuted, properties confiscated, and practices prohibited. All qigong groups were then disbanded or deregistered, their practices considered illegal (though by 2004 certain groups were beginning to make a comeback). Since Falun Gong is not considered a religion, it is not protected by China's legal guarantees of religious freedom. As Yang notes, the "practice of qigong in the park in the morning, once a universal scene all over China," quickly disappeared.[55]

In October 1999 special additional measures were enacted by the NPC Standing Committee outlawing heretical sects and activities. The measures attacked activities that "under the guise of religion, qigong or another name disrupt social order or harm the people's lives, financial security and economic development."[56] Falun Gong is allegedly a danger to China's social and political stability (and CCP power), both of which have eroded substantially in the face of economic problems, such as urban unemployment, income disparities, and rural poverty. The government maintains that they are also a threat to the Chinese people themselves. While the practices themselves are not dangerous (though perhaps some are strenuous), Li Hongzhi's insistence that members not take medicine or use modern doctors, but use qigong healing practices instead, allegedly resulted in 1,400 deaths by the time of the crackdown.[57]

In December 2001 a National Work Conference on Religious Affairs was held with the original intention of discussing the anti-Falun Gong campaign, but by the time it was held such a strong consensus against Falun Gong had emerged that there was little left to discuss. Instead, the conference turned into an opportunity to consider further ways of adapting religion to socialist society. Jiang Zemin, who was nearing his term as leader, even argued that the Party and state could "guide" religion to meet the needs of socialism. He further encouraged officials to continue to stick to policies on religious freedom, refrain from using administrative force to eliminate religion, and accept that religious belief would be an integral part of Chinese society for the foreseeable future.[58]

What was planned as a meeting to discuss developments regarding the violent repression of a religious group, therefore, resulted in the Party recommitting itself to religious freedom, albeit within the established framework of the government-sanctioned "patriotic" religious associations. But as Yang points out, to the extent that legal religious groups are restricted and illegal groups are suppressed, a "gray" market of religious providers will emerge to meet the needs of believers. In such a gray market, "individuals resort to informal religious practices and spiritual alternatives" and engage in religious activities that are illegally performed by registered religious groups, or in religious activities performed by legally registered secular entities.[59] He also argues that the gray market provides a fertile ground for NRMs and is difficult to regulate and impossible to enforce, given its large size and volatile nature in heavily-regulated societies like China.[60]

Of course, regulating any state of religious affairs in a country as large as China is nearly impossible, and if the government deregulated the religious market overnight, the religious economy would become immediately flooded with all sorts of purveyors of various religious and pseudo-religious offerings. Apparently such a move is not a viable option to even the most liberal-minded Chinese official. But perhaps the gray market is the answer to China's festering religious freedom problem. If the state continues to allow the gray market to expand, the realm of religious freedom will be opened. If the state identifies dangerous actors in the gray market of religion (such as exist in most any society, including child molestation by clergy, violent acts carried out in the name of religion, etc.) they can respond as appropriate, just as they can permit other gray groups to flourish insofar as they prove useful (or at least not dangerous) to society. This is not the ideal way to extend religious liberty, of course, but as Deng himself said, "it doesn't matter if the cat is black or white, as long as it catches mice."

Religion in China Today: Patriotic, Political, or Intolerant?

As just discussed, China's process of religious liberalization has certainly seen its share of ups and downs over the past three decades, but it is beyond dispute that the system as a whole has been greatly liberalized over the course of China's period of *gaige kaifang* (reform and opening). Whereas meeting as a group of believers to read the Bible was a dangerous proposition under Mao, an ambitious group of house church Christians in Shanxi Province recently almost got away with constructing a huge eight-story mega-church that could serve nearly 50,000 worshippers. While in the end the Chinese government did intervene and shut it down for the group's failure to obtain the proper building permits, the penalty they will pay for such a blatant act is far from what it would have been decades ago. Indeed, such a construction project would have been stopped at the first shovel full of dirt.

Over the past few years in particular, the Chinese government has been extending a greater sphere of activity to house churches, even allowing a conference on the rise of house churches to be held in Beijing in the fall of 2009. While Chinese authorities seem to be growing more tolerant of house churches quietly renting facilities for their services in the name of ambiguous or even fraudulent entities, apparently constructing a monstrous sanctuary—even in far off Shanxi—could not go unanswered. In a country like China, recovering from decades of authoritarian rule, one must measure liberalization by the type of intervention the state takes into the realm of religion, not by whether or not it intervenes in the first place.

As liberalization progresses, religious belief and practice are booming. Churches and other religious institutions are reopening all over China, and their attendance is beginning to swell. As these joint processes of political liberalization and religious revival continue, the political efficacy of China's believers will become increasingly significant. The problem is, we don't know what this will mean. Aikman has suggested that by 2050 China will be "Christianized," that is, a society in which a quarter or more of the population professes Christianity. Jenkins, whose work on the global spread of Christianity, reaches a similar conclusion. But for Aikman, a Christianized China will be a China that engages in politics and international relations quite differently from the way it does today.

While we have no way of knowing how large China's Christian population will be in the next quarter century, or what the implications of such a development would be, there are several other significant questions that are more amenable to empirical analysis. For example, will Chinese Christians become a leading force in the liberalization process, or will they remain docile and other-worldly focused? After years of persecution, will they exhibit tolerance to others, regardless of their faith preference? And finally, how will they view the proper relationship between church and state? While certainly not the last word on the issue, the J. M. Dawson Institute of Church-State Studies has been conducting a survey of attitudes toward religion, politics, and tolerance that can shed significant light on these issues.[61]

Politically Apathetic or Efficacious?

Only recently have we begun to get a real sense of what China's religious revival looks like, and we still know precious little about what Chinese themselves feel about church-state issues. Quite a bit of anecdotal evidence suggests that they are politically apathetic. Are China's believers today apathetic simply because at this point that is the safest course of action? If we mean by apathetic that they do not care at all regarding state policies, then hardly any believers in China can be categorized as such, for almost all wish freedom to practice their faith. One should be careful not to fall victim to the idea of the political apathy of Chinese believers, however, given the linkage of the theological currents among Chinese believers and the nature of the contemporary regime. Moreover, world historical experience—from Asia as much as from other parts of the globe—indicates that religion is often connected with political, economic, and social liberalization, if not outright revolution. Religious attitudes are related historically and cross-nationally with a variety of other attitudes, from the embracing of human rights to tolerance for others of different faiths and even democracy. Of course, religious convictions are also just as often associated with intolerance, extremism, and violence.

As far as the Chinese government is concerned, the dominant position is that religion is not politically apathetic, or apolitical, but rather directly related to issues of political instability. As Ye Xiaowen, long-time director of SARA who was replaced last year, commented, "religious leaders always manipulate and control believers to challenge political leaders," using religion to penetrate into the political realm and promote separatism. "The Protestant meeting pots [sic], Catholic underground forces, Tibetan separatist organizations," and separatist forces in Xinjiang are "all sources of religious problems in China."[62]

Outside the Party itself, certain scholars sympathetic to the official position agree with such sentiments. As Gong and Sun phrase it, "the religious problem is not only a spiritual problem, but also a huge socio-political problem," they argue, further pointing out that the religion question is "a hot-button issue" the world over.[63] Others, like Fang Wen, point to a "believ-ers-citizen paradox," which he argues is "a very urgent" issue in China's social transformation and can "become a serious threat to nation-building." For Fang, the "believers-citizen paradox" relates to the "extreme religious identity" of some believers, particularly those who identify or sympathize with the Tibetan and Xinjiang independence movements.[64]

This latter position illustrates the close connection between religious and ethnic identity in China, particularly in regard to Tibetan Buddhists and the Muslim Uyghurs of Xinjiang. But not only do long-held anti-Christian sentiments persist as well, as clearly exemplified by Ye Xiaowen's assessment above, but Christians seem to be becoming increasingly politically con-scious. The traditional line from the house churches, as stated in the *Jiating Jiaohui Xinyang Gaobai*, "We are against the unification and adulteration of church and state. We are against the church's dependence on foreign pow-ers to develop itself. We are against the church's participation in activities which will undermine the integrity of the country and the unity of ethnic groups."[65] Such a position shows great deference to the Chinese party-state that not all that long ago was calling for the eradication of religion.

Similar attitudes are expressed in a document published after the *Jiating Jiaohui Xinyang Gaobai*, where it was stated that the members of the house churches pledge to "uphold the Constitution of the People's Republic of China, as well as the leaders and the government ordained by God." This document even refers to its own persecution, though not in order to blame the government for its actions. "Although we are usually misunderstood and repressed by the government," they write, "we do not hold any anti-government attitudes or activities." Such a position was arrived at by the house churches after four large house churches were labeled as "evil cults" by the Chinese government in 1996, with the situation resolved a few years later once a group of house church leaders convinced the government that they should not be viewed in such a way. Following this episode, their plea was simply that China's leaders would "have more wisdom and skill to gov-ern the state, understand the benefit of the Gospel to the people, and protect religious freedom according to the Constitution."[66] Hardly apathy, but not very politically efficacious, either.

One need not look far for bolder statements calling for Christians to engage the political realm. As the *Jidutu Weiquan Shouce* states, "church-state separation does not mean that Christians, clergy, and churches cannot participate in public political activities." As this important tract makes clear, while a political struggle on the part of the church is futile, "indifference or taking an apolitical position actually supports the injustices of the status quo." It is a "Christian's duty," therefore, "to engage in political delibera- tion and protest," they argue.[67] These are rather strong words coming from a statement that originated from a pastoral conference.

Li Fan has recently pointed out that two eras in the political orientation of the Chinese house churches can be discerned by comparing statements from the 1990s with more recent ones. Fan suggests that the earlier, more apolitical, statements were made in order to avoid governmental repres- sion and only sought protection for religious freedom.[68] "The publication of the *Christian Handbook for Rights Protection*," however, Li points out, "shows a significant change": the house church has begun to call for greater protection of rights and now seeks to redefine the relationship between Christianity and Chinese political development, a change which, Fan sug- gests, "indicates that the house church has become a powerful social insti- tution" which can fight for its own interests. Such a transformation means that the house church "will necessarily influence Chinese politics" in the coming years.

In this same article and a more recent paper, Li has also argued that the house church may positively impact Chinese democratization.[69] Christianity—especially Protestantism—will "directly influence China's democratization," Li states. "Their approach," he adds, "is one of directly participating as a main force in the movement for rights protection." To Li, the development of Christianity in China is compatible with world culture and also positive for China's future.

Chinese Attitudes on God and Religion

As we mentioned above, it has only been quite recently that scholars have begun to get a real sense of what China's religious revival looks like, while we know even less about Chinese attitudes toward church-state issues. A quantum leap forward in this regard was made with Baylor's Empirical Study of Values in China (ESVC) survey, on which I was a co-principal investigator. That survey gave us insight into the nature of belief in China today and its social correlates, though it is not without its shortcomings and limitations.[70] Among its most important findings is that the percentage of Christians in China today may only be 2.5 percent of the population. The numbers suggested by some others, including Liu Peng, David Aikman, and the *World Religion Database*, far exceeds this estimate, though it is close to the official estimate of the Chinese government. Liu Peng puts the number at

50 million house church Christians, and an additional 16 million members of the Three-Self Patriotic Movement churches, for a total of 66 million Christians in China.[71] At the extreme high end, the *World Religion Database* puts the percentage of Christians in China at 7.76 percent, or a just above 100 million, but this number is most certainly an overestimation.[72]

Perhaps just as interesting is the finding that, although 58 percent of those interviewed in the ESVC survey responded that they did not believe in such a thing as "god," 9 percent said they did, even though they themselves were not believers. Of course, such a question reflects Christian beliefs more accurately than beliefs such as Buddhism and Taoism, in which belief in a personal god is non-existent. Responses to more general questions, however, such as whether or not religion is important in one's life, offer great insight into the religious beliefs of people of all different faith traditions. Of those surveyed, 9 percent responded that religious belief was somewhat important in their life, while nearly 3 percent (2.7) responded that religion was very important. To the vast majority of Chinese, however, religious belief was not important, with 19.8 percent responding that is was somewhat unimportant, while 62.5 percent said it was not important at all.

One set of questions from the ESVC survey that lends some truly unique insight into Chinese beliefs on religion relates to the "foreignness" or appropriateness of Christianity to China and the traditional religions of China (see Table 7.1). Despite some rather strong anti-Christian attitudes (and policies) throughout China's history, only a quarter of those surveyed felt that Christianity, as a Western religion, is not suitable for the Chinese people, while nearly 44 percent explicitly disagreed with such a statement. Likewise, roughly the same number of people thought that the "three teachings" (i.e., Buddhism, Taoism, and Confucianism) were best suited to the Chinese people, while 42.6 percent disagreed. These responses were almost identical to those received when asked specifically whether Confucianism is best suited to the Chinese people, even though nearly 54 percent felt that Confucianism was not even a religion.

Table 7.1 Chinese Attitudes Toward Religion

	Agree	Disagree	Don't Know
Christianity is a Western religion and not suitable for Chinese	24.6	43.8	29.5
Is Confucianism a religion?	18.2	53.8	26.9
The "three teachings" are best suited for the Chinese people	23.7	42.6	31.4

Chinese Attitudes on Church-State Relations

The data made available from the ESVC survey continues to yield great insights into religious belief and values in China today, but it sheds very little light on issues more directly related to church and state. One survey that does offer such insight, however, is the Pushi Institute's survey of Chinese Religion and Harmonious Society, directed by Liu Peng of the Chinese Academy of Social Science and sanctioned by the Center of Development and Research of the State Council of the PRC. The sample for this survey was quite excellent, drawing upon 30 different sampling points from nine provinces. Although conducted in 2007–2008, the results have not yet been published.[73] The data from this innovative survey will contribute to our knowledge of church-state relations in China unlike any previous study, as even the early findings already offered by Liu illustrate.

Among these findings, one of the most interesting is that believers favor independence for religious organizations, with 57.9 percent of Protestants and 50 percent of believers of other traditions (Catholicism, Buddhism, Islam, etc.) responding that religious organizations should be in charge of religious affairs in China, rather than the law or the government. Protestants, as a matter of fact, were much more likely to be *against* the state's regulation of religion in this regard, with only 15.8 percent favoring such an arrangement, whereas 34.6 percent of other believers supported governmental regulation of religious affairs. Protestants were more supportive of the law and the courts providing such regulatory functions, however, with 26.3 percent responding thusly, whereas only 15.5 percent of other believers felt similarly. We can thus see that most believers want religious affairs to remain independent of government control, and that they do not even trust the rule of law, given the lack of juridical independence in China.[74] And in comparison with other religions, Protestants are more skeptical of governmental control, a fact that could pose a great challenge to China's policy of intervening in religious affairs in the name of public administration.

During the summer of 2009 the Dawson Institute began to run a new, small-sample survey of church-state issues in China. As this book was going to press, we had only completed the first wave of the survey, totaling 401 respondents from ten different sampling points chosen from among the five regions of Guangzhou, Zhejiang, Wuhan, Liaoning, and Beijing. Though the data must be analyzed with caution given the sample with which we are working, the preliminary results are quite interesting and can be used to further refine future survey research on similar issues in China. While it is not necessarily representative of all of China's diversity, it does provide a pretty accurate representation of the Chinese heartland, from the north of the country to the south, and from the eastern coastline into the central plains. Analysis of the responses indicates that our sample somewhat over-represents urban areas and those with a higher-education. In fact, 41.6 percent of respondents had some university education or had completed college, while another 31.4 percent had attended graduate school. Only 20 percent had a high school education or less.

The sample may also somewhat over-represent females, though probably not by much. Of those who identified their gender, 53.9 percent identified themselves as male, while 46.1 percent were female. In fact, the survey is probably over-represented by females, since 24.2 percent did not identify their gender, and the surveyors observed that the majority of those who failed to give their gender were in fact female. In terms of the ages of the respondents, China's younger generation was slightly over-sampled, with slightly more than half of the sample (52 percent) between the ages of 18–25, with 37 percent of respondents between the ages 26–40, and another 10 percent over 40 years of age. One of the primary reasons for such an age distribution among our respondents was the unwillingness of many of the older generation to take part in the survey. It is not simply due to incorrect sampling methods, therefore, but to a very skewed response rate.

While this sample does not mirror the general population, which is more evenly distributed across the various age ranges, there is a benefit to over-sampling China's youth; they have been less impacted by the anti-religious propaganda of the PRC state and therefore their attitudes are more representative of Chinese attitudes on religion and politics today, as opposed to during the Mao or even Deng eras. And by over-sampling among China's better-educated population, we get a picture of the attitudes and beliefs of China's middle class and socially-mobile members, the social groupings known for being the most active in participating in—and leading—social movements for political change.[75]

Governmental Support of Religion in China

Under a system of church-state separation, the success and failure of religious organizations is in the hands of the people, not the state. That is, which religious groups will form, establish themselves, and survive is determined by the actions of those involved, including their financial contributions to help pay for the necessities of maintaining religious facilities. The state's role is simply that of providing a system of religious liberty while also ensuring

Table 7.2 Attitude Toward Religious Sites

Attitude toward growth of religious sites:	
Very positive (somewhat positive)	17.1 (25.6)
Somewhat negative (very negative)	17.6 (2.3)
Government should help pay for religious sites:	
Should pay (shouldn't pay)	60.5 (39.5)

the public welfare. In American church-state parlance, the state should protect the right of free exercise, not become unnecessarily intermingled, and ensure that—as with any other social institution—religious institutions abide by the law and are not a danger to the public welfare. In addition to a state willing and able to take on these functions, such a system of church-state separation also requires a citizenry supportive of the state limiting its involvement to these functions.

In this regard, a majority is not prepared for such a system. More than 60 percent of those interviewed as part of our survey responded that the government should help pay for religious sites (see Table 7.2). Only slightly more than 40 percent, however, felt positively about the growth of religious sites in China, with one quarter of those surveyed expressing a "very positive" attitude.[76] In China, most property is public property, and in the case of religious sites, most are run as tourist sites, with the government collecting revenue from visitors. Thus is makes perfect sense that the state should help pay for their operation.

The very strong support for some state financial support of religious sites stands in stark contrast to the U.S. model of separation. It is not, however, actually very different from other parts of the developed world, including Europe, where governments often provide financial resources to churches and other religious sites which serve as something of a "public utility," as Davie has argued.[77] In such a situation, the state ensures that such religious institutions are there to provide "religious" services that often fill a somewhat secular purpose as well, even for those who are unattached to the church or even outright confess they have no belief in God. Such services range all the way from baptisms, which serve as communal acknowledgement of a birth, to funerals, which commemorate the passing of a community member, both regardless of whether or not those holding the service or being memorialized in such a way profess(ed) any religious belief. The degree to which Chinese support for religion may resemble such a situation is certainly an area ripe for future research.

When it comes to which religious sites the state supports, certain preferences and prejudices become apparent (see Table 7.3). A clear preference exists

Table 7.3 Attitude Toward Growth of Churches

	Positive	Negative
Protestant churches	23.2 (24.5)	11.1 (4.5)
Catholic churches	14.4 (23.7)	12.8 (5.1)
Taoist temples	15.1 (25.1)	11.6 (4.6)
Buddhist temples	19 (28.8)	10.1 (4)
Islamic mosques	10.2 (20.7)	15.6 (7.8)

for Protestant churches and Buddhist and Taoist temples, all with more than 40 percent of respondents expressing a positive attitude (calculated by combining both the "very positive" and "somewhat positive" responses). While the very high level of positive responses regarding the growth of Protestant churches is surely related to some over-representation of Protestants in our sample, the even stronger support for Buddhist and Taoist temples confirms our suspicion about the "public utility" function of certain traditional religious sites in China.

The other part of the story is the deep degree of prejudice felt toward Islam apparent from the responses to this question. Table 7.3 clearly illustrates distinctly lower levels of enthusiasm regarding the spread of mosques in China, a finding which illustrates a more general phenomenon prevalent among most Chinese, a topic further explored below. At this point, we can simply note that, not only were the fewest positive attitudes toward the growth of religious sites registered for mosques, but the largest number of negative attitudes were likewise associated with the spread of Muslim places of worship, with nearly a quarter of respondents harboring negative attitudes in this regard—the largest number of negative responses for any of the religious sites listed.

Islamophobia and Religious Intolerance

If these data lead us to suspect that Islamophobia may be present in China today, the data in Table 7.4 not only further confirms this suspicion, they point to its cause. While two-thirds of those surveyed initially responded that religion is not associated with violence, when subsequently asked about the peacefulness of specific religious traditions, the picture came more clearly into focus. Of course, structuring survey questionnaires in this way is a prized technique of the survey researcher, allowing one to compare responses to general phenomena with more specific ones, forcing the respondent to stop thinking abstractly and to consider real-world issues about which s/he is likely to hold strong opinions, albeit opinions

Table 7.4 Peacefulness of Different Religions

Religion is associated with violence:	
True (not true)	33.8 (66.2)
Han Buddhism:	
Very peaceful (somewhat peaceful)	46.7 (23.2)
Somewhat violent (very violent)	1.6 (0)
Tibetan Buddhism:	
Very peaceful (somewhat peaceful)	13 (24.9)
Somewhat violent (very violent)	23.9 (4.2)
Taoism:	
Very peaceful (somewhat peaceful)	34.9 (24.1)
Somewhat violent (very violent)	2.9 (0)
Catholicism:	
Very peaceful (somewhat peaceful)	17.8 (29.7)
Somewhat violent (very violent)	12.3 (1.6)
Islam:	
Very peaceful (somewhat peaceful)	10.8 (17.8)
Somewhat violent (very violent)	24.9 (10.2)
Protestantism:	
Very peaceful (somewhat peaceful)	29.7 (23.2)
Somewhat violent (very violent)	10.2 (1)

which on a day-to-day basis the individual may keep packed away in his or her subconscious. Prejudice, intolerance, and fear are precisely these sort of attitudes.

The religion which Chinese seem to fear the most is Islam. While nearly 30 percent considered Islam peaceful (again, summing the two positive responses), 35 percent believed it was a violent religion—a response only on par with that of another vilified ethno-religious group in China—the Tibetan Buddhists. In the latter case, 28 percent believed Tibetan Buddhism was violent, though only 4.2 percent believed it was very violent. As discussed in Chapter 6, Tibetan Buddhism is clearly distinguished from the Han Buddhism of the Han people. Indeed, just how clearly the two are disassociated from one another in China is seen by the fact that Han Buddhism was considered the most peaceful of any religion listed, while Tibetan Buddhism was a close second to Islam as the most violent.

Taoism likewise took a close second to Han Buddhism as a peaceful religion, with not a single respondent in our survey feeling that either tradition was "very violent." The middle ground was occupied by Christianity, with Catholicism, and Protestantism being seen by around half of those surveyed as either very peaceful or somewhat peaceful, illustrating that the histories of these religions in China and their association with colonialism is not forgotten. But the perceived violent nature of these traditions pales in comparison to those of Islam and Tibetan Buddhism.

Just what is it about Islam and Tibetan Buddhism that makes them so prone to violence in the minds of our survey respondents? While in the United States or Europe, events such as 9/11, the July 7, 2005 London tube bombing, or the 2004 murder of Dutch filmmaker Theo Van Gogh by a Muslim come to mind, in China Islam is associated with violence that has occurred closer to home. These include acts of violence associated with the East Turkistan Islamic Movement, a separatist group seeking the independence of China's Xinjiang territory whose acts include the 2000 bombing of a student cafeteria at Tsinghua University, all the way to a 2008 incident in Kashgar in which two Muslim Uyghurs rammed their truck into a police post and tossed grenades at the officers.[78] It also includes daily interactions among China's majority Han population and migrants from Xinjiang and Tibet working in traditionally-Han populated territories, where they often engage in menial, if not illegal, activities.

To our Chinese respondents, surprisingly, it is not Islam's or Tibetan Buddhism's theology or religious doctrines *per se* (or at least not solely) that lead to their propensity for violence. The responses summarized in Table 7.5 illustrate that this perceived association between these religions and violence is more closely related to the manipulation of religious leaders and the influence of foreign actors than any theological doctrine or belief. More than 50 percent of respondents felt the underlying causes of religious violence in China were due to the manipulation of religious leaders and the influence of foreign organizations. Similarly, more than 50 percent attributed this phenomenon to the problematic implementation of religion policy in China.

A study of the role of Islam in Russia's Chechen War illustrates quite well how these factors are seen to operate in cases of ethno-religious violence. As Wang Guanyu argues, some of the main causes of the Islamic extremism in the Chechen conflict are related to the "penetration and support of Islamic extremist forces from abroad" and Russia's mistakes in implementing its religion and nationalities policies.[79] Moreover, our survey respondents

Table 7.5 Causes of Religious Violence

Theology or essence of the religious belief	29.2
Ethnicity or national character of the people	39.7
Manipulation by political leaders	40.4
Manipulation by religious leaders	52.6
Foreign influence	54.4
Problematic implementation of religion policy	51.6

attributed lower levels of significance to the ethnic and national character of specific groups in regard to religious violence, with just less than 40 percent feeling that such factors were among the causes of the association between religion and violence. But since our question did not flesh out distinctions between the role of ethnicity and specific religious traditions, we are not able to determine whether or not the ethno-national identity factor correlates with Islam and Tibetan Buddhism. We must remain cautious, therefore, about concluding from our data that Islamophobia—or "Tibetophobia"— exist in China. The situation is certainly sufficiently complex, however, to warrant deeper investigation.

Religion and Social Harmony

At the Sixth Plenary Session of the sixteenth Central Committee of the CCP, President Hu Jintao delivered an important speech in which he emphasized the positive role believers can play in promoting a harmonious society in China. President Hu said, "[we shall] intensify the unity between believers and non-believers, as well as the unity among people who believe in different faiths, and let religion play its positive roles in the construction of a harmonious society."[80] Then in his report to the seventeenth National Congress of the CCP in 2007, President Hu stated that, while the goal of CCP leadership is the "development of socialism with Chinese characteristics," social harmony, along with scientific development, is necessary to achieve that goal. "One is integral to the other and neither is possible without the other," Hu argued. The concept of a "harmonious society" (*hexie shehui*) quickly became the new buzzword in China, in many ways replacing the phrase "socialist construction," used so often to justify CCP policies during earlier eras, though one can now see the two phrases used in combination.

This focus on social harmony stands in sharp contrast to earlier phases of CCP rule, when turmoil and even revolution were justifiable methods in achieving policy objectives. This certainly described the situation with religion policy during the Cultural Revolution, for example, when temples were destroyed and sacred texts were burned. But social harmony has another side as well; not only does it imply some degree of tolerance on the part of the state, it also implies a degree of support for the state's objectives on the part of religious organizations. Some fear this is a new litmus test, and that organizations that cannot prove that they can contribute to social harmony in China will be discriminated against or even shut down. Evidence seems to indicate, however, that the measure being used is that of a lack of disharmony, that is, religious groups must shy away from overtly revolutionary behavior, and perhaps even peaceful political behavior that is counter to the leadership of the CCP.

In a June 2008 meeting between the sociologist Peter L. Berger, myself, and then-SARA director Ye Xiaowen, the topic of discussion turned to the issue of "harmonious society." Minister Ye asked Prof. Berger in what ways he thought religion could contribute to social harmony in China. In asking his question, Minister Ye expressed genuine interest in the topic. In fact, he may have known that the purpose of our visit to China was to deliver a co-authored paper on this exact topic at a conference on "Religion and Rule of Law: The Legal System and Religion in a Harmonious Society," organized and hosted by the Institute of World Religions of the Chinese Academy of Social Sciences (and co-sponsored by the J. M. Dawson Institute of Church-State Studies, the Law and Religion Program at Brigham Young University, and the Council on Faith and International Affairs). Prof. Berger, therefore, was quite prepared to answer the question.

Prof. Berger suggested to Minister Ye that those who equate jihadist violence—or for that matter any sort of fanaticism—with the resurgence of Islam are distorting the reality of the subject. Of course, there are reasons to be concerned about the radical versions of Islamic ideology and to take measures to counteract its violent expressions, but the great majority of Muslims in the world are not fanatical or violent. Rather, Prof. Berger explained that the resurgence of Islam is brought about by millions of people finding meaning and direction in their lives by adhering to this faith. Prof. Berger raised a second point that the global explosion of Evangelical Protestantism, especially Pentecostalism, bears an uncanny resemblance to the Protestant ethic which Max Weber credited with a causal role in the origins of modern capitalism in Europe and North America, suggesting that Pentecostalism may play a similar role today. Little did either of us know at the time that Chinese scholars and policymakers have been keenly interested in this relationship, and that the perceived economic benefits of Christian belief may be one factor driving the increased liberalization of China's religion policy. Toward the end of his retirement, former president Jiang Zemin is even supposed to have said when asked, "if you could make one decree that you knew would be obeyed in China, what would it be?" that he would make Christianity "the official religion of China."[81] As Aikman recently pointed out in recounting the story to a public audience, when he expressed the idea Jiang apparently had in mind the economic benefits of the faith.[82]

The Chinese are quite right to be concerned with the implications of the resurgence of Islam and the spread of Evangelical Protestantism for social harmony. Religious resources can contribute in both positive and negative ways to social harmony, with greatly different results deriving from various contexts. Where political grievances exist, for example, quite often religion can be drawn upon both to unite a group together and to establish a dividing line between "us" and "them." Moreover, in the competition for scarce resources—or even larger shares of wealth in a rapidly modernizing society—social class and economic position can become blurred with religious difference, often with disastrous consequences. Where this does develop, it is usually in multi-confessional societies—especially those in which ethnic lines are roughly coterminous with religious ones. Such facts suggest that China should be cautious about the rapid spread of any religious tradition in China.

In a nuanced manner, Prof. Berger pointed out that another situation that may disrupt social harmony is when a political and/or cultural elite seeks to impose its secularism on an often passionately religious populace, which very often resembles a "secularist" fundamentalism. Prof. Berger suggested that Turkey today dramatically illustrates such a conflict, and offered Israel and India as further examples—both attained independence under the leadership of secular elites, and more recently have confronted rebellious religious movements, respectively representing conservative Judaism and conservative Hinduism. The fact that the CCP has promoted a "scientific worldview"—including through the publications of SARA's own publishing house—was not mentioned, nor did it need to be.

While all of this may sound quite depressing in terms of religion's relationship to social harmony, overall the impact of religion on social harmony is probably more positive than negative. As Berger's work has shown, under conditions of modernity, individuals choose not only to believe or not to believe, but what to believe, and in making their selection they are accepting a set of moral and ethical precepts that offer very many positive functions for society as a whole. In this way, religion not only instructs its members how they should relate themselves to God, but also to other members of society. And since religions that seek to destabilize society are few and far between, this means that religion contributes in a fundamental way to social harmony.

Data from the ESVC survey clearly illustrates that religion's role in China can be positive in this way. First, Chinese society appears to exhibit a healthy level of respect and tolerance for religion—less than 10 percent of respondents exhibited any serious negative feelings toward religion's role in society, and that number even dropped considerably among those who professed a religious belief themselves. The most negative attitudes toward religion were actually associated with concern for one's fellow man—that it might give bad people the opportunity to defraud others. Of course, anyone familiar with religion in any part of the world knows that it is indeed susceptible to such manipulation, and examples can be drawn from any country, including among the most developed and law-based societies. On balance, respondents were also more positive about religion than negative, and the negative responses most often given related to fraudulent activities and religion being a waste of financial resources, not a practice that contributes to social instability in any way.

Likewise, the data analyzed here from our survey of church-state issues in China further suggests that religion does not seem poised to be a destabilizing factor in Chinese society and politics. Granted, issues of Islamophobia and "Tibetophobia" may be present, but more often than not they seem related in significant ways to calls for national self-determination and "splittism," as the Chinese government refers to separatism. As the collapse of Communism in Eastern Europe and the Soviet Union illustrated, such calls for separatism indeed lead to social disharmony and hardship, perhaps even more often than democracy, with the former Yugoslavia and many parts of the former Soviet Union—including present-day Russia—well illustrating the point. These are, of course, lessons not lost on the Chinese themselves.[83]

One lesson clearly drawn from the Soviet debacle has been that a well-formulated religion policy can go far in preventing ethno-religious conflict and containing flair-ups as they occur. The data analyzed here is such that we cannot identify all of the ways in which religion may negatively impact social harmony in China, but by being able to identify some ways in which religion makes a positive contribution to social harmony, policymakers can feel secure about liberalizing bureaucratic control in those areas and invest their limited resources in monitoring and addressing the activities of groups that are the most likely to destabilize China's social order, while continuing to grant greater religious liberty to those that pose no threat to political stability and social harmony.

Renegotiating China's "Great Wall" of Separation

While challenges certainly continue to exist in terms of religious liberty, so much has changed in the area of church-state relations in China that an emerging area of concern is that of religious establishment and/or preferential treatment for particular religious groups. While 30 years ago religion was seen as a backward practice that was incompatible with socialism and therefore had to be eradicated, as the CCP realizes that religion may contribute to social harmony and perhaps even economic productivity, they may eventually conclude that "more is better," and actually seek to promote the further spread of religion in Chinese society, whether that be through a Christianization, as Aikman sees on the horizon, or a more prominent role for China's most popular religious tradition—Buddhism.

Should this be a cause of alarm? If one looks at the post-Communist societies of Eastern Europe and Central Asia, we see that shortly after the end of scientific atheism as the *de facto* state religion, in most places religious liberty and pluralism lasted only a few short years before religious establishments or quasi-establishments returned. With Communism gone, many societies picked up where they had left off, as with the Russian Orthodox Church's return to primacy, as discussed in the previous chapter. Is there the chance that China might follow a similar path? Might China promote one of its traditional religions, such as Buddhism or Taoism? While Buddhism has certainly come into vogue lately, with China even funding Confucius study centers at U.S. universities, Chinese nationalism has yet to become attached to a particular religion or set of religions. As religion becomes more generally accepted by both citizens and the state, however, one must bear in mind that the "separationist" model of church-state relations followed by the CCP may come into question as well.

An interesting example both of how far religious tolerance in China has come and how the ideal of church-state separation may be renegotiated relates to state support for land for religious organizations. The situation with which the Chinese are confronted is an interesting one, and one which elicits sympathies. With the rapid development in China's urban areas, not only are urban areas sprawling into new territories at an amazing rate, but the cost of land in these areas is likewise skyrocketing. This puts believers of all faiths in a difficult situation; as families move into new areas, there are no churches, mosques, or temples nearby where they may worship. While the state is naturally involved in developing the necessary infrastructure in such areas—including roads, sewers, schools, and hospitals—what should be its role in facilitating the development of spiritual life in the new communities?

In the West, as well as in countries in other parts of the world, this is typically handled by private communities, not the state. Established co-religionists from other areas, usually within the same country if not the same region, often provide assistance in planting a new church. For example, a Lutheran church may attempt to "plant" a new church in an expanding part of a city, or Texas Baptists may help get a Baptist church started in Siberia. When the state does choose to get involved, as in some parts of Scandinavia, publicly-owned lands can be set aside for auction, with allotments for each religious group, and with the highest-bidding religious group winning the bid.

In both cases, China faces limitations. First, since China's religious revival is still relatively recent, many believers are not yet wealthy enough to fund the development of plant churches in neighboring areas. Simple math illustrates that, with a rapidly-growing religious population, there is often a lag in terms of membership and church finances. In China, religious belief—particularly Christianity—is rapidly expanding among migrant workers, rural inhabitants, and the poor, although it is certainly not limited to these groups. Secondly, there is the issue of foreign ties. Under its policy of "three-self's," Chinese religious organizations are not permitted to be under the direction of foreign entities, and this makes all foreign ties suspect. Although the Chinese government has certainly softened its policy on foreign assistance and relations between Chinese religious groups and foreign entities (ranging from mission agencies to the Vatican), it is still highly problematic for a Western church to fully sponsor the building of a church on Chinese soil (or for Wahhabis to fund the construction of a mosque there, for that matter).

Faced with this situation, one rapidly-growing city in China is debating a very interesting solution—a state-funded land bank.[84] The idea is that the city would lease property at a subsidized rate to religious groups, thus giving a head start to these churches. After a while, they could become self-sufficient and eventually purchase their own land. How far the tolerance of religion has come in the past few years that something like this is even being debated! It is certainly commendable that a Chinese governmental agency wishes to help in this way, but from the position of separation of church and state, this is a bad idea for several reasons.

First of all, if the state owns the land, it can at any point evict the religious group if it disagrees with its message or some other activity. Secondly, how can this be done without giving preferential treatment to one group over another? When I presented this point to the drafter of this proposal, he argued that they could make land accessible to all who wanted it. Of course, to carry out any scheme like this would require criteria, and the first of these would be official recognition. In the case of the Catholics, for example, this would mean that land would go to the recognized Catholic Patriotic Association but not the underground Catholic Church connected to the Vatican. In this way, they would be giving preference to the former and discriminating against the latter. Certainly, one can see that certain forms of Christianity are preferred to others (three-self churches to house churches, for instance), and that groups such as Falun Gong, Xiang Gong, and Dongfang Shandian are not likely to be on the list for land from any land bank.

In a lecture delivered at Renmin University of China during our visit, Prof. Berger pointed out that religious plurality is enhanced if there is a legally-guaranteed freedom of religion in a society. But even if political authorities try to prevent such plurality, Berger argued, it will creep in nevertheless—unless the authorities successfully stem all the forces of modernity. This is very difficult to do without undercutting modernity itself, and the benefits that go with it. It is commendable that China has progressed so far in liberalizing its religion policy and is now to the point of debating issues such as a land bank and state-funded renovation of religious buildings. But the answer to their dilemma is greater religious liberty, not state-sponsorship. If religious life is allowed even greater latitude, then religious communities will flourish, individual believers will prosper financially, and foreign assistance will pour in. The state will of course need to regulate many of these activities, but religion's contribution to social harmony will only be maximized when religious liberty is guaranteed.

Notes

1. Lü, 1981, p. 13.
2. Jonathan Chao, "China's Religious Policy," *China and the Church Today* (May-June 1979), p. 2.
3. Yan Sun, *The Chinese Reassessment of Socialism 1976–1982* (Princeton: Princeton University Press, 1995). See also Marsh, *Unparalleled Reforms*.
4. Chao, 1979, p. 1.
5. "Zongjiao he fengjian mixin," *Renmin Ribao*, March 15, 1979. Chao incorrectly gives the title of this article in English as "Religion and Superstition." All subsequent quotations are from this document, which is a single page long. Keston Archive, <China/RelChiTod/1979>.
6. Ibid.
7. Chao, 1979, p. 2.
8. See his several articles in *Renmin ribao* and *Wenhui Bao, inter alia*, between January 1963 and June 1964.
9. Liang Hao and Yang Zhen, "Zongjiao conglai jiushi renmin de yapian—yu Ya Hanzhang tongzhi shangque," *Xin Jianshe* (December 20, 1965); and Bing Quan, Xiao Fu, and Yu He, "Zhengque lijie 'zongjiao shi renmin de yapian'—yu Ya Hanzhang tongzhi shangque," *Wenhui Bao* (June 23, 1964). See also You Xiang and Liu Junwang, "Makesi Liening zhuyi zongjiaoguan de jige wenti," *Xin Jianshe* (September 20, 1963).

10. Lü Daji, "Zhengque renshi zongjiao...," pp. 1–3.
11. This quote comes from Zhang's article, but the translation here is from MacInnis, doc. 8.
12. Zhang Ji'an, "Dui 'zongjiao shi renmin de yapian' zhege lunduan de chubu lijie," *Shijie Zongjiao Yanjiu*, Vol. 2 (1981), p. 11.
13. Lü, 1981, p. 13.
14. Lü Daji, "Shi lun zongjiao zai lishi shang de zuoyong," *Shijie Zongjiao Yanjiu*, Vol. 4 (1982), p. 93.
15. Zhang, 1981, p. 9.
16. Ibid., p. 11.
17. Jonathan Chao, *Wise as Serpents Harmless as Doves: Christians in China Tell Their Story* (Pasadena: Chinese Church Research Center, 1988), p. xxiii.
18. Ibid., p. xxiii.
19. Ibid., p. xxv.
20. Alan Hunter and Kim-Kwong Chan, *Protestantism in Contemporary China* (New York: Cambridge University Press, 1993), p. 72.
21. Chao, 1988, p. xxv.
22. *Economist* (November 18, 1989), p. 13.
23. Hunter and Chan, p. 95
24. Pittman Potter, "Belief in Control: Regulation of Religion in China," in Daniel Overmyer, ed. *Religion in China Today* (New York: Cambridge University Press, 2003), p. 15.
25. Hunter and Chan, p. 100.
26. Ibid., pp. 100–1.
27. For Deng Xiaoping's refutation of Western nations using human rights as an excuse to exert pressure on China, see "First Priority Should Always be Given to National Sovereignty and Security," December 1, 1989. Available online at: http://www.humanrights-china.org
28. See, for example, Rui Bian, "Xifan tuixing 'heping yanbian' de zhanlue mubiao," *Banyue Tan* 19 (October 10, 1989), pp. 56–59; and "Xifan tuixing 'heping yanbian' de shoufa," *Banyue Tan* 20 & 21 (October 25 and November 10, 1989), pp. 57–9 and pp. 56–7.
29. Tian Juanbao, "Jiekesiluofake," *Jingri Sulian Dongou*, No. 3 (1990), pp. 17–21.
30. Sabrina Ramet, *Nihil Obstat: Religion, Politics, and Social Change in East-Central Europe and Russia* (Durham: Duke University Press, 1998), p. 40.
31. Sixiang Lilun Bu, *Zhongguo qingnian bao*, "Sulian zhengbian hou zhongguo de xianshi yingdui yu zhanlue xuanze," (September 1991). Reprinted in *Zhongguo Zhichun* (January 1992), pp. 35–9.

32. Ye Xiaowen, "China's Current Religious Question: Once Again an Inquiry into the Five Characteristics of Religion," March 22, 1996. This document is reprinted in *China: State Control of Religion* (New York: Human Rights Watch/Asia, 1997), pp. 116–44.

33. Ibid., p. 133.

34. Ibid., p. 130.

35. Ibid., p. 133.

36. Luo Shuze, "Some Hot Issues in our Work on Religion," *Qiushi* 5 (1996). This document is reprinted in *China: State Control of Religion,* pp. 65–70.

37. Ibid., p. 65.

38. Ibid.

39. Ibid.

40. United Front Work Department of the Tongxiang Municipal Committee of the Chinese Communist Party, "Opinion Concerning Carrying Out the Special Struggle to Curb Illegal Activities of the Catholic and Protestant Christians According to Law," 1997. This document is reprinted in *China: State Control of Religion,* pp. 71–9.

41. "Opinion Concerning Carrying Out the Special Struggle to Curb Illegal Activities," p. 73.

42. Marsh, *Unparalleled Reforms.*

43. David Palmer, *Qigong Fever: Body, Science, and Utopia in China* (New York: Columbia University Press, 2007).

44. Yu Guangyuan, *Fan renti ye gongneng lun* (Guiyang: Guizhou Renmin Press, 1997).

45. Fenggang Yang, "The Red, Black, and Gray Markets of Religion in China," *Sociological Quarterly,* Vol. 47 (2006), p. 112.

46. Ibid., p. 111.

47. Ibid.

48. Ibid.

49. Human Rights Watch, *Dangerous Meditation: China's Campaign Against Falungong* (New York: Human Rights Watch, 2002), p. 18.

50. Interview with members of Falun Dafa, Austin, Texas, October 23, 2002; Confirmed in interview with Falun Gong representative, Rowan University, March 15, 2009.

51. *Renmin Ribao* (June 20, 1999). Cited in Human Rights Watch, *Dangerous Meditation,* p. 19.

52. Ming Xia and Shiping Hua, "The Battle Between the Chinese Government and Falun Gong," *Chinese Law and Government,* Vol. 32, No. 5 (September/October 1999).

53. Human Rights Watch, *Dangerous Meditation*, p. 19.
54. "Wang Zhaoguo On Fight Against 'Falungong'," *World News Connection* (July 23, 1999).
55. Yang, p. 113.
56. Potter, p. 25.
57. Human Rights Watch, *Dangerous Meditation*, p. 18.
58. Potter, pp. 17–18.
59. Yang, pp. 98–99; pp. 108–9.
60. Ibid., p. 99.
61. This project centers on the Dawson Institute Survey of Religious Tolerance, conducted between 2009–2010. The initial results of our first-wave survey were recently published as Christopher Marsh and Zhifeng Zhong, "Chinese Views on Church and State," *Journal of Church & State*, Vol. 52, No. 1 (Winter 2010).
62. Ye Xiaowen, *Zongjiao Wenti: Zenme Kan, Zenme Ban* (Beijing: Religious Culture Publishing House, 2007), pp. 220–1.
63. Gong Xuezeng and Sun Ruihua, *Ma Kesi Zhuyi Zongjiao Guan yu Dang de Zongjiao Gongzuon Fangzhen* (Beijing: Central Editing and Translation Publishing House, 2007), pp. 5–6.
64. Fang Wen, "Zhengzhiti zhong de Xintu-Gongmin Kunjing: Qunti Zige Lujing," *Beijing Daxue Xuebao Shezhe Ban*, No.4 (2009).
65. *Jiating Jiaohui Xinyang Gaobai*. Available at: http://www.shengshan.org/article/jiaohuizhili/20081024/9.html
66. *Jiu Jinshan Gongshi*, December 8, 2008. Published in *Jidu Ribao* (December 15, 2008). Available at: http://www.gospelherald.ca
67. *Jidutu Weiquan Shouce*. Available at: http://www.shengshan.org/article/ziliaoxiazai/20081029/94.html
68. Fan Li, "Jidujiao Fazhan dui Zhengzhi de Yingxiang," paper presented at 2008 Christianity and Harmonious society conference on House church issues, November 21–22, 2008.
69. Fan Li, "Jidujiao Fazhan dui Zhongguo Minzhu Fazhan de Yingxiang," paper presented at the center for the study of contemporary China, Keio University, Japan, July 18, 2009. Available at: http://www.cssm.gov.cn
70. For more on the ESVC, see Elisa Jiexia Zhai, "Contrasting Trends of Religious Markets in Contemporary Mainland China and in Taiwan," *Journal of Church & State*, Vol. 52, No. 1 (Winter 2010). See also, Elisa Jiexia Zhai, Raymond Huang, Byron Johnson, and Rodney Stark, "China's Christian Millions: Empirical Speculation of Protestant Christianity in Contemporary China," working paper, Institute for Studies of Religion, Baylor University, 2009.

71. Liu Peng, *China Daily* (December 9, 2009).

72. *World Religion Database.* For more on the speculative nature of this database regarding China, see Robert Woodberry, "*World Religion Database*: Impressive—but Improvable," *International Bulletin of Missionary Research*, Vol. 34, No. 1 (January 2010), pp. 21–2.

73. The information presented here comes from Liu Peng, "China's Religious Investigation—Church-State Relations," invited guest lecture delivered at the J. M. Dawson Institute of Church-State Studies, Baylor University, March 5, 2009.

74. For more on this topic, see Jin Ze, "The Functions of Religion in Constructing a Harmonious Society: A Chinese Perspective," *Review of Faith and International Affairs*, Vol. 7, No. 3 (2009), pp. 21–6.

75. See, for example, Charles Tilly and Sidney Tarrow, *Contentious Politics* (Boulder: Paradigm, 2007).

76. For more on the rise of churches in contemporary China and the state's involvement in providing land and other resources for their development, see Christopher Marsh, "Revisiting China's 'Great Wall' of Separation: Religious Liberty in China Today," *Journal of Church & State*, Vol. 50, No. 2 (2008), pp. 205–12.

77. Grace Davie, "The Persistence of Institutional Religion in Modern Europe," in Laura Woodhead, with P. Heelas and David Martin, eds. *Peter Berger and the Study of Religion* (London: Routledge, 2001), pp. 101–11; and "Vicarious Religion: A Methodological Challenge," in Nancy Ammerman, ed., *Everyday Religion: Observing Modern Religious Lives* (New York: Oxford University Press, 2006), pp. 21–36.

78. Edward Wong, "Town in China Returns to Normal a Day After a Bold Attack," *New York Times*, (August 6, 2008), p. A6.

79. Wang Guanyu, "Chechen yisilan jiduan shili xunshu pengzhang de genyuan," *Eluosi Zhongya Dongou Yanjiu*, Vol. 2 (2003), pp. 34–40.

80. "CPC Central Committee on building a socialist harmonious society and a number of decisions on major issues," *Xinhua* (October 18, 2006). Available at: http://news.xinhuanet.com/politics/2006–10/18/content_5218639.htm

81. Aikman, p. 17. In his source footnote to this statement, Aikman provides no documentation and states that he cannot reveal the identity of his source. In a review of the book, Jinghao Zhou raised serious concerns over this issue, pointing out that "Jiang Zemin's record over the last ten years suggests he is firmly opposed to religion" (*Journal of Religion & Society*, Vol. 7, 2005). Given the gravity of the statement, certainly others at the banquet would have recalled it as well. Chinese sources I consulted

acknowledged hearing of the incident, but believe it to be nothing more than a rumor, if not an outright joke.

82. David Aikman, "Jesus in Beijing," lecture delivered at the J. M. Dawson Institute of Church-State Studies, Baylor University, April 17, 2010.

83. Christopher Marsh, "Learning from Your Comrade's Mistakes: The Impact of the Soviet Past on China's Future," *Communist and Post-Communist Studies*, Vol. 36, No. 3 (2003); and Christopher Marsh and Nikolas Gvosdev, "China's Balkan Nightmare," *The National Interest*, No. 84 (Summer 2006). See also Marsh, *Unparalleled Reforms*.

84. Interview with official of regional RAB office. City, name, and date withheld to protect confidentiality.

Conclusion: Man, the State, and God

But, as we have already seen, men, foolish as they are, thought little of the grace they had received, and turned away from God. They defiled their own soul so completely that they not only lost their apprehension of God, but invented for themselves other gods of various kinds. They fashioned idols for themselves in place of the truth and reverenced things that are not, rather than God Who is, as St. Paul says, 'worshipping the creature rather than the Creator.' Moreover, and much worse, they transferred the honor which is due to God to material objects such as wood and stone, and also to man.[1]

—*Athanasius (d. 373)*

Throughout recorded history, in all parts of the world, every known society has had some set of values and beliefs—however primitive—that can be understood as religion. Predating the development of writing by millennia, religion must have emerged once language had evolved sufficiently to convey complex ideas. Certainly, as man's mind evolved from *Homo Erectus* into *Homo Sapiens*, it began to develop an awareness of itself. As he witnessed death all around him—mostly relating to his hunting for food, with either beast or man falling in the process—man became aware of his finite existence and the fragility of life. Thus was born the need for religion, the need to answer the questions of "why am I here?" and "what is my relationship to the rest of creation?"

The cave paintings at Lascaux, France, are an excellent illustration of the emergence of religious belief among primitive man.[2] The hundreds of decorated caves in the region date back as far as 30,000 years ago, long before the emergence of the first writing systems. Through the use of image, these prehistoric people were able to represent the travails of life, both of triumph and defeat, and preserve them for posterity. Most scholars agree that these caves were sacred places for the performance of some kind of ritual.[3] Indeed, the French Ministry of Culture and Communication refers to the paintings as "iconography," and the Lascaux cave as a "prehistoric Sistine Chapel."[4] Scholars can only speculate, however, as to the role played by these labyrinths below the earth in the rites of passage that must have been part of their primitive culture. Young men would enter the caves as boys and, once taking part in prescribed rites and rituals, leave as full-fledged members of the community and sufficiently prepared for the hunt. Thus was born religion as a set of rituals guiding the handling and care of the sacred, as distinct from the profane. The caves at Lascaux, so deep below the ground and set apart from the surface hundreds of meters above, separated the profane world above ground from the sacred chambers hidden below.

One particular painting at Lascaux, located in the "Shaft of the Dead Man," depicts a fallen human figure. In sharp contrast to the bison which stands before him, this man is depicted by a very rudimentarily drawn stick figure. Atop the man's head is a bird-like mask, while on the ground next to him rests a rod topped by another bird-head. Similar paintings throughout France and indeed even in Africa suggest that this man is probably a shaman.[5] Thus was born the sacerdotum, the class of religious *virtuosi* who mediate between this world and the next.

From the archeological to the zoological, and from prehistory to today, man seems to desire communication with the transcendent. This has led many observers—theologians and social scientists alike—to conclude that man is *Homo Religiosus*, that is, he is by his very nature a religious being. If nothing else, the failure of the world's most ambitious forced secularization programs proves that there is great truth to this idea. Not only has man historically been religious, but uprooting these beliefs is no easy task. He will often fight to the bitter end to preserve his faith, and many will willingly go to their death at the hands of the state for their God.

Religion after Atheism

How ironic it is that as Western intellectuals lament the evils of organized religion people the world over still fight against authoritarian regimes that seek to limit their freedom of belief. Though I am sure they would balk at the comparison, the idea that religious organizations are detestable and that they take advantage of unsuspecting, feeble-minded people is one with which Marx, Engels, and Lenin would certainly agree. If they had their druthers, rather than proclaiming that "God is not Great" or that there is a "God Delusion," secularists such as Dawkins, Hitchens, and certainly Newdow might even entertain the idea of implementing similar anti-religion policies in the West. But could such methods even be effective? Certainly the U.S. Constitution put some strict limits on the influence of religion in American society, while at the same time limiting the state's ability to control religious groups. That combination has led to one of the most religiously vibrant societies in the world. At the other end of the spectrum are those societies that violently attacked religious organizations and even individual believers, including the Soviet Union and the People's Republic of China during its Maoist heyday.

When those regimes were willing and able to attack religion systematically, they proved they could be quite successful. In the Soviet Union during the late 1930s, only a few hundred out of more than 20,000 churches remained in existence. China was even more successful than that, and during the Cultural Revolution every single religious establishment in the country was effectively closed. These historical examples show that it can be done. Hitler's invasion of the Soviet Union turned the tide there, however, and starting with gestures by the Church toward Stalin and the Soviet state, a *rapprochement* was reached a mere 5 years after the USSR's period of most severe repression. In the case of China, its religious revival began still during the Cultural Revolution, admittedly though in its later years. No sooner had the Red Guards slowed their parades through the streets or their confiscation of public facilities than groups of believers began to meet secretly in each other's homes for Bible reading and worship. Both cases of severe repression were effective only as long as the repression continued; as soon as repression diminished in intensity, religion came back.

We, of course, must also take into account the more private side of religious belief. Destroying every church, temple, and mosque in China is not the same thing as converting people to atheism; that was an even greater abject failure. People like Xu Yun, Georgi Vins, Aida Skripnikova, Moses Xie, and countless others stood against the most brutal onslaughts by the Soviet state and Maoist regime as they refused to succomb to the most violent acts. Stopping someone from worshipping publicly is one thing; getting them to abandon their faith is quite another.

Ironically, persecuting religious believers may be one thing that can *halt* natural processes of secularization. Both the old secularization theorists as well as proponents of the new atheism suspect that natural processes of epistemological secularization will eventually do the job, as religion becomes less able to provide satisfying—or plausible—answers about one's existence. But trying to force the process seems to work in reverse to a certain degree. Theologically, this seems particularly true for Christianity and Islam, though undoubtedly there are aspects to Buddhism and Taoism that might work similarly. It will take someone better versed in those traditions, however, to flesh out that process. For now, it is quite apparent that forced secularization—particularly brutal crackdowns—draw quite easily upon apocalyptic elements of Christianity, and probably Islam as well. In the case of the former, throughout history regimes that attacked Christians were immediately condemned as the anti-Christ. Such a tradition is found not only in Rome, but can be found in Russia and China as well, and long pre-dates the arrival of Communism. Tsar Peter the Great was labeled such by several groups, including most strongly by the Old Believers. In China, it was the Taiping rebels who saw their anti-Christ in their Qing overlords.

The eponym was most fitting, however, for Russians and Ukrainians, two peoples with a long history of looking to the Bible for clues to their past and future. At least as far back as the *Primary Chronicle*, the *Rus'* looked to scripture for such clues and found them from Genesis to Revelations. They were the descendants of Noah's third son, Japheth, giving themselves direct lineage to the diluvian period, and they were of the tribe of Magog (or Gog), in the land of Rosh. The implications of such identity as expressed in Revelations, where the Gog and Magog were both thrown out of heaven, apparently didn't matter to those drawing these lines. Ancestors were found in the Bible, and that was enough. And if that wasn't enough, St. Andrew had visited Kiev and blessed the land and its inhabitants as early as the Apostolic period. Clearly, this was a land blessed by the Lord and the *Rus'* were a cho-sen people, much like the Jews of the Old Testament.

It was two events in particular, however, that resonated most saliently with believers—and even *then* non-believers—during the final days of the Soviet Union. The first was the disaster at Chernobyl' which was quickly pointed out as rather clearly predicted in the Book of Revelations, where the waters of "wormwood" (*chernobyl'* in Ukrainian), turned "bitter." Anyone who has gotten a taste of hydrogen peroxide can immediately connect the idea of hydrogen-based nuclear energy fallout with bitter water. Such was seen by many as a sign of the Apocalypse.

The next connection was that of the millennial celebration of the Baptism of *Rus'*. One of the most important numbers in New Testament eschatology is the number one thousand, probably being used by as many different groups throughout the history of Christianity to predict the Second Coming. The simultaneity of the millennium of Christianity and *perestroika* and the lib-eralization of Soviet religion policy had a unique effect. Those who had been weaned on Soviet atheist propaganda even began to wonder which was truth; the scientific atheism propagated by the Soviet regime, or the "false" beliefs of Christianity that they had attacked for 70 years? Even the most convinced Party member had to give pause and think twice, especially as he watched Mikhail Gorbachev standing beside Patriarch Pimen speaking favorably about the Russian Orthodox Church. Here was the Church being glorified by the party-state that had preached against it for 70 years.

That "preaching" did not work very well. It had many notable successes, including the conversion of some seminary students in the early Soviet period, including one man who went on to have his own atheist radio show in Leningrad. But in the end there was no large-scale abandonment of faith by one-time believers due to their coming into contact with atheist literature, and certainly not with scientific knowledge, as Lenin, Trotsky, and Yaroslavsky had expected. Where propaganda would have its greatest effect would be with the youth. Even if one were raised with faith in the home, he or she would be bombarded by contradictory information the rest of the time, including at school, in the youth organizations, and often among friends. While Party leaders hoped these very same youth would turn against their parents, hardly any ever did. If they found the truth to rest with the Party, most simply chalked the whole thing up to their parent's still not having a scientific worldview, and that they were duped by old-time superstition. In those cases, filial piety trumped loyalty to the Party.

In other cases, generational replacement was a failure as well, as children were raised with sufficient faith at home that they were able to retain their faith in larger atheistic society. This they could do by feigning atheism, which was done often, or by living outwardly as a person of faith, a lifestyle that came at great cost sometimes. In fact, the cost could be as high as being removed from the home of one's parents' and placed in an orphanage. Even this monopolization of a child's education and development most often had no effect upon his or her faith. Once the seed of faith had been placed in a young child's heart, it was quite difficult for the Soviet regime to dislodge, at least by the methods they employed. Hardship, loneliness, detestable conditions; the environment they offered was hardly conducive to one's rejection of their parents and their home life. Most likely, it had the opposite effect, on both parents and children. At least this was what happened in one of the most celebrated cases, that of the Siberian Seven, three parents and their four children who had been so taken, who made a dash for the U.S. embassy in Moscow and then stayed there for 5 years as they sought asylum in America. Their release came only 2 years before Gorbachev ascended to the USSR's highest post and began an about-face on Marxist-Leninist policies. Very quickly, religious repression would cease and Russia's religious revival would emerge from its own ashes.

Religion's Survival and Revival

Perhaps nowhere in the modern world has the determination of man to preserve his faith been more forcefully challenged than under Marxist regimes seeking to eliminate the "opium of the people." In particular, the cases of Soviet and Chinese religious repression represent the two most severe, large-scale, and prolonged examples of persecution of religion the modern world has ever witnessed. In both cases the similarities—as the previous pages have shown—do not end there. The ideological motivation behind these persecutions was based on Marxism-Leninism. In the case of the Soviet Union, Lenin proposed pragmatic policies toward religion that would serve his political agenda, as would his successor, Joseph Stalin. As for the Chinese, they took their starting point on issues of religion from Stalin's Soviet Union and Mao's own thoughts on the subject, though eventually the writings of Marx and Engels would become influential during the early period of liberalization.

Despite similar bases and theoretical arguments, the Soviet and Chinese approaches to religious repression are actually more different than they are similar. The Soviets never tried to adopt a Chinese-type approach to religious affairs, while the Chinese more or less dismissed the relevance of the Soviet model of religion from the start. In the area of atheism promotion, Chinese efforts were so meager by comparison that they are hardly worth mentioning. The Chinese did, however, apparently learn some lessons from the Soviets in terms of managing religious affairs. The TSPM, CBA, and other associations resemble Soviet grouping such as the Union of Evangelical Christians—Baptists and other groups that were used to harness religions together in the Soviet Union. In this, the Chinese found them similarly useful during periods of repression, and similarly problematic during periods of liberalization (cf. the struggle in Russia over the Russian Orthodox Church Outside Russia and the Orthodox Church of America, on the one hand, and the struggle in China over the TSPM churches and the unregistered house churches).

When it came to repression, the Soviets probably eliminated more clergy than the Chinese, even when we adjust for population. There were many years when the number of clergy rounded up ran into the thousands, though in China there were only two similar periods—1951–1953 and the years of the Cultural Revolution, particularly 1966–1969. The same can be said of believers, with more believers incarcerated and/or killed by the Soviet state than by China; one only need lay the annual volumes of *Religious Prisoners in the USSR*[6] alongside the lists of names of Chinese believers suffering repression.[7] The only exception here would be that of the Cultural Revolution, an event in Chinese church-state relations wholly without parallel in Soviet history, or probably any other country. The catastrophe that was the Cultural Revolution is unfathomable and the cost of human life inestimable, but it certainly exceeds that of the Soviet Union during any period, with only the period of the 1930s and the purges coming a distant second.

In at least one important way, moreover, the two cases of state persecution of religion examined here represent diametrical opposites. Russia is one of the most religious societies in the modern world, and perhaps the most religious society in Europe, while on the other hand, for most of the modern period China has been one of the least religious societies (at least according to traditional definitions of religion). So, although this study only included two historical examples, in many ways they can be generalized beyond themselves to other parts of the world, and provide insight into man's religious propensity, for they represent extremes of belief and unbelief, respectively.

In some ways, the relationship between religion and atheism can be seen as proportionally related; the stronger the religious tradition, the stronger was the attempt to eradicate religion. Of course, stronger atheist policies would be required to kill off a strong religious tradition. This would explain why in China we observe weaker religious adherence being coupled with a weaker implementation of atheistic policies. And insofar as the CCP attacked religion, these attacks were again commensurate with the relative degree of embeddedness of the tradition within Chinese society. While the CCP did not even consider Confucianism a religion, and Taoism was folk superstition at best, Buddhism, Islam, and Christianity each had connections to other political factors (Tibetan separatism, Uyghur separatism, and *heping yanbian*) that can equally be seen as the cause of their being targeted for attack.

It may be this factor that explains the overall pattern of change in religiosity during the phases of suppression, survival, and revival. From such a perspective, we can understand each regime's persecution of religion as being based to some degree on proportionality to its pre-Communist religiosity. Russia's severe attack against religion, therefore, was proportionate to its deep religiosity before the Bolshevik Revolution, while likewise China's more mild attack on religion was commensurate with its own lower level of popular religious adherence before Mao and the CCP took power. Additionally, it was in deeply-religious Russia that persecution was more fiercely resisted, while defiance against state persecution in China was of a lower level than in the USSR.

It could simply be that a lesser attack on religion engenders a lower level of resistance, while a more severe attack mobilizes a stronger resistance movement, but the evidence here does not seem to support such a conclusion. As repression reached some of its highest levels in the USSR under Khrushchev's crackdown, for example, resistance was low, only reaching its peak under the subsequent Brezhnev-era relaxation on church destruction. Likewise, in China during the Cultural Revolution, there was virtually no resistance during the high point years of 1966–1969, and while belief and organized religious behavior returned once the repression relaxed, one still cannot speak of the period as one of resistance. Under conditions of totalitarian social control, the relationship between severity of repression and strength of resistance is most certainly trumped. But when overall levels of social repression are sufficiently relaxed, as under Brezhnev, Gorbachev, Deng, and Jiang, resistance movements—and individual acts of defiance—become more emboldened.

The liberalization of religion policy in both countries was tied up with the overall liberalization of political, economic, and social life implemented by leaders who sought to humanize socialism and make it more viable. In this area, China was the leader, liberalizing religion policy nearly a decade before the Soviets. But once Gorbachev decided to move on the religious front, things progressed rapidly, and limited liberalization of religion under Deng was quickly passed as *perestroika* and *glasnost'* saw a rapid renaissance of religious belief and an equally rapid resurgence of the Russian Orthodox Church as the *primus inter non-pares*. Just as the Soviet persecution of religion was severe, so too was the religious revival that followed its cessation. Once suppression weakened and halted, popular faith and religiosity almost immediately returned, and returned with a vengeance. As for China, the liberalization of religion there has been truncated by waves of persecution and periodic attacks against specific religious groups. Meanwhile, the revival is simply unprecedented, with religion not only returning to pre-1949 levels, but exceeding those levels significantly. And religious "fever" in China is far from over.

The Desecularization of Russia and China

The revival of religion in Russia and China following decades of repression is an example *par excellence* of desecularization. As discussed in the introduction, there are probably two ways of operationalizing Berger's concept of desecularization, the first of which results in our defining desecularization as *the process by which sectors of society and culture are brought under the domination of religious institutions and symbols.* This is a high standard, as the term "domination" requires that the sacred dominate over the secular. Such a relationship could only be achieved at a very high price in modern society, though groups such as the Taliban and Al Qaida propose such an ideal nevertheless. Even in Russia, where desecularization has gone the farthest, it is difficult to point to sectors of society and culture that are now "dominated" by religious institutions and symbols.

One component of society that has seen rapid and profound infiltration by religion is that of Russian national identity and its defense. The whole post-Soviet concept of Russian national identity, the articulation of Russian national interests, and the behavior of the state organs charged with their defense has become imbued with Orthodox symbolism. Atheists define themselves as Orthodox, the KGB has a chapel on its grounds, the military has Orthodox priests "volunteering" in it, and military and police units go into action under the banners of patron saints. Still, it would be too much to say that such "comingling" equates to dominance. Even in the area of education, where prior to the Bolshevik Revolution the Russian Orthodox Church played a powerful role, in post-Soviet Russia the Church cannot be said to dominate. Not only does the number of religiously-affiliated schools—though impressive for such rapid growth—pale in comparison with public schools, the introduction of religion into the latter has only resulted thus far in the teaching of one course, and even that has not yet been carried out in all public schools.[8]

Clearly, a standard that requires domination for desecularization to be seen as occurring is too high. As the preceding pages clearly illustrate, if desecularization exists, the case of Russia must meet its criteria. A superior method of operationalizing desecularization is that offered by Karpov. He suggests that desecularization can be understood as "a process of counter-secularization, through which religion reasserts its societal influence in reaction to previous and/or co-occurring secularizing processes."[9] Karpov's definition brings into the equation religion's reassertion of a formerly-held position and it recognizes the potential for continued efforts at secularization within the same society. In the case of China, this has clearly been the case since the 1970s. While atheism is still promoted, policies restricting religious belief have softened, and all the while religious belief has blossomed. Moreover, that blossoming has remained confined to the field of personal religious belief, and as of yet has not branched over into the public square or political institutions, nor is it likely to do so in the foreseeable future.

On the contrary, Russia has seen a quite different form of desecularization. Religion is strongly reasserting itself into Russian politics, culture, society, and even the arts, as it attempts to regain its historical (sometimes even an "imagined" or invented) influence. Of course, the previous secularizing process was the Soviet policy of forced secularization, but it must include as well the secularizing trends underway in late imperial Russia. Looking at Russia's religious resurgence as a reassertion is useful, for it pinpoints the areas in which religion is likely to be most active, that is, those in which it previously wielded influence. This most clearly points to institutions of politics, society, and culture, and much less so to economics and foreign policy. In these two latter realms, religion's involvement has remained mostly symbolic and of little consequence. While Orthodox beliefs may impact believers' economic values, the Church has done little to involve itself in the economy. One of the few clear examples of such involvement was the formulation of a *Collection of Moral Principles and Rights of Business*, but even this was formulated by a lay group of believers and was of little effect.[10]

In the foreign policy and national security realm there seemingly has been more reassertion, but that, too, remains mostly symbolic. The construction and consecration of a Russian Orthodox Church in Havana or Pyongyang does little to expand Russia's foreign policy interests, but are significant symbolic acts of the Church's (and the state's) global reach. The same can be said for such moves as Putin having the Patriarch bless the passing of the nuclear football (the briefcase containing secret launch codes), having him bless Russian troops before military maneuvers, or designating a saint to be the protector of a government agency, as was done when St. Seraphim of Sarov was named the "spiritual patron-protector" of Russia's nuclear arsenal. While such acts may infuriate Western observers and lead them to conclude that the ROC is now "entrenched" in Russian politics, they are of little real effect.[11]

Of much greater concern are the legal restrictions placed on religious groups which pose no threat to the Russian state but which face undue restrictions on their activities. Having religious publications such as the Jehovah's Witnesses' *The Watchtower* placed on the government's list of extremist literature is simply a blatant act of intolerance, and most likely one which has ties to the Russian Orthodox Church and its hatred of "sects." Similarly, the recent development whereby the Russian Orthodox Church will have an opportunity to review draft legislation before it is brought to the floor of the Duma for voting is such a violation of all international legal norms that there is probably not even a term to describe it. It is a breach of much more than separation of church and state, and leans toward theocratic rule. The same can be said, but to a lesser degree, regarding the frequent "meetings" that are now taking place between the ROC and various government ministries, including the Ministry of Foreign Affairs. Such developments are worrisome on so many levels that even the problem of state financial assistance to the ROC pales in comparison with it. If this is not a case of "religion reasserting its influence" it is only because the ROC never had such influence in the past. Indeed, if any case for desecularization can be made using our first definition, that of sectors of society coming under the domination of religious institutions and symbols, it is in regard to these areas of Russian politics.

China's desecularization is of a quite different magnitude. Its greatest development has thus far been in the realm of private religiosity. Beginning in the early 1970s—several years before the official closing of the Cultural Revolution—small groups of believers began meeting together in their homes for worship and Bible study. Thus was born the house church movement, the most clear sign of desecularization in China. But in China TSPM churches are also overflowing today, while Buddhism is experiencing a prolonged revival as well.

Much of Christianity's revival has remained limited to private religiosity and "private" (i.e., non-public) gatherings of believers (admittedly often quite large). Buddhists and related native traditions, however, have entered the public square more visibly—in the case of Falun Gong, both figuratively and literally, as they gathered by the thousands off Tiananmen Square in April 1999. While the state quelled their attempt to show their presence publicly, they have been more welcoming to Buddhism. Former director of SARA, Ye Xiaowen, appeared quite sympathetic to China's largest religious tradition.[12] The state also welcomed assistance from Buddhists and international Buddhist organizations (though of course not recognizing Buddhists from Taiwan as "international") following the recent wave of earthquakes that have shaken the country. Though these events still fall shy of religion "reasserting" itself, the state is continually permitting opportunities for Buddhism to participate in the public life of the nation that are unprecedented during the history of the PRC.

The concept of desecularization is fully appropriate to the post-Communist world. Perhaps no other societies better exemplify the change of course, from secularization to the resurgence of religion, than Russia and China. As scholars continue work on fleshing out a theory of desecularization, the post-Communist world will offer critical cases for analysis.

The Impossibility of an Atheistic World?

If forced secularization only eventually resulted in desecularization, then what real possibility exists for the success of natural secularization? Much of Western scholarship and debate centers on issues such as the God "illusion," the culture wars, and even secular government as a violation of religious freedom, with various groups promoting or lamenting the inevitable secularization of the world. But while the failures of forced secularization should give solace to those who wish to see religion emerge victorious from this fight, one cannot simply conclude that the end of forced secularization in the Communist world means that atheism has lost and that the battle against belief is over.

It is tempting to conclude from this analysis of the Soviet and Chinese secularization experiments that atheism was a failure. Insofar as this is true, it is only generalizable to atheism as a forced policy and it was only a partial failure at that. It was relatively successful for many years at curtailing religious belief among millions of people, many of whom can simply never believe in religion, even though some wish they could. I have interviewed many people in Russia who take part in some church activities and even urge their children and grandchildren to believe, even though they themselves say they simply cannot. One young woman in Russia told me how her grandmother is always buying her icons for various occasions and that she practically pressures her into attending church, all while she does not believe herself. "Her Soviet education left her with no doubt that nothing beyond this world exists," she laments. This can be explained as another form of a mother consoling her child, where, as Berger explains, a mother lulls her child back to sleep, lying that everything is all right.[13] It also probably shows how one's spiritual thirst beckons when unquenched, and as such illustrates a lasting impact of forced secularization. It is interesting and significant that even some of the cases of success do not wish to pass that success on to their descendants. China, with its minimal promotion of atheism, probably has not witnessed such a phenomenon, but many Chinese are open to religious beliefs, and others are outright seekers.

Though forced secularization failed in the end, this period will not be easily overcome. There is no return to the *status quo ante*. These societies, like all societies, are path dependent, and their past will continue to impact their future. This is particularly true for China, where the effects of atheism will long plague Chinese society. The CCP attack against religion was more anti-clerical than it was about promoting atheism *per se*. It was effective, however, at leveling the playing field of China's religious economy. With no religious worldview commonly accepted—not necessarily believed, but simply recognized as the dominant spiritual explanation for man's existence and worldly mission—people did not even have a religion that they didn't believe. That is, a religion that existed as the "other" and juxtaposed to the secularity of the ordinary citizen. If man has a basic need for religion, a need for cosmological significance, then the environment created by the CCP was unnatural for man. Under the Cultural Revolution in particular, the situation became one in which man's religious thirst could not be quenched. The long-term effect of CCP religion policy means that China's religious economy was void of any brand to which most people were loyal, or which served the function of a public utility.

It is probably this fact which has changed China's religious economy so fundamentally that we are seeing the rise of Christianity there unlike at any other time in its 1,300 year existence in the Middle Kingdom. With Confucianism and Taoism more or less purged from Chinese culture, Christianity is now competing more effectively than ever before and gaining millions of converts. In the past, Chinese did not have to choose a religion. They simply chose whether to believe or not to believe, to take part in one or more of the three dominant religious traditions or not to take part. In such an environment, no choice was necessary and the *sanjiao* was sufficient to meet the spiritual needs of most Chinese. Now, without any taken-for-granted religion, a choice is necessary, and that choice is increasingly Christianity.

The Soviets knew better about how to go about wiping out religion. Not only did they attack the church ruthlessly and promote atheism enthusiastically, they also did their best to stop the socialization of religion at home by not allowing parents to raise their kids with religion. While the Chinese attempted similar policies, they were meager in comparison, and only in the Soviet Union were children taken away to orphanages if their parents were found to be raising their children in a faith tradition.[14] Simultaneously, the youth would be "properly" socialized as model Soviet citizens through the schools and various youth organizations, such as the Young Pioneers and the Komsomol, all of which pledged loyalty to scientific atheism. And if anyone had a question or was confronted with an idea that might spark some sort of doubt in the veracity of atheism, there were plenty *karmanii slovar' ateista* ("pocket dictionary of atheism") on hand.

But in the end, these measures still proved insufficient to the task of creating an atheist society. Stories abound of believers participating in Soviet youth organizations while still retaining their faith—if not outright coming to faith because of such involvement. A Russian Orthodox priest confided to me that it was in reading the Bible in order to refute it that he came to faith suddenly, while another mentioned how he would wander behind the movie screen in a converted church and look at the icons stacked back there. Before long he was kneeling and praying before them.

Even when children were taken from their parents, such acts only embold-ened the parents and probably only strengthened the desire of their children for religion; how could time spent in a Soviet orphanage—notorious for hor-rid conditions—lead a child to conclude that they had been saved by the Soviet state? After all, they did not take children who had only briefly been introduced to religion—they took kids who were believers and enthusiastic about their faith. It is very unlikely that such an experience broke their faith, with the case of the children of the Siberian seven being a case in point.

Atheism's Limited Success

Despite the many failures of forced secularization, one must admit sev-eral successes. The number of atheists in both countries is certainly larger today than it would have been had this episode never unfolded. As Bishop Hilarion rightly points out, atheism was already very influential in Russia long before the onslaught of Soviet atheist propaganda.[15] The degree of unbe-lief in Russian society today, therefore, cannot even be entirely attributed to Soviet policy, and of course the very fact that the Soviets came up with atheist policies shows that atheism's appeal and spread was a native move-ment. For China, however, while religious belief was limited and there was a strong anti-religion and anti-Christian movement in the 1920s and 1930s, these were more anti-Western than they were about the liberation of people's minds from a false consciousness.

This leaves us with one group that is quite numerous in both societ-ies, those who do not believe, do not really care either way, and are more or less satisfied with the situation. Does their existence prove that secu-larization is possible? The answer to that question is no, for there have always been non-believers. These particular non-believers, moreover, have been exposed to a powerful stimulus, and we cannot conclude any-thing about how they would have reacted without such a stimulus, and by extension how others without that or a similar stimulus will develop. We can conclude that there are probably fewer such non-believers in Russia than in China, since Russian national identity has become so connected to Orthodox identity over the past decade or two (and oftentimes not even related to belief in God or religion per se). In China, though, many people—indeed the majority—do not believe in religion nor do they hold sincere atheist convictions. Rather, they are simply materialists. While their atheism is probably closer to what Marx and Engels had in mind when they envisioned an atheist world, the global resurgence of religion must force one to question how long they will live without religion, particularly when groups of believers are increasingly free to share their faith and motivated to do so.

Calvin argued in his *Institutes of the Christian Religion* that God put a sufficient desire in man's soul to want to commune with him; as he phrased it, God was "engraved on our hearts." Though by no means a theological study, the evidence presented here suggests that man's religious impulse is very strong and difficult to extinguish. Empirical scholars of religion, including Berger, argue that man finds comfort and strength in religion. Though life is bearable without religious belief, it seems much more pleasant when one has it. As the French existentialist Albert Camus once said, "I would rather live my life as if there is a God and die to find out there isn't, than live my life as if there isn't and die to find out there is."

If we accept for a moment that—given the proper resources, time, and isolation—an atheistic society could have been developed in the communist world, would this then mean that the entire human race—again with similar campaigns and resources—could be made atheistic? The evidence presented here from the examples of forced secularization lead us to conclude otherwise. In addition to the historical evidence provided here, consider two more points. First, it is impossible to disprove the existence of the supernatural. The field of neurotheology provides conclusive evidence that man attributes certain neurological abnormalities to the supernatural, and that there is no indication that those abnormalities will disappear as man further evolves. To the contrary, they are likely to become more common.[16] Secondly, in some sense the science that has proven this also proves something else; that even the wealth of scientific knowledge that documents the neurological forces at work in the human brain and how they relate to religious sentiment does not compel everyone who knows of this science to abandon religion—not even a majority of the scientists working in the field are atheists! If science does not necessarily disprove the existence of the soul and God to leading scientific minds, how can it do so for the average man on the street, who lacks the scientific sophistication to even comprehend the science behind neurotheology? Even if science could dismiss religion as nothing more than a psychological abnormality, there would remain holdouts, just as there remain holdouts who believe that secularization is happening despite the overwhelming evidence to the contrary.

The two cases examined here are different in many ways, both in the manner in which religion was repressed in an earlier period and the manner in which it has recently revived. But both cases demonstrate that even the most determined efforts to wipe out religion in the public sphere will not necessarily finish the job in eradicating belief in people's hearts and minds. What is more, as soon as the period of repression diminishes or is brought to an end, people almost immediately turn back to religion again. If one has religious faith oneself, one will interpret these facts as only to be expected—at the core of religion is truth, and truth will always come out again. The social scientist, committed to staying with falsifiable empirical facts, cannot make such a statement (even if he is a believer himself). The truth about God cannot be either proved or disproved by the methods of empirical science. However, what the social scientist *can* say, without putting on a theological hat, is that any effort to eradicate religion is likely to be exceedingly difficult—even in societies as different from each other as Russia and China. A regime, no matter how secular in its official ideology, would be well advised not even to waste its resources on such an effort.

Notes

1   Athanasius, *On the Incarnation* (Crestwood, NY: St. Vladimir's Seminary Press, 1996), p. 38.

2   George Bataille, *The Cradle of Humanity: Prehistoric Art and Culture* (New York: Zone Books, 2005).

3   Karen Armstrong, *The Case for God* (New York: Alfred Knopf, 2009), p. 5.

4   French Ministry of Culture and Communication, http://www.culture. gouv.fr/culture/arcnat/lascaux/en/da2.htm; accessed October 20, 2009.

5   Armstrong, p. 5.

6   This publication was produced annually by Keston College in collaboration with various human rights organizations as well as dissident groups from inside the Soviet Union. Keston Library and Archive.

7   The best list is kept by ChinaAid (http://www.chinaaid.org). Falun Gong also regularly publishes lists of their persecuted believers, though it is apparently not available through their website (http://www.falundafa. org).

8   Elena Lisovskaya and Vyacheslav Karpov, "Orthodoxy, Islam, and the Desecularization of Russia's State Schools," *Politics and Religion*, Vol. 3, No. 2 (2010).

9   Vyacheslav Karpov, "Desecularization: A Conceptual Framework," *Journal of Church & State*, Vol. 52, No. 2 (2010).

10   Christopher Marsh, "Counting One's Blessings: The Economic Values of Russian Orthodox Christians" in *Markets, Morals & Religion*, Jonathan

B. Imber, ed. (New Brunswick, NJ: Transaction Publishers, 2008), pp. 179–89.

11 Blitt, pp. 707–37.

12 See, for example, his essay "Building a Harmonious Society and Calling for Joint Efforts to Create a Harmonious World," in *A Harmonious World Begins in the Mind* (Beijing: Religious Culture Publishing House, 2006), pp. 1–14.

13 Peter Berger, *Rumor of Angels: Modern Society and the Rediscovery of the Supernatural* (New York: Anchor, 1970), pp. 67–8.

14 Tatiyana Nikol'skaya, "Deti i Gosateizm," *Evangel'skaya Gazeta 'Mirt'*, No. 6, Vol. 31 (2001).

15 Metropolitan Hilarion (Alfeyev), "Atheism and Orthodoxy in Modern Russia" (no date). Available at: http://bishop.hilarion.orthodoxia.org/. Accessed March 5, 2009.

16 Michael Trimble, *The Soul in the Brain: The Cerebral Basis of Language, Art, and Belief* (Baltimore: Johns Hopkins University Press, 2007). See also Jay Feierman, ed., *The Biology of Religious Behavior: The Evolutionary Origins of Faith and Religion* (Westport, CT: Praeger, 2009).

Index